ABOUT THE EDITOR

Over the last thirty years, Jenny Quealy has been on a path that would eventually lead her to becoming the compiling editor of *Great Australian Rabbit Stories*. Her journey began when she decided to study geography, Australian literature and government as part of a Bachelor of Arts degree at Sydney University. Jenny then went on to work with the community Landcare movement, from its beginnings on the national scene in 1990 and for the twenty years that followed.

2009 saw the 150th anniversary of the release of wild rabbits into Australia, and Jenny was selected by the Rabbit Management Advisory Group (RMAG), supported by Australian Wool Innovation (AWI) and the Invasive Animals Cooperative Research Centre (IACRC), to create and manage the RabbitScan initiative, a national community science project, helping to map the current spread, density and impacts of rabbits. Meanwhile, after speaking with the IACRC CEO and RMAG, ABC Rural radio decided to collect rabbit stories from across the nation. Jenny worked with ABC Rural radio and the IACRC to develop and judge the 'Rabbiting On' storytelling competition. Jenny then took the wonderful stories that came out of 'Rabbiting On' to ABC Books, in the hope that they would publish these stories as part of their Great Australian Stories series.

The publication of this book makes these invaluable stories of Australian social history accessible to all.

Great Australian
RABBIT STORIES

Great Australian RABBIT STORIES

Jenny Quealy

The ABC 'Wave' device is a trademark of the Australian Broadcasting Corporation and is used under licence by HarperCollins*Publishers* Australia.

First published in Australia in 2010
by HarperCollins*Publishers* Australia Pty Limited
ABN 36 009 913 517
harpercollins.com.au

HarperCollins*Publishers*
Level 13, 201 Elizabeth Street, Sydney NSW 2000, Australia
31 View Road, Glenfield, Auckland 0627, New Zealand
A 53, Sector 57, Noida, UP, India
77–85 Fulham Palace Road, London W6 8JB, United Kingdom
2 Bloor Street East, 20th floor, Toronto, Ontario M4W 1A8, Canada
10 East 53rd Street, New York NY 10022, USA

National Library of Australia Cataloguing-in-Publication data:

Great Australian rabbit stories / editor, Jenny Quealy.
ISBN: 978 0 7333 2808 4 (pbk.)
Series: Great Australian stories
Rabbits–Australia–Control–Anecdotes.
Country life–Australia–Anecdotes.
Australia–Social life and customs.
Quealy, Jenny.
Australian Broadcasting Corporation.
636.9322

Front cover photograph by Jenny Quealy
Back cover photographs: (*left*) courtesy National Library of Australia; (*middle*) courtesy Ron Rees; (*right*) courtesy Peter Bird; (*spine*) courtesy National Library of Australia
Cover design by Priscilla Nielsen
Photograph of Jenny Quealy by Norman Plant
Typeset in 11/16pt AdobeCaslon Regular by Kirby Jones
Printed and bound in Australia by Griffin Press
70gsm Classic used by HarperCollins*Publishers* is a natural, recyclable product made from wood grown in sustainable forests. The manufacturing processes conform to the environmental regulations in the country of origin, Finland.

5 4 12 13

Thanks to all the
great Australian storytellers
who made this book possible

CONTENTS

FOREWORD

One hundred and fifty years after the deliberate import and release of just twenty-four wild European rabbits (*Oryctolagus cuniculus*) onto an Australian property around Christmas 1859, a community science project called RabbitScan began, asking Australians to help map how far the descendants of those original rabbits had spread. Scientists needed to have an accurate understanding of where rabbits were, across Australia, and in what numbers to plan the next steps in the long battle with the pest. Farmers and scientists were once again concerned that rabbits were on the increase, after years on the wane.

The rabbit most urban dwellers are familiar with nowadays is cuddly Peter Rabbit of the songs and stories. But we are not talking 'cute' here. The wild European rabbit, released into Australia for sport shooting, is the mangy, destructive, highly resilient and adaptable vertebrate pest. He's the rascally one; the one that causes about a billion dollars in lost agricultural production every five years. The one that has caused massive flora and fauna loss, at a cost we haven't calculated. Ask anyone trying to keep them out of vineyards, vegetable gardens and cropping fields or off ovals, dunes, bushland and World Heritage Areas.

The lead-up to the RabbitScan project included a simple idea, to run a rabbit storytelling competition. The idea started with an interview by ABC Rural journalist Sarina Locke with Professor Tony Peacock, CEO of the Invasive Animals Cooperative Research Centre. Their chat led to discussions with the Rabbit Management Advisory Group and the group's support of an ABC Radio storytelling competition called 'Rabbiting On', as part of the national reflection. The theme, endearing in this sense, was promoted to invite people to tell their memories – tall stories but true – involving the rabbit. 'Rabbiting On' ran over four months, from December 2008 to March 2009.

The steering committee had no idea of the depth of feeling about the rabbit they were about to unleash. Their invitation released a flood of stories about rabbits and what they've meant to Australians. The project tapped into pent-up memory banks, ready for the asking. Hundreds of stories came in from all over the country. Stories flowed in from men and women looking back on their childhoods, from people with still-vivid recall of the plagues before the 1950s, people whose lives and landscapes were changed by the rabbit. The range was astounding; some came as hard-to-read letters with challenging handwriting from those in their nineties; others via the web as emails or blogs, with digital photos attached. All seemed to have a record to tell: best price; first shot; quickest skun; largest haul; longest drive. The competition judges knew they were too good to simply leave in the ABC archive. This was history!

The result is this delightful, frightening and fascinating collection of just some of the stories from 'Rabbiting On'. There are stories from the people who encountered the rabbit in their everyday

'The Prince at the Rabbit Warren, Barwon Park' showing Prince Alfred, Duke of Edinburgh, with his hunting party during a visit to Australia in 1867.

lives, but accounts also from scientists working behind the scenes to keep rabbit numbers low and prevent the devastation of earlier years.

Australia has seen rabbits in plague proportions – in their billions before 1950, and plaguing again up to the mid-1990s. But most of us have forgotten about the rabbits over the last fifteen years. The numbers had seemed to dwindle; the plague levels were no longer being reached. The last bio-control, rabbit haemorrhagic disease virus (RHD or RHDV, known then as calicivirus), had reduced the rabbit population to less than five per cent of their plague numbers. The relief felt was immediate and seemed to be lasting. The national attention shifted. Priorities changed. Programs closed or were dramatically wound back.

In the 1950s, with myxomatosis, then in the 1990s, with RHD, Australia's scientists successfully released biological control of rabbits; other countries with similar problems followed our lead. At both times there was a huge and immediate relief from damage caused, and landholders, the scientific community and agencies relaxed. (Possibly a few bilbies, bandicoots and quolls relaxed as well – and there was, perhaps, some confusion among the predator foxes and cats too!)

But some scientists and land managers never stopped being vigilant and aware of the potential damage from just small numbers of rabbits, and the potential for a resurgence in numbers. They knew when to look for the telltale signs of immunity or recovery by the species from the controls (a virus is 'good' for only so many years before the target species begins to fight back successfully).

Luckily for Australia, this country has always had a handful of the world's best scientists on the case of the rabbit. They have been supported by the agricultural industries which felt the brunt of the rabbit plagues: the wool, meat and livestock groups, and landholders.

These stories are a reminder that we need to continue to keep a hop, skip and jump ahead of the rabbit, to ensure the damage inflicted on Australia's fauna, flora and productive landscapes does not again escalate and to reflect on how times have changed. Four questions hover: are rabbits on the increase again? Are the previously successful biological controls failing? Is the rabbit's most significant impact – on our environment – continuing unchecked? And why don't we see that even one rabbit per hectare is a plague in its own little way – that it can destroy new growth and new plants, and devastate complex ecosystems?

These stories were so important to gather – particularly as those contributors with first-hand experiences and stories are in their retiring years (or close to). Most have never had their stories told and published publicly. This collection is important as it records their stories and thus their irreplaceable, first-hand knowledge of the rabbit's impact and potential for escalating damage.

These stories also tell us how we've practised farming and animal husbandry for the past 150 years, and give fascinating insights into how Australians lived over that time as well. There are rabbit stories of the Depression; of hats, furs and fashion; of murder; of the raising of boys; of the loss of much-loved working dogs and horses as casualties of the rabbit battle; and, of course, of the catastrophic losses of Australia's native plants and animals.

But it isn't all serious! The collection contains a great many laughs to balance the more sobering stories. For example, the story of the sand goanna and the trapper's horse, and the tale of the church organ startling both a newly inhabited burrow into a dusty stampede and the congregation into shock.

The stories also contain a rich and broad lexicon, like these snippets: 'the paddocks were a moving mass, like maggots on a dead sheep', 'the scrub was so thick the dogs had to run out to the road to bark', and this evocative line, 'It was an honest gate, but no longer straight.' You are about to embark on a wild ride, on the back of a collection of Australia's yarns and yarn-spinners, and will easily imagine them being told to family, a mate or a crowd, in pubs, kitchens, wherever people gather, by a fascinating collection of contributors.

The rabbit might seem to be an animal with a soft footprint; these stories show otherwise. These days, with all the talk on reducing ecological footprints, the best we can do is to keep this pest animal at particularly low numbers, and to keep aware of where they are and whether they, or we, have the upper hand. While the rabbit remains, even in small numbers, our flora and fauna are at risk.

Let's all reflect on the 'rabbiting on' of our peers and forebears, as evident in these stories, and listen carefully each day for the renewed patter of millions of rabbits' feet. The trials and efforts of our preceding generations demand respect and action, if only to save what it is they were saving. Perhaps after these stories we'll all prefer to buy chocolate bilbies at Easter to help fund continued research into managing the very resilient rabbit, as the need for new bio-controls will to be with us for the next 150 years. Of that we can be sure.

INTRODUCTION: A FIVE-GENERATION STORY

It may seem a rare thing for five generations of the one family to have the same little furry animal nemesis, the destructive enemy of generations. But the gentle-looking rabbit has been the cause of much strife, expense and work. Rabbits have greatly changed our unique, ecologically complex, beautiful and productive landscapes. Their impact has been huge. Mostly we relate this to agricultural losses and costs. But the rabbit's impact on Australia's native species, which have been evolving since this place was Gondwanaland, has been largely overlooked.

In just 150 years the rabbit has quietly achieved massive change in the fauna and flora of much of southern and central Australia. Yet for all this, most Australians under fifty think of the rabbit as a childhood pet, or an occasional gourmet restaurant meal, or the key material of the iconic Akubra bushman's hat, or a story from the older folk. Rabbits are thought of more with fondness than fear of their destructive potential.

But not for one family: the Lords, who are not unique in their generational experience of battles with the rabbit. On the Lord run, Thackaringa, in western NSW, just south-west of Broken Hill, the rabbit's impact has been felt continuously throughout their 130-plus years of settlement, starting with John Vivian Lord (or 'JVL' as he was known and as the old stock brand attests) at The Pinnacles, now part of Thackaringa Station. While in mid-2009 there were only small numbers of rabbits evident on Thackaringa, the knowledge that as few as one to two rabbits per hectare are able to stop native perennials (plants) sprouting, sees an ever-vigilant family as ready as their forebears to keep those rabbit numbers low.

For the Lords, rabbit plagues are still in living and vivid memory, and have been a costly and constant battle. Rabbits have added to drought conditions by removing native and other vegetation, and have impacted on native fauna. Like the Lords, the best of Australia's land

One night's catch on Thackaringa, circa 1934.

managers and scientists are in awe of the rabbit's resilience as a species, and its ongoing adaptation to wildly differing and harsh Australian conditions – some of which the rabbits have probably caused.

The tools of this multi-generation struggle are mostly a clanging collection of inventions, each representing a different age and method for removing rabbits. Many of them are still on the property; some are rusting and rustic (and 'worth a pretty penny' no doubt to rural antiques enthusiasts and historians). They provide a unique insight into five generations of trial and error, success and toil in Australia's war with the rabbit. Early rabbit-proof fencing sits coiled alongside a 'poison cart', a sulky, and dozens of traps and other well-worn tools. They lie where they have been for years, in easy reach of the homestead and sheds. Nearby, early tractors and the hopper that dispensed poison-laced oats still sit. In the sheds are motorbikes, GPS units and the larger tractor used to pull a ripper that closed in over 28,000 warrens over a two-year period; rifles are locked away, safe, but ready.

But the more recent and successful tools of the battle are not evident, like the vials which once housed virus-carrying Spanish fleas, and the mosquitoes and flies that spread viral infections. The most powerful and successful tools take up no shed space and provide little material for future archaeologists – they'll have to dig instead with forensic abilities and microscopes. As with most advances, the latest tools to fight rabbits have become precision-based, highly potent bio-controls which mimic or use natural systems. Fleas, mosquitoes and flies have been the vectors for biological controls that have enabled the Lords to get back to the other things they do well: growing wool and meat for a world market, while caring for a unique rangelands landscape, an area that is iconic to Australia.

Right now, three generations of Lords live on the station; the oldest, John Lord, is eighty-six and the youngest, Hugh Lord, just twenty-one. Both rate the rabbit as an amazing animal but a real pest, a costly distraction from what they and previous generations settled there for: running sheep in a beautiful, yet often harsh, landscape and climate.

What is remarkable about the Lords is the resolve and generosity of the family, who not only tackle the problem on their own place, but also voluntarily spend months – even years – of their time working beyond their property gates and the rabbit-proof fences that run through and beyond their property, to find an answer to the rabbit problem as a community service.

But the notable thing about the Lords is that they are loath to grandstand – they have simply got on with the job. But while doing it, they got noticed and were asked to give of their time and to help take a message and a passion for protecting Australia's fauna and flora and productivity right to the top of Australia's government, and to the centre of our community and industry. The three current generations of landowners – John, David and Hugh – share a confidence and drive to spread the word of the catastrophic environmental impact of rabbits, including drought and dust storms. Each also shows a love for the place and the drive that is so characteristic of people who know their country and would fight tooth and nail to protect it.

Yet they are not natural hunters, nor the usual caricature of a seasoned shooter. The burden of needing to cull destructive invasive animals shows, as does the resolve to ensure Australians don't forget how quickly invasive animals can reach plague numbers and why this must be prevented.

JVL's great-great-grandkids, Charlie, Emma and Hugh Lord, are typical of the current generation of regional Australia. They are reaching their early twenties – the age at which their grandfather, John Lord, was singlehandedly managing Thackaringa and two other family properties, a holding of over 66,000 hectares. Raised on the land, able

The Lords: David, John, Emma and Hugh have been active all their lives in rabbit control, to protect the landscape and the wool industry.

to muster, draft and otherwise manage stock and the landscape, Charlie, Emma and Hugh are also typical 'young moderns': tech-savvy, well-educated and keen for a full and fun lifestyle. On breaks home from school in Adelaide, they each helped log rabbit warrens – totalling over 28,000 – on GPS units, as a mapping task prior to the massive rabbit management program that was needed between the two great rabbit diseases, myxomatosis and RHD.

Now Charlie is away with his wife, Rhiannon (Annie), both geologists and Emma is in finance in Broken Hill, often using her days off to help out at Thackaringa when the pressure is on. Hugh is home, working alongside his dad at times, but also working sheep on a friend's place up north, or at another property down south as time and opportunity allow.

They have each also sat alongside their dad offering comments and support as he hosted visits from scientists, the media, other landholders, students and politicians of all persuasions keen to learn from the Lords' experience, given generously. David's dad did the same in the 1960s and 1970s, taking university geography students (like me) through the property; all at their cost.

The Lords as woolgrowers are representative of the sheep industry, but seem as focused on rabbits as they are on sheep. Of course they are in the business of sheep, but they are also managing landscape conservation (water, vegetation and soils) and invasive animal control. Hence the whole family is multi-skilled. They are also collaborative, keeping pace with science, policy and innovation, and a large and varied network of people from all walks of life.

The Lord men might, as one of them (Ken Lord, now in his eighties) says, all have 'characteristic wild, long eyebrows' and the ability to have a laugh at themselves. But looking a little deeper into this family, one is struck by a common and deeply held love for this country and a deep resolve to protect and care for it, to keep it productive and to repair the damage the rabbit and droughts have caused. There is a serious temperament at work here; perhaps they developed such strength and resilience by their focus on containing the rabbits and their impact over such a long period.

In many ways the Lords epitomise the history of the epic struggle between farmers and rabbits – a struggle that is detailed in the stories that follow. But they also represent the new breed of farmer, dedicated to preserving the Australian landscape – indeed, to fight for it.

THE DAMAGE DONE

This collection needs a warning. Many of the stories are quite graphic in their description of how Australians have gone about killing wild rabbits over the last 150 years. Farmers, trappers, scientists and even kids used a range of methods, many of which are now considered to be cruel, as they often meant a long and painful death for the rabbit. Many of these methods also had a negative environmental impact.

Readers need to reflect on a few issues here, including the lack of choice at the time and the sheer desperation of those fighting this mighty pest. The poisons and early virus controls that were used are now unacceptable to us, and scientists continue to modify and find new biological controls that are quicker, more effective and less damaging to other animal species, the native flora, the land and our people. One wonders at the amount of chemicals and poisons laid out across the land and handled – without today's safety precautions – by our forebears.

The most encouraging trends of the last couple of decades have been the use of more acceptable virus controls, and the intense and important focus on farm, landholder, community volunteer and agency officer health and safety. It is vital that we not allow rabbits to return to plague proportions. We must understand that even at small numbers rabbits can have a devastating impact.

Many of the practices and products described in the stories are no longer appropriate for rabbit control. For information on the best controls, speak to your local council, livestock health or catchment office, or Landcare group. Alternatively, you can contact RabbitScan (www.rabbitscan.net.au) or the Invasive Animals Cooperative Research Centre (www.invasiveanimals.com).

An Imperial Chemical Industries researcher examines carbon-monoxide foam used for rabbit control, 1963.

1.

TRAPPERS, RABBITOHS, BUYERS AND SELLERS

This chapter gives the reader a rich brew of real characters from across Australia and over time, with arguably the most evocative imagery and language of the collection. Here were people making a living from a job that was tough and necessary, but a bit 'on the nose'; the rabbiters or rabbitohs, as anyone in the trade was known. In the words of one contributor, rabbiters were at one time seen to be 'worse than shearers' – alluding to both as unsavoury types, and perhaps referring to fellows like the trapper so well-described in winning contributor Barry Hadlow's story, 'Old Burt the rabbit trapper'.

These stories show that, over time, rabbiters were a varied lot, with most families seeming to have at least one rabbiter in their midst, be it grandfather, dad, son, mum, aunt or sister. Often the rest of the family helped out in some way. Scratch the surface of your parents' or grandparents' memories and there are stories of relatives who were part of the rabbiting tradition and who helped save the farm, feed the family or supplement the family income.

Mostly rabbiters were needed, welcomed and even heroes. While others were infamous for keeping a few kittens (young rabbits) in their pockets, which they might let loose in areas rabbits had not yet reached, to keep the trade going.

Many of the rabbiters in these stories were hard-working, long-travelling blokes (or the occasional 'sheila'). They were away from home for long hours, even years, and missed out on being with their families and seeing them grow. They were adept at handling dogs and ferrets, as well as snakes, possums and other 'bycatch' of the rabbiting task! They knew the country well: the landscapes; the way to read a place; tracking and trapping guided at times only by the stars and the moon. The rabbiter might be a trapper, a driver, a seller, a buyer, a trader, a chiller-operator or a trap-maker. There were so many roles developed as the rabbits plagued. Many left their other jobs and homes, or created their first job, and many found a way to make a real quid from rabbiting on. Just some of them are captured here.

Whatever people thought of them, rabbiters made money (but I'll bet the tax records wouldn't be able to track the market accurately). Here are glimpses of a few of Australia's first entrepreneurs who built rabbiting into an industry important to most of Australia, and a major part of Australia's economy at its height. Interestingly, early attempts to bring in known virus controls were delayed in favour of the industry and its perceived contributions, as rabbits became a major export product of Australia. What appeared to be forgotten in those debates was the impact on native fauna and flora, on soils and waterways, and on people's health. But here are the stories and the rabbiters' records, of the numbers and prices, which range into the legendary. Wherever the rabbiter went a unique Australian story was possible and, thanks to these contributors, some of their stories have been captured.

OLD BURT THE RABBIT TRAPPER

BARRY HADLOW

Not everyone had a problem with the rabbit invasion. Some industrious people made a tidy living out of trapping, skinning and selling the rabbit carcasses. There was a ready market for the skins to be made into ladies' gloves and the fur into felt hats for men. It took between eight to thirteen rabbits to make an Akubra hat and no man would dream of being seen outside without his felt hat in the 1920s and 1930s.

One industrious soul was Old Burt the rabbit trapper, who visited our district in the late 1930s and early 1940s. He would come around every six months or so, generally in the winter months when the rabbits had their best fur growing. The old dray was something to behold. His horse was ancient with a tired look in its eyes and would stop walking without a moment's hesitation. The horse also had a lazy bottom lip which sort of gaped, and we would watch, fascinated, as flies popped in to slake their thirst. The dray's sides were festooned with rabbit traps and the wire sleeves for drying and stretching the skins. Everything clinked and rattled in rhythm with the slow progress of the dray.

Seated on a plank across the middle of the dray was Old Burt with his own very old battered Akubra jammed on his head. Old Burt didn't believe in shaving very often and it was difficult to see where the brown of the nicotine stain started and ended on his wispy beard. When Old Burt turned up at your farm you always checked the wind and positioned yourself to avoid the smell. Old Burt himself smelled of drying rabbit skins. Add a few dead bunnies on the floor of the dray heaped together with his unwashed clothes, and let's just say we could smell him coming.

Burt had a couple of dogs with him and they were always well fed, feasting on rabbit carcasses. When Old Burt asked where all the rabbits were, the farmer was only too glad to point him in the right direction. Old Burt would head off and you would see him the next day or the day after with a whole pile of rabbit skins stretched on the wire sleeves. As soon as they were dry he would tie up bundles and send them to Elders Smith.

Old Burt never stayed more than a day or two and although all the farmers would have welcomed him to stay and really clean the population of rabbits right out, he would merely mumble, 'Well, I'll be back next year!'

RABBIT'S RESPITE

JOHN IVE

'Bloody geezer … #@$%$ … Hell!!!' That is an abridged version of my grandfather's confronting outburst as his horse and gig, complete with contents, took off at breakneck speed across the lignum flat. Such outbursts were not uncommon from the retired British merchant seaman who, at eight, had run away from home to become a cabin boy, only to be sunk twice by German U-boats during the First World War. What was noteworthy about this particular outburst was the incident that precipitated it.

My grandfather had become the district rabbiter in the Benjeroop area of northern Victoria after my father returned to our farm following the Second World War. It was March 1950, rabbit numbers were at a pre-myxo peak and landholders were utterly desperate. The mosaic of dryland and irrigation farming provided a nutritious smorgasbord year-round for the ever-increasing rabbit population. The native lignum which covered flood-prone areas in the near-flat landscape provided excellent cover for rabbits.

It was in such an area that Grandfather had spent another long and successful day rabbiting. By day's end the gig was heavily laden with rabbits – some skun, some not – and all the paraphernalia used for rabbiting: traps; rusty fencing wire; shovels; mattocks; axe; crowbar; poison pot; firearms; tuckerbox; water bag; and, at foot, a pack of tired dogs ranging from fleet-footed greyhounds to tenacious little fox terriers – about ten in total.

As if to provide a bit of light-hearted relief to end a tiring day, the dogs bailed up a sand goanna – a fine specimen about 2 metres in length and well engorged on the endless supply of rabbit kittens. The goanna immediately hit top speed, as its straightened legs propelled its raised body ahead of the closing dog pack.

The natural instinct of goannas facing danger on the ground is to seek refuge up the nearest tree. But alas, the lignum flats of Benjeroop were treeless and one-metre lignum bushes were not a safe alternative. At around 18 hands high at the wither, the horse offered the tallest possibility within the sprinting limit of the engorged goanna. The goanna shot up the horse's front leg and quick as a flash was perched between the horse's ears – albeit precariously. Startled by the events, the horse bolted, instantaneously reaching top speed and then more, as the goanna dug in its claws to avoid losing its grip, upon which its life now surely depended. The gig's contents started flying in all directions, along with my grandfather's notorious outburst!

Three days later the horse was found nursing numerous lacerations from fences and the like encountered in its frenzied run, still dragging the shredded remains of the harness that once hauled the gig. The largest gig pieces recovered along the run were the steel rims from the wooden-spoked wheels, which had shattered along with the rest of the gig.

No doubt many a rabbit along the run rejoiced at the respite the incident was to provide. My 74-year-old grandfather 'retired' from 'bloody rabbiting' forthwith.

WITH MY PACK OF SIXTY TO SEVENTY DOGS

MARY KILMARTIN, AS TOLD BY ERNIE KILMARTIN

In the year 1949 my mother and father were sharefarming at Maffra in central Gippsland, Victoria. My mother saw a job advertised in the *Weekly Times*, so they answered the ad for a father and son job on a large sheep and cattle station in the Western District. Banongil East was just outside of Skipton, an hour from Ballarat. We got the job and headed off in the old black Buick to meet the owners of the property. We were told I was to be the rabbiter; I was fourteen years of age when I began the job.

There was a stone fence all around the boundary, 5500 acres. I had to mend the fence with stones and wire to keep the rabbits out. We lived in a little house on the station, on the road from Skipton to Lismore. I would leave home at 7.00 am each morning with lunch and water, and would be out all day, returning home around 5.00 pm.

I travelled around in a four-wheeled buggy, with Brownie the horse. He was a good carthorse I could leave grazing for long periods with no fear of him taking off. I had a pack of sixty to seventy dogs who worked, including fox terriers, spaniels, greyhounds and staghounds. Some days the dogs would catch up to 200 rabbits.

We also used a large wire-netting fence to drive the rabbits into. Local footy clubs would use this as a fundraiser. Fifty men, women and children would all join in, driving the rabbits into the wings and then into a narrow enclosure. When they had them trapped they would knock the rabbits on the head rather than shoot them, so they could be sold. On a good netting day we would get 2000 rabbits.

Some of the dogs in my pack were able to get down in the burrows, or I would dig them out with a mattock or shovel. The rocky terrain made it extremely difficult to dig into the burrows. Some of the rabbits were able to be sold if they were not bruised. The rabbit buyer would pay me fifty shillings a pair.

Rabbit skins were sold by weight; winter coats were the best price. I trapped all year round for seven years. Over the years I also used traps and the shotgun to cull rabbits.

The dogs often got fired up and chased and killed foxes as well. Managing a pack of dogs as big as mine was dangerous at times. They would fight each other and it was often safer to leave them to it, rather than pull them apart. The dogs would indicate which section of the warren the rabbits were in at the time. The scent of the rabbits and the heat radiating from their bodies gave their

Boundary rider Harry Reynolds with his supply cart, Burracoppin Depot, Western Australia, 1926.

hiding spots away. Some of the larger warrens may have had twenty or more exit points.

The 'moving hill' we often saw in the distance was in fact a rocky barrier or stony rise covered in hundreds of rabbits. My younger brothers and sisters loved to clap their hands and see the rabbits scatter with their fluffy white tails bobbing along. Dad would often go mad at them when they brought baby rabbits home to play with.

The destruction that the rabbits would leave behind them was dreadful. The land would be bare of any vegetation, leaving the property useless for running stock. The stock would not feed on the land where the rabbits had been as they had soured it. Rabbit-infested land would halve the amount of stock that could be run. They ate more feed than the cattle. Rabbits are very quick breeders and their warrens were massive.

'BERT USED TO SAY HE WAS BORN WITH FUR UP HIS NOSE'

MELVA GRAHAM

My mother's stories always started this way, then she'd go rabbiting on about her life as a trapper's mate in the late 1930s. Dad was still trapping rabbits for a while after he came back from the war, and I would follow him around while he set traps at the entrance to burrows. He would dig a hole with his trap-setter (a small hand hoe and hammer head combined), set down his trap, hammer in the chain attached to it, hold the plate with a worn-smooth setting stick while he tore a piece of paper from the neatly cut square wad pinned to his shirt, place the paper over the trap plate, sprinkle a little soil over the paper, and cover the lot with soil. Then in the ground nearby, he would scratch the number of traps set. Mum and I would help carry his trap supply.

My mother's parents were not ecstatic about their daughter's marriage to a lowly rabbit trapper. However, Dad was probably earning more money than they were out on Misery Farm in the Millewa. From his earnings he bought a new Dodge truck, complete with helper springs for carrying large loads of rabbits, and started a rabbit carting business.

My mother would continue, 'We were picking up rabbits from trappers out at Ned's Corner, north-west of Mildura, and taking them into the chillers in Mildura. The trappers would bleed and gut the rabbits, pair them up by slitting their legs and hang them in a hessian screen to protect them from flies. We carried three tiers of paired rabbits suspended on horizontal rails bolted to our truck tray. At the exporter's chiller, the rabbits would be graded and paid for by the rabbit buyer. Then we'd fill up two 44 gallon drums with water to take out to the trappers, together with their ordered food supplies, when next we picked up their catch.

'When the rabbits petered out around Ned's Corner in the hot, dry summer of 1938 to 1939, we heard that there were "rabbits at Port Augusta ... millions of them!" So we set off, taking a couple of trappers with us. The rabbits were really there, and in their millions, and we soon had twenty-two trappers on our round. We paid the trappers cash "on the stump" there, which meant that if we didn't get the rabbits into the chiller on time, we suffered the loss. Once we got bogged in one of the creeks, so Bert skun 360 pairs of rabbits so that we would at least recover some money for their skins.'

Although these were the years of Depression with unemployment and near-starvation, the rabbit industry gave men like my father an independence and way of earning a living. It was fortunate, too, that Mum was a creative rabbit cook. As one farmer said, 'Although the rabbits were a pest, we would'a damned well starved without 'em!'

A GOOD SENSE OF DIRECTION

ALAN SCHEER

In the Depression, my father went to a farm belonging to the Gotthold Pfeiffer family in Brinkley, South Australia. At the edge of a scrub, he built his camp out of kerosene iron. I don't know why it was called that. I'm guessing that they were cut out of kerosene drums. It had a wooden door, wood stove and the floor was dirt. He had three beds held from the roof by chains; he was worried about scorpions getting into the beds.

My father then trapped rabbits for a living. In those days, rabbit buyers would go to the farm to buy his rabbits. At night he had a Tilley lamp to check his traps and used a hoe to make a line to follow, to know where he set his traps.

As a child in the late 1950s, my father taught me to set traps. On some weekends, I'd ride my pushbike out to Pfeiffer's farm or my grandpa's farm near Murray Bridge. I'd carry twelve traps on the bike. At times my father would drive me out to check my traps. I hated this. If I'd set a trap in the wrong place, he'd shake his head, then give me a lecture.

We'd eat some of the rabbits I caught; the rest I would sell for a shilling each. Later on in life, in the early 1970s, I gave up slaughtering in the meatworks in Murray Bridge to collect fowl eggs on the weekends with my partner at the time. I'd also go near Meningie trapping for two days each week with 100 traps. I slept in the car and used a torch to check my traps at night. I had a good sense of direction, remembering which direction every trap was. I'd check my traps at 5.00 am, then 8.00 pm and at midnight, usually getting about eighty to ninety pairs of rabbits which I sold to the rabbit buyer at Tailem Bend. Nowadays trapping rabbits is banned, but I still have the memories.

UNCLE CHARLIE MY HERO

BARRY BELL

My mother's brother Charlie worked on a western district station as a rabbiter. His job was to control the rabbits on the station with every means possible, and feed the station sheepdogs with rabbits. He was supplied with a house, a horse and cart, dozens of steel-jawed Ace rabbit traps, a number of ferrets and rabbit nets and a number of crossbred whippet and greyhound mongrel dogs. He was paid a small wage and kept the money from the sale of rabbits to the butchers' chiller and the sale of dried skins, at two shillings and sixpence per pound, with nine to twelve skins per pound.

During school holidays my sister and I would stay with Uncle Charlie and Aunty Jean and go rabbiting every day. Summer was the best time to poison rabbits. We would sit under a big red gum with a board and knife and a bucket full of apples or carrots and cut them into small pieces (rabbit bite-size). A ploughshare was fitted under the cart to make a fresh furrow in the soil; we would then drop the bait down a tube into the furrow.

Uncle Charlie would give the rabbits two free feeds of fresh bait and the trail would go for miles. On the third day he would lace the bait with strychnine and place the poisoned bait in the furrow. The next morning we would be up early to pick up the dead rabbits (hundreds of them). Most would be close to the trail and the dogs would find the distant ones and bring them back to the cart. All afternoon was spent skinning the rabbits while they were still fresh and pegging the skins out on a clay-pan or on a wire frame. We would go home at night exhausted, and with the strong smell of dead rabbits all over us.

Uncle Charlie would put ferrets down the burrows with rabbit nets over the holes to catch the remaining rabbits. When the rabbits ran out we had to catch them and wring their necks before they escaped, then gut and leg them on a wire across the back of the cart under a hessian screen to stop the blowflies.

When the ferrets came out we would roll up newspaper, push it down the burrows and backfill with soil. The paper would deter outside rabbits from digging in. The dogs were always ahead, hunting the rabbits into the burrows before the ferrets went in. Then Uncle Charlie would set a steel trap on the filled-in burrow to catch any stray rabbits digging in.

The next morning we would all collect the rabbits caught by the traps, skin them and keep the best ones for the table. Many settlers lived on rabbit meat cooked in many different ways. The best skins were made into fur coats and the rest used for Akubra hats. Only for the rabbits in those tough times, many families on the land would have starved. Uncle Charlie was my hero with his horse and cart, ferrets and dogs.

HORSEBACK HUNTING

AUB SHAW

Aub was born at Galong, NSW, in 1921 and feels he was rabbiting since the age of seven until his retirement from farming and being a lifelong 'apprentice rabbiter'. From this early age he learned to dig out burrows and hunt the rabbits down with dogs. He recalls men on horseback hunting rabbits down with stock whips on Bobbara Hill outside Galong. Later the famous old grey Fergie tractors with rippers attached were very effective in ripping out the rabbit burrows.

Aub came to live at Glenelg, Little Billabong, in 1949. The absence of men all over rural NSW, due to the war, had allowed the rabbit numbers to increase to plague proportions. This was the situation on the Shaw property along with neighbouring properties. Rabbit control began in earnest: Aub employed three station hands and had a large pack of dogs – about twenty. This pack consisted of greyhounds, terriers and beagles. As you could imagine, there was no processed dog food at that time. Aub recalls wanting to go back to Galong for Christmas but being concerned the dogs would go hungry. The morning of his departure he went out early and shot fifty rabbits within the hour; the dogs were right for their Christmas dinner.

Over the next three years, Aub and his workmen continued to work on ridding 1500 acres of rabbits, repairing many fences and making them rabbit-proof. Hundreds of bottles of Lavacide were used, other times strychnine. Baits were made by pulling up black thistle roots from the ground, washing them and cutting them into bait-size pieces. These pieces were then placed in a billy can and sprinkled with vanilla (to tempt the rabbits) and strychnine. Baits were speared out of the billy with a needle and placed around burrows. This method worked extremely well with 500 to 600 rabbits being poisoned in one night! The remaining 2000 acres of the Shaw property was still infested with bunnies. Myxomatosis was introduced about this time and rabbit numbers were definitely on the decline.

As if the rabbit plague was not enough for farming families, in 1952 fire completely destroyed the 3500 acre property and many others in the district. Fencing was destroyed. The fire did assist with trying to beat the rabbit by burning lots of the fallen timber that had provided shelter for the rabbits and destroying the food source of the rabbit. Gone also was the pasture for the Shaw stock. Aub and his workmen had to rebuild fences using netting and continue their pursuit of the rabbit. The wool industry in Australia was nearly wiped out due to the rabbits eating the grass.

The purchase of a 'Nuffield' tractor with a ripper attachment certainly made the rabbiting job easier. Rabbit skins were pegged

A good sulky load of rabbits, Moruya, New South Wales, circa 1890.

out on wire frames to dry prior to being purchased by a skin buyer. Winter skins were more valuable but even then the remuneration was small.

The Methodist Church in Holbrook received the proceeds of rabbits for its building fund. In the Kyeamba district, a lane was fenced across the Wagga Road and the rabbits funnelled into an area around a dam where poison was laid; it killed thousands. Aub is not a fancier of rabbit, as you could well imagine; he can only recall eating it once – once was enough!

RABBITING TURNS TO GOLD

ROB CALDWELL

On a rabbiting excursion to Kings Plains near Blayney in NSW, I met up with a mate, Sutt. His dad was a gold prospecting fanatic, to the point where he convinced his son and a couple of mates to help out with a mining enterprise. The deal was that he would pay us for the gold we retrieved. This was potentially more lucrative than rabbiting. We rode our bikes 5 miles out of Blayney to a place that was simply a ploughed paddock. In the bottom corner of this paddock was our goldmine, a place where we dug shafts 6 feet by 2 feet and down 22 feet through topsoil, clay and ironstone to the alluvial gravel of an old creek bed.

I hadn't got rabbiting out of my system in view of the prospects of gold, and I convinced my mates Sutt and Fuss that we should hedge our bets and set a few traps on a hill across the creek, where the rabbits were plentiful. As mine shafts and rabbit traps are not really dog-friendly, our days of cycling around town to borrow dogs had to be curtailed.

So our rabbiting techniques changed somewhat. At the end of the goldmining day, we set a round of ten to twenty traps and some noose snares at fence holes before returning home. The next morning we would go around the traps, collect the rabbits, re-set and go for gold.

Most people who have experienced the Blayney climate would understand that we could still get the dead rabbits to the chiller at night without any deterioration in the quality of the product!

It wasn't too far down the track (in 1958) that the goldmining proved to be more lucrative than rabbiting. The physical effort was harder, though. Once we had dug down to the dry creek bed, we dug tunnels – called drives – to follow the alluvial gold. The drives were up to 30 feet long, and were about 3 foot, 6 inches high by 2 foot, 6 inches wide – the swing arc of a miner's pick from a kneeling or crouching position. The gold-bearing material, called wash, was put into buckets, slid back along the drive to the shaft, and then windlassed to the surface for washing and recovery of gold.

Yes, we had gold fever all right; we learned to divine with a piece of 8-gauge wire. This proved to be an essential part of this type of mining. Before selecting a site for the next shaft, we would do divining cross-sections of the paddock, placing a stone wherever the divining rod indicated a change. The stones mapped the course of the buried creek bed, and the shafts were sunk on the downstream end of the inside of a bend; the most likely area of deposits of alluvial gold. So rabbiting became a subsidiary business, as far as pocket money was concerned.

THE BEST RABBIT TRAPPER – MAX'S STORY

NOEL COWCHER

'I may not be the best rabbit trapper to ever set an iron trap, but I certainly haven't heard of any better.' Such is the claim from retired farmer, shearer and hunter, Max Cowcher, my dad, as he reflects nostalgically on his rabbit trapping years around Quindanning in the upper Great Southern region of Western Australia.

With a face that hides generations of stories from a time when life seemed simple and every day an adventure, a larrikin grin emerges and a glint in his eye suggests pride in his mastery of trapping and a fondness for the tales he has to tell of a youth well spent.

Max's first account of trapping tells of two weedy brothers balanced across a spring trap on a tree branch, the combined weight of the runty six- and seven-year-olds providing just enough force to pry the jaws open. With some nervous apprehension the trap was set, carefully placed in the well-scraped hole and then covered with fresh dirt filtered through a hand at a tantalising height and fingers just daring the trap jaws to have a snap.

During the war years, as was so often at the time, families were sent in different directions to complete their schooling. Max boarded at the Toodyay Convent, and he and a few of the boys there would set traps around the town to hustle the locals for a little extra pocket money in hard times. Living away from home at a tender age and completing the chores of the convent, like chopping wood and milking cows, could seem like hard times for a young boy, but there is nothing but delight in his eyes as Max recounts his nightly toilet visit.

The rabbits were on the rise in the war years, and one could rely on spirited young boys to do their bit to reduce their numbers. The boys received a severe chastising the morning all of the shoes went missing. Walking along a two-storey balcony to reach the toilets, the only ammunition the boys could raise to have a shot at the rabbits below was, of course, their shoes. The next morning saw the grass littered with shoes – and the occasional injured rabbit.

On leaving school, Max took to the shearing shed at another time when the rabbit population had begun to swell. Trapping in the off-season became a lucrative earner for a young man and before long Max was setting up to 250 traps in a night and morning shift. Traps were set on warrens, dungheaps, pads and set grain lines. Interestingly, the old roo dogs, which plodded behind the trappers all day and all night, became most adept at avoiding the dangerous jaws. Max recalls only one time when a dog was injured from the traps; they were moreover great company and handy when it came to finishing foxes that had investigated an iron trap too closely.

Max's record for one night's trapping was 176 pairs and from such lucrative returns he managed to buy his first car in the early 1950s. He recalls larger catches from trappers in the district that set water traps: up to 1500 rabbits, but believes his 176 pairs from 250 traps stands as a record in the district.

A LIFELONG CAREER

BLUEY STANCOMBE

In 1918, aged twelve years, my father left Maldon Catholic School in Victoria to begin his lifelong career as a rabbiter. He walked the hills with his rifle, then hawked the rabbits around town. He later got an old horse out of the pound for two bob, and with rope reins and an old cart was able to travel further afield.

He trapped and ferreted, keeping the rabbits alive in an old dairy until he had a killing night. The rabbits were sent, in crates on the goods train, to Bendigo. The price paid was fourpence for a large pair (four pound, gutted) and tuppence a pair for small and rejects. Sometimes no cheque was returned, because the buyer at the other end said they were unfit for human consumption, and there was no comeback.

In 1945, Harry Portelli, a rabbit trader from Kyneton, started to buy rabbits in our area. Dad then had a killing night and drove the cart to Chewton, about 13 miles, where he was met by Harry. In 1950, Harry built a chiller in our yard. Its walls and floor were sawdust, one foot thick, and it had a ceiling of about 3 feet. Each time he came in the truck to pick up the rabbits he brought a truckload of sawdust from the saw mill. We not only caught rabbits, but bought rabbits on commission for Harry. Prices slowly went up and then they were two bob a pair. Harry connected the electricity to our place and the chiller was converted and then it ran silently, without the continual noise of the old petrol motor.

Dad mainly ferreted and trapped. We worked about 100 Lanes Ace traps. He was amazing, finding the traps at night, in the rocks, trees and couch grass with only the aid of a hurricane lamp. He always had a pack of dogs and heaps of ferrets housed under the peppercorn tree.

In the summer, I would help Dad yarding rabbits. At night they came down from the hills through holes in the wire-netting fence to drink and feed. We would put a stone on the post where the hole was, then at midnight we would sneak out and block them in. At daybreak we would drive them, but they couldn't get home and we would shoot and dig them out, getting hundreds of pairs. Sometimes there were so many driven into the burrows, the last ones were smothered.

My father persisted with his horse and cart. In his words, 'It was cheap, didn't bog and the horse could feed while I'm working.' Rabbiting was his life. His only needs were good dogs, ferrets, a sharp penknife and an occasional bottle in the chaff shed. He was the last of the full-time rabbiters in our area.

RABBIT BUSINESS

CATHIE MACARTHUR

My husband's family settled in the heart of rabbit country in the late 1940s. They started off buying the rabbits from whoever went out and caught. Oberon is high on the Blue Mountains in NSW and winters there are very, very cold. Snow covers this icy region for weeks on end. The rabbit-catchers delivered their cache of rabbits to my father-in-law's home and he and his sons gutted, skinned and boned the rabbits before transporting them to Sydney. The meat was to go into factories for making into delicatessen meat such as devon and salami, and the furs to the wool and skin buyers.

Business boomed and Arthur, my father-in-law, built a freezing works so rabbits could be handled and stored in good condition. The family handled up to 25,000 pairs of rabbits per week. For many farmers, catching rabbits was the only way to survive.

Professional rabbit trappers, farmers and prisoners from the nearby prison farm used to bring hundreds, even thousands, of rabbits in and hang them on sticks to await processing. Many times I have gone around knocking the carcasses with a stick to get the maggots out of them.

A large shed was also used to store the rabbit skins; my husband, Ian, and his friends used to have races to see who could skin the rabbit the fastest. Ian remembers skinning 2000 rabbits a day but others could be doing around 2500. The skinners used to sit in this shed skinning for hours, with the windows open and wind, rain and snow blowing through; a hard way to earn pocket money.

I was left to mind the business one day when the family had business away, and I was to receive any rabbits that came. But instead I got a call to go to a tiny village many miles away to collect some. Fine; I could do this as I had a brand-new station wagon, so off I went.

When I met up with the hunter he had quite a lot of rabbits, which we packed into my car. Finding he needed the room the passenger seat was taking, he put the seat-back down and kept on packing the rabbits in. It was getting dark so I started back to Oberon, with the windows open to let in fresh air, as the smell was so strong. The weight in the back made the front of the car very light, so driving was not easy. Snow started falling and the windscreen blades worked hard to give me some sight of the road. I did get home without any accidents, but I decided not to try that again; it took a long time to clear the smell from my lovely new car.

One of my treasured possessions is a rabbit-skin rug which Arthur had made. He collected the very best of the thick winter skins and took them to a furrier who then sorted again and made up the rug using the best of the best rabbit furs.

Amateur shooters with shotguns and rabbits, Winchelsea area, Victoria, circa 1958. Wild European rabbits had first been released in Barwon Park, Winchelsea about 100 years earlier.

LOADED UP, HE NEARLY DROWNED

FRED TUDDENHAM (WOOL CLASSER)

A story about Bob Kerger (Kerg) and his wife, Eva May Kerger (Cook), and their life with rabbits.

My boss, Kerg, and his wife, Cook, worked the rabbits from Birregurra to Geelong and back for some twenty years. Cook was the transporter to markets in Geelong and the supplier of food.

Kerg camped out two to three weeks at a time, trapping and ferreting. He would carry 100 rabbit traps on his back. Once he nearly drowned when he fell into a flooded creek loaded up with traps. He would always go to the owner of a property to ask permission to trap. Sometimes he would get a feed or a cup of tea and was always made welcome. He would shear sheep between shifts.

I recall him telling me about when he went on strike at the Bon Accord Café in Geelong. He and his mate Jordy wanted a raise from a halfpenny a pair to a halfpenny a rabbit. The strike lasted only five minutes – the quickest strike in history!

Kerg could set a trap with one hand. He would start out about 100 yards from the rabbits' warren, moving in about 20 yards at a time, shifting his traps. His theory was the big rabbits were out there, and the little ones he would get next time. He never trapped a fence line or a burrow. It was too easy for foxes to take the catch. He would set two or three traps close together in the hope of getting a fox. Quite often it worked.

Kerg was not allowed to go to war as rabbit trapping and shearing were deemed essential services. Rabbits' felt was made into diggers' slouch hats. Kerg always regretted having to stay home and not going to war with his mates.

Shortly after buying the farm, they got a 3-acre dam made for wildlife. It became home to many types of birds and wildlife. Kerg and Cook neither drank nor smoked and had good health nearly all their lives, eating rabbits for twenty years. Both died in their eighties, and their property sold for a million dollars. They had no children, but always looked after others. Kerg was a great supporter of local football and a great fireman. He had a stainless-steel rabbit trap made to go on his headstone and it is still there thirty years later. And so are the rabbits. I reckon their immune system genetics could be a cure for cancer. Look at how they have survived!

DAD'S MATE DIVI

GARRY KNIGHT

My dad was a prolific hunter of rabbits, using ferrets and nets, and as an eager thirteen-year-old, I was always in tow when a ferreting expedition was underway. So, too, was one of Dad's buddies, Divi Johnson. I knew Divi was not his real name, but it seemed to suit him. According to Dad, Divi had the best ferrets in town.

Divi was a large, rotund man and only ever rode a pushbike, not possessing a car or driver's licence. This may have been just as well, as he enjoyed a beer at the RSL after a hard day's work, and would sometimes admit to Dad that he'd 'had the quota last night, Syd'. Even at my tender age, I knew what this meant.

Divi painted houses for a living and he always wore his trademark paint-stained white bib overalls, even when ferreting, and no matter what the weather. He would walk up and down hills for miles lugging ferrets, nets and rabbits. Often, he would set out alone on his old Malvern Star bicycle, ferret box and nets slung over his shoulder, and long-handled shovel tied with hay band across the handlebars. Fortunately rabbits were plentiful then and he never had to travel too far from town.

He once called in to our place on the way home from a successful day with ten pairs of rabbits strung over the shovel, swaying to and fro as he navigated up our gravel driveway. It was quite a sight to see the bike loaded up, with Divi struggling to steer a straight line because of the weight of the rabbits. The frame creaked and groaned and the tyres on the old bike bulged under the weight. I half-expected them to explode any time, but they never did.

When it came to rabbits, no one knew more than Divi. His ability to assess whether a warren housed bunnies was unmatched, and his ferrets worked hard all day, determined to find any prey that might be hidden away in the warren.

Our best-ever ferret, a black and yellow one, was a doe we purchased from Divi. She was a champion. Quick, agile and she lived to chase rabbits. Sadly, she was bitten by a snake in a burrow and staggered out like she was drunk. She died minutes later and Dad and I each privately shed a tear that day.

Dad had immense respect for Divi, and I followed suit. Anyone who can ride a bike loaded with twenty rabbits swinging from a shovel across the handlebars had to be admired by a lad of thirteen.

WHAT THEY COST THE COUNTRY!

A. PENGLAZE (SUBMITTED BY ANNE MILES)

This is a treasured piece of writing from my relative A. Penglaze.

I was a bit of a trapper myself, but could never hold a candle to Jim. These are a few memories of our trapping days. Rabbits came into Fernbank, Gippsland, Victoria, in 1907. It was a long drought year. The rabbits were over the other side of the Mitchell River before that, but there was always enough water in the river to hold them back. Anyway, they eventually came over and we quickly found out about it.

By 1910 they were everywhere. Trappers were then about in numbers, as well as buyers operating in most railway stations. The price of a pair of rabbits was never much more than one shilling, top price; often less. During the summer months the rabbits were sent to Melbourne each day of the week, but during the winter months and cooler periods they were sent three times a week.

The buyer's name was Arthur Richardson; he bought for Angliss who exported frozen rabbits to England. I have seen 130 crates leave Fernbank in one morning. Each crate held twenty-two pairs of rabbits. That's over 5000 rabbits! This was in the winter period and represented two days' catch. I made a lot of money around that time out of trapping. The general wage at that time was ten shillings and tenpence per day for all bush work. My best catch for one night was fifty-five pairs out of ninety-six traps! Price was one shilling and one penny per pair.

A trapper would check their traps before dark, then again at 10.00 pm and stay up till 2.00 am. I had a kerosene lantern to see by. I remember setting thirty-three traps at one burrow and in the morning getting sixteen pairs.

The rabbits made work for people. But what they cost the country would be impossible to estimate: the wire netting; the fencer; the man to clean up the rabbits inside. The rabbits held their own until myxomatosis came.

RABBITS SO THICK

IAN BRAID

Rabbits were in plague proportions on a property known as Armistead, near Kimberley in Tasmania. Folklore has it that several trappers arrived to catch the vermin. The rabbits were that thick on the ground they had to kill two dozen rabbits to make enough room to put down their traps so that they could start to trap them.

FIVE-STAR SAND HILL'S RESORT

JOHN AND VERA RAYSON

There is nothing easy or glamorous about shooting rabbits and living in outback Australia in the middle of summer. I knew that from the many letters and tapes he had sent me, but my friends and relatives back in Germany thought I was embarking on a great adventure with the love of my life. After my arrival in Australia, in December 1979, we made our way to Naryilco Station in Queensland's Channel Country. His camp was at an outstation 70 kilometres from Naryilco Homestead. There were three more camps scattered around, well away from the noisy diesel motors powering the big chillers which housed the thousands of pairs of frozen rabbits, picked up fortnightly by the rabbit buyer.

On approaching the shooters' camp he said, 'Welcome to five-star Sand Hill's Resort.' My introduction to Clarry, Bluey and Ray was brief; not just because of my limited English, but these were typical Aussie bushies and sceptical of a 'sheila' in their midst. After the introductions it was time for me to inspect my new home. Watching me carefully as I entered his weatherbeaten tent, he said, 'Improvements can be made.' I hoped so, because all it contained was an old army bed, a makeshift table, a camping chair and a one-burner gas cooker. Hanging from a tree branch was a rusty bucket to which a shower head was attached.

I was surprised how easily I adapted to my new home amid sand hills and native vegetation, but I had trouble with the extreme heat, the fine bulldust and gutting rabbits. My job was holding the spotlight, picking up the shot rabbits and throwing them onto the truck. Not used to the heat and working at night, I would fall asleep. Also, the smell of gutting rabbits made me feel sick. He could shoot more rabbits on his own than with my 'big help', so it was decided I should stay at the camp.

Alone with a box of books, one caught my attention. The pictures told the story: rabbits, fence-high; crops and native vegetation eaten away; land once green was now bare. Suddenly I understood why these cute-looking animals were considered a pest in Australia.

Three months later the rabbits got scarcer and skinnier, as myxomatosis had finally caught up with them. No longer able to make a living at Naryilco, the camp was moved to Pine View Station near Broken Hill in NSW, where there were still plenty of rabbits and no myxomatosis.

Not only was the weather becoming more bearable for me but, due to the station owner's kindness by letting us use the showers in the shearers' quarters, life was a little more civilised.

But soon we had to move again. Myxomatosis was rapidly moving in, and by the middle of 1980 we had shifted our camp to Anna Creek Station, near the Simpson Desert. By the end of that year it was all over. Myxomatosis brought me back to urban living.

MY HUSBAND THE BUYER

LORRAINE POLGLAZE

My husband, while travelling around Ivanhoe, NSW, as a rabbit buyer in the late 1950s, regularly collected rabbits from trappers to take them back to Melbourne to sell in the market. On one occasion he called in on one of his regular trappers and his sons, where he was often invited to join with them for a meal. He generally did as he only carried tinned food with him; he always looked forwards to the meal and the company.

The procedure was to first sort the rabbits into pairs to make sure they were suitable for sale. While sorting, he came across a pair that were flyblown. As he threw them aside, the trapper asked what the problem was. My husband said they had turned green. The trapper picked them up, threw them to his son and said, 'Here is another pair for the pot!' My husband spent a couple more years buying, but never ate at this trapper's table again.

THEIR ONLY COMPANION

NORM CRUICKSHANK

In 1930, bunnies went a long way towards saving the sanity of many a poor bugger struggling on starvation rations. But the farmers were driven mad as they dragged millions from their burrows with the help of those with a trap.

Skins were sold to buyers at the roadside each week for a shilling a pound, and fashion wearers paid a little more for lustrous fox tails undamaged by gunshot.

Steel traps set flat in shallow, soft earth beside a burrow spelled rabbit hell: hair-triggers locking teeth onto legs when stood upon. Men shouldered bags of heavy traps across hill and dale, their only companion by necessity a well-trained dog. Trapping, skinning, cleaning and drying hides during frosty cold winters remained a bloody hard slog when sold for small reward.

Boundary riders Ovens and team, Dromedary Hills, Western Australia, 1926.

Chiselling a shallow hole, gently covering the trap's deadly teeth with a piece of paper and a light sprinkle of earth fooled Br'er Bunny as steel jaws claimed another victim.

Half-asleep trappers yawning to be home in a nice warm bed sat out the night by the light of a small fire, their dog-eared mate ever alert. Stumbling over rough ground in the low light of a smoky old hurricane lamp, his seeing 'ears and eyes' four-legged friend responded to a quiet pat and hushed 'thanks' as a small reward.

After collecting an early first few, there was time for a bit of 'shut-eye' on Mother Earth's bloody hard ground, as close to the fire as possible, an old grey blanket offering small comfort. All too soon a billy of tea was brewing from a few grey ashes, as dawn's fitful hour arrived; then time for getting out and about with the dingo and fox breakfasting on bunny, though luckily the night is good and the count worthwhile.

A well-worn pocketknife from off the belt peels the bunny from his winter wear, which is then stretched wide on a U-shaped bow of number 10 fencing wire, then days in the sun, and a family of hungry kids in the neighbourhood eat meat and survive.

THE OTHER SIDE OF THE STORY

VAL LIGHTBODY

1949: Nihill and Vera Lightbody decided to get out of the rat race in Melbourne and move to Kerang in northern Victoria to live. Nihill was a refrigeration mechanic who hoped to establish a refrigeration sales and service business from his new home. An acquaintance, Jack McCraith, heard Nihill was moving to the country and asked if he would put one of his rabbit chillers in his premises; Jack would supply a truck for Nihill to establish a rabbit run to collect the fresh rabbits from the farms on specific days. One day he would travel to

Sandhill Lake and the Lake Charm area; another to Appin. This proved to be a very satisfactory arrangement. Word spreads very quickly in a small country town. People were soon arriving with their rabbits. Men who worked for the Lands Department called after work, farmers came and at weekends the local lads would be out having fun with their ferrets and nets to make a few shillings pocket money – their transport, bicycles! They would receive one shilling and sixpence for a pair of rabbits. Everyone was happy to receive a supplement to their income. This would be fifteen cents today. The adult wage may only have been three pounds ten shillings or so a week, which would be seven dollars today. The rabbits were not to be caught by dogs as that would cause bruising.

1952: Nihill and Vera's son Ron came to town to join the family, he had just finished his apprenticeship in Melbourne as an electrician and Dad hoped they would be successful business partners. Nihill and Vera decided to go on a six-week trip to Cairns and leave Ron to collect the rabbits and look after the home. I had known Vera for the time they had been in Kerang, through my employment. She encouraged Ron to meet me and then through local dances we became friendly. Unfortunately, Nihill was involved in a fatal accident. Vera returned to Kerang. Ron had kept the rabbit run going and Vera took over on her return. The rabbit run was the beginning of Ron's electrical business as the farmers he called on had heard of the new equipment for farmers called '12-volt' or '32-volt' lighting plants. This was the beginning of the business *R. S. Lightbody – Electrician – Kerang*.

1954: Ron and I married. Later that year, due to the rabbits being under control, Mr McCraith no longer felt it viable to keep the chiller in Kerang; the end of an era. Mr McCraith had numerous chillers in northern Victoria and southern NSW; he was a very successful exporter and known as 'the Rabbit King'.

LIFE THEN

MRS SHIRLEY MAYFIELD

When I was twelve years old, in 1950, my dad got a job at Werai Station, 30 miles from Deniliquin in NSW, to help control the rabbits on the property. We were living in an old caravan pulled by a Chev ute. Our family consisted of my mum, who was pregnant at the time, Dad and my older brother Jim, who was fourteen. We arrived at Echuca on an evening in January, and went out to Werai the next day.

Dad started work and we moved into the shearers' quarters 3 miles from the homestead. We were given two cows for Mum to milk; most of the milk going in to the homestead. Jim and I would help Dad with the rabbiting. He had a group of eight dogs to chase down the rabbits. The dogs were a motley crew, ranging from a greyhound and a whippet to a cocker spaniel. One day when they were chasing rabbits the cocker spaniel ran under a tree and caught his back on a branch. He ripped the skin open for about 6 inches, and Mum had to sew him together with a strong thread.

The shearers' quarters were very basic. There was no stove, so Mum had to cook in a camp oven over the open fire. We slept in the long row of shearers' rooms. The dogs were fed on boiled rabbit. These were cooked in a 4-gallon tin hung over the fire. I spent a fair bit of time skinning the rabbits and stretching the skins on wire frames to sell for pocket money. When the skins were eventually sold, I only received a few shillings for them as they were infested with weevils.

We spent a couple of months catching rabbits with the dogs and then, as the rabbits were so bad, the bosses decided to put out 1080 poison. Several of the workers dug a huge hole measuring about 3 metres square, by the same depth. We helped to run out the trails of poisoned carrots and then took several days with the horse and cart going around picking up dead rabbits. When we filled the cart we would take them to the hole and throw them in. By the time we finished, the hole was nearly full of rabbits. While at Werai Station, Jim and I continued with our correspondence schooling.

Mum went into Deniliquin to have the baby. Heavy rain fell over the next few days and we were flooded in. Werai was cut off from Deniliquin. We were surrounded by water and could not even get to the homestead. On the twenty-third of March Mum returned home with the mailman. The roads were still flooded, but he knew the way so well, he was able to get through. Baby brother Robert was ten days old. After the flood went down, the mozzies came in huge numbers and Dad decided to leave Werai. We moved out on the ninth of April and our rabbiting days were over.

'THERE'S A QUID IN RABBIT SKINS'

HARRY HILL

At the start of 1944 I obtained a job as office boy with a local business. It was to be a permanent position and if I did a correspondence course in accountancy I was assured I'd rise in status and remuneration. After about two months I received word that I'd been awarded a Teacher Trainee Scholarship by the NSW Department of Education, but I wouldn't start the course until June.

I thought I should advise the business manager that I'd be leaving in a couple of months. His reply was a bit alarming: 'No you won't. I took you on as a permanent employee. You'll leave at the end of the week. I want someone I can rely on.' Thus, I found myself out of work with no cash flow – quite a predicament for a seventeen-year-old.

After a football game I made my situation known to my teammates. One, Jim, said, 'There's a quid in rabbit skins.' Jim lived on a dairy farm about 3 miles out of town and, as his presence on the farm was not essential, he suggested we set up a rabbit trapping camp. He knew where there was a farm crawling with rabbits and he'd get the owner's approval.

We pooled our camping and trapping resources – a tent and fly; setter and axe; rabbit bows; cooking and eating utensils; blankets and food; about forty rabbit traps; and my dog, a fox terrier called Digger whose life revolved around rabbits.

We had to get to the trapping site which was on Sandy Creek, about 13 miles from town. My gear was taken out to the farm when Jim came in to football training and from there everything was loaded into a horse-drawn sulky which continued the trip. Jim's brother came with us on horseback and returned with the horse and sulky.

Jim and I needed the rest of the day to cut tent poles, erect the tent and fly, then cut more poles to knock up pole-and-corn-bag beds for both of us. We had just enough time to walk up the creek and assess the trapping potential. What we saw delighted us: warrens, burrows and dunghills everywhere; rabbits popping down burrows and scuttling into the scrub. We were so impressed that we raced back to camp and collected about a dozen traps to get them set before it was dark. Digger was in ecstasy and I promised him fresh rabbit for his breakfast.

After a feed we sat in the firelight talking and making prophesies. Our reverie was shattered by a terrible howling and commotion coming from further up the creek. I looked for Digger. He was missing. A lantern was lit and we hurried towards the noise. As expected, Digger was caught in a trap. He'd been unable to control his rabbit killing urge and had gone to check the trap line. He was embarrassed but not badly hurt. I let him out of the trap and he alternated in licking his injured foot and apologising to me by licking me. In case he had another lapse I tied him up for the night.

Early next morning we went round the traps to find that our catch in twelve traps was nil. Two more traps had been sprung and all the other traps were exactly as we had set them. We moved the whole forty traps further up the creek and set them in the most ideal of locations.

I watched Jim setting a trap and was a bit surprised to find he was lacking in the finer points of trap-setting. It was necessary to support the plate of the trap to stop it activating while being carefully covered with fine dirt. This was done by poking a finger under the jaw and supporting the plate. When the finger was removed, there was a small hole in the dirt that had to be filled in. Jim used a small stick to do this.

My father, a 'professional' rabbit trapper, had shown me how to use the side of my little finger to brush some dirt into the hole. I thought I should show Jim how to do it. When I was sure I had his full attention I demonstrated. Result – the trap sprung, I got a face full of dirt and my little finger was between the trap jaws. Jim thanked me for my coaching.

The next morning our feelings were a mix of apprehension and anticipation. We became glum as we checked the trap line. We had provided a meal for a hawk or eagle (part of a rabbit still in the trap), another meal for a fox (severed foot still in the trap and heaps of fur), but we did get two rabbits.

There was little improvement for the rest of the week. Our total catch was less than twenty rabbits. The rabbits had become 'trap shy': from recent trappings they had picked up enough knowledge to avoid traps. We then found that all our skins were flyblown. Remedy: put the skins on an ants nest and allow the ants' to help themselves to the maggots.

After a week of testing the theory 'There's a quid in rabbit skins' I surrendered my share to Jim and went to Sydney to be trained in an occupation that actually paid a quid.

TROTTING ON

PAULINE PENINGTON BROWN

I was expecting a proposal of marriage, but instead he told me he was off to Gippsland to fight the rabbit plague. It was 1947 and I had lost my heart on the practice putting green at General Motors, Fisherman's Bend, to my Second World War hero. He'd been wounded at Bardia then, after discharge, was an RAAF rear air-gunner with a NEI squadron in the Pacific area. He had dreams of

Two men processing rabbit meat at McGrath's, Melbourne, 1957. Australia had so many wild rabbits that a thriving industry grew quickly, employing many.

adventure, plus he was sure he'd earn more money than the draftsman's wage he earned from 'the General'. That rabbit plague nearly wrecked my marriage plans, but in the end I had more staying power than the rabbits.

The truth was that Keith had aspirations to become a farmer, and catching rabbits seemed like a good way to get started. According to Keith, the most economical transport would be horse and wagon (he'd joined a Lighthorse Militia unit at fifteen years of age and knew horse management), so he bought Captain the horse, a wagon and camping equipment. The problem was, when all set to go, no rabbit traps were available. Finally the 'trapper' was helped by a disbelieving but influential acquaintance finding some in Tasmania and having them flown to Melbourne in a hurry.

It was my privilege to be taken on a few trial journeys. Keith lived in Black Rock and I was at Brighton, so in those days we didn't have to venture far in most directions to come upon bushy parts. Sadly, Captain foundered and was replaced by Toby – beware the dodgy horse-dealer! Eventually the day came to depart for Foster, where Keith had arranged with a farmer to clear rabbits. He promised to write and left his golf clubs with me, so if he needed money I could sell them and send a postal order. No way would I have sold them. I was determined we'd have a few more rounds together.

It took the wagoner much longer to get to Foster than anticipated. When the hills were too steep he unloaded part of the cargo, drove Toby and the wagon to the top, then walked back and carried the load up himself! Friends of mine who had set out for a day trip to Gippsland the day after Keith left told me that not far from Dandenong they passed him going, and saw him again when they were coming home; he hadn't made much progress. Undeterred, Keith and Toby trotted on.

Unfortunately the trapping wasn't exactly successful. The farmer turned out to be a 'mean old bugger', he had a fierce bull that had to be avoided, the weather was lousy and the rabbits scarce. However, always hopeful, Keith packed up and went down to Fish Creek where he felled timber with his prized Plumb axe, but before long headed for home. Toby and the rabbit traps were left with good people. His wagon and possessions were trucked home, and Keith took a drafting job on the Thompson Dam project.

Later, when married and playing golf again at General Motors, he told me the Thompson Dam would mean Melbourne would never again be short of water. Like elimination of the rabbits with myxomatosis, and the war to end all wars, that proved to be wrong too.

LIVING OFF A PEST

DAMIEN VELLA

We headed due north towards Kyneton in Victoria's Macedon Ranges. We drove out of town and turned left at Barron's shop about 4 miles out. Our final stop was another mile at a place called Resedale Junction. Mum was horrified: 'Where have you brought me to?' That was her only comment! We had arrived in Australia.

Dad and his cousin trapped and ferreted in the areas of Baynton, Mia Mia, Pipers Creek and Pyalong. They would be invited by the farmer of a particular property to trap and keep the rabbits down. This they tried to do with 200 steel rabbit traps. The vehicle used was a 1926 single-seater Chevrolet which he had converted into a utility.

Dad had a system as to how he conducted his trapping. They would start to lay the traps along selected fence lines at about 5.30 pm. Then between 11.30 pm and 1.00 am they would clear the evening run. The next morning, starting about 5.30 am they would clear the fence line of all the rabbits and traps. Bleeding, gutting and cleaning then took place and the rabbits were hung under a tree covered in long hessian bagging. The next part of their system was to work the same area with the ferrets until 1.00 pm. Another system of trapping was the Rabbit Drive. Every year one was conducted to raise money for the schools.

The rabbit price varied from one shilling a pair to a very high price of two shillings and sixpence a pair. At the top end of the price Dad used to be very pleased and in later years use to say that they sometimes made twenty-two pounds in a week and it was the biggest wage he earned in those times.

The rabbit was and still is a very serious pest to the man on the land. However, at the same time this pest enabled some people to survive during the Depression and also gave our family a start in Australia. I don't remember how many times a week we ate rabbit, but it was there most of the time.

EVEN WORSE THAN SHEARERS

GLORIA JARICK

'A story about rabbits? I'll have to think about that,' the ex-shearer and rabbit trapper replied. Without any thinking, though, he said, 'You know, Uncle Jerry and Ronnie are long since dead. But they were trappers. It was the middle of summer; it was bloody hot, it was. But it didn't stop them. Rabbit trappers were the scum of the bush in those days; even worse than shearers! If you didn't have two bob to rub together you'd go trapping.

'Ronnie and Jerry built their rabbit cart out of an old wooden crate. Refined it they did, even had supports for the bicycle wheels and made wooden shafts. It carried their traps or the rabbits. It must have been the middle of summer, because it was bloody hot. Ronnie managed to get a couple of days with a Pastures Protection Board to gas rabbits. This was Queensland, y'see.

'It couldn't be done today of course, but he was given canisters of poisonous gas. I just can't remember the name of the gas, but it was bloody poisonous. He had to put holes in the canisters and put them down the burrows, then block the opening to the burrow. There was no protective gear in those days, nothing. Anyways, Ronnie just blocked the burrows. Don't know what he did with those canisters. Probably threw them in un-punctured. The name of the gas will come to me in a minute. It was easy for Ronnie and Jerry to trap those rabbits. They thought it was pretty good lurk. Everyone was happy. The P. P. Board got its rabbits killed. Ronnie got paid for killing them, and Ronnie and Jerry got paid a second time for the rabbit skins.'

TRAPPERS' TRICKS

FRANK McCARTHY

After Australia came under the influence of the rabbit, the financial pendulum swung away from the landed gentry towards the battlers. The end of 1948 saw the creation of a government marketing scheme known as the Australian Rabbit Skin Board to stabilise and allow fair money to the trapper, dealer, broker, exporter, hat manufacturer and fur dresser.

In 1938 and 1939 the quantity of rabbit skins exported from Australia was 4,433,000 pounds at a value of £429,000. In the five years ending 1947/1948 exports averaged 12,650,000 pounds, representing £5 million in value. But many of the skins were used in Australia by Akubra and other hat manufacturers, therefore were not included in these figures. Also not taken into account were the frozen rabbits exported to the United Kingdom.

I had a six-year involvement in the rabbit trade, buying rabbits from trappers from Lamaroo (South Australia) across to Foster

(Gippsland, Victoria). I used to sell rabbits to Jack McCraith, Frank Simmonds, George Dohr, Dave Mullholland, A. McCarty, Harry Portelli, Smorgons and Borthwicks. Jack McCraith was the first to introduce the mobile rabbit freezer to the trade. He had seventy-three freezers in Victoria, sixty-five in South Australia and forty-eight in NSW. In 1949, McCraith exported 205,000 crates, or 6 million rabbits, to England. Jack McCraith ceased operations, as the bureaucracy made it too difficult to operate; this from a man who in thirty years exported 130 million rabbits to England.

Trappers were very cunning men. One old chap I knew carried a pickle bottle with him and upon gutting a doe (female) rabbit, he would inspect her bladder, any fluid was saved in the bottle, sometimes collecting half a bottle full. When next setting up his traps, he would sprinkle some of this female urine to attract the buck rabbits.

There were many trap manufacturers: Lanes Ace, Downey, Bunyip, and Tonks to name a few. In the early 1950s, Angus McKenzie had three commercial diesel semitrailers transporting frozen rabbits from Hawker, Copley, Lyndhurst and Flinders Ranges for Smorgons. They would do a trip each per week.

BREEDING LIKE RABBITS

MURIEL BIRD

I married my late husband, Stewart, in 1949 and as his lawful wife I followed him with his work. After marriage Stewart found his early work as a rouseabout and rabbit trapper on the Ball family's station at Bowmans Creek, near Singleton, NSW. We settled into a work cottage on the property and Stewart went about his tasks. As the rabbit population began to soar, Bowmans Creek became our base, and from there we travelled to other Ball properties at Upper Rouchel and Rouchel Brook. On these properties, Stewart and I camped in huts, and Stewart's sole occupation became 'rabbit trapper'.

The days (and months) living in these huts were solitary – Stewart's day started before daylight and he returned to the hut after dark. Stewart would rise and have breakfast, saddle up and pack his two faithful horses, Dodger and Blue, before setting off on his rabbit run with his two dogs, Pat and Mick and a packed lunch. The rabbit run would involve checking 120 rabbit traps, killing the trapped rabbits (usually by screwing and cracking their necks – Stewart didn't have a gun) and resetting the traps. As Stewart dismounted from his horse to check the traps, he could just drop the reins and the quiet horses would stand and wait patiently for their master. The horses had 'wallets' across their backs, which were two corn bags sewn together. This was where the dead rabbits were kept until Stewart returned to the hut.

Seeing a white bunny's tail bobbing up and down from a distance was a good indication of a rabbit trapped. Another indicator was a squealing rabbit. If any rabbit managed to escape from a trap as Stewart tried to retrieve it, the two dogs were waiting and ready to pounce. It was important for Stewart to remember the landmarks and location of his traps (trying to find a trap in the bush is similar to trying to find a needle in a haystack!). The two dogs must have had a good idea of trap locations, as neither of them ever got caught in a trap.

On returning to the hut, using a kerosene lantern to provide light, Stewart would painstakingly skin the rabbits with his pocketknife and bow them out to dry (we had special shaped wire bows for this purpose). Skinning the rabbits provided extra income, as we were able to sell the skins to a hide and skin buyer (P. C. Bird at Newcastle) – it was about a pound (two dollars) for a pound of good skins. And there were about six to seven skins in a pound. Quality was determined by the thickness of the fur – the thicker the better.

As areas were cleared of rabbits, we would use a mattock to fill in the old rabbit burrows. We did the best we could with the simple tools that we had (no machines those days). Filling in burrows was an important task as it reduced the likelihood of valued horses and cattle laming themselves. Once this task was complete, Stewart would set his traps in a new area.

I rarely did the rabbit run with Stewart as the days were long and slow and I was expecting my first child. So instead my days were spent in the single-room hut, with no power or phone. The hut had one bed, a small table, a cupboard and a few chairs. If the nights

Jack with rabbits, 1932.

were cold we would pull a few extra corn bags over us to keep warm. I spent my time washing (all by hand in a tub), writing letters to family, knitting and crocheting. If I needed food supplies I would travel by horseback. All my cooking was done outside. I had a small fireplace protected by an old water tank. Here I cooked vegetables, meat and sweets. Our meat was stored in a meat safe, keeping it free from blowflies. We also had 'bully beef' (tinned meat) and powdered milk. There was a small water tank on the hut, otherwise we carried a water bag or got water from the dams or creek if we wanted to boil the billy. Of an evening I would be waiting for Stewart's safe return. And it was only when I could hear the sound of the horse's hoof or Stewart's whistling that I knew that all was well. I knew, however, that his day was not over – there was rabbit skinning to be done!

I'll never forget the sight of the rabbits moving in masses over the then dry and barren ground. They were just everywhere. The rabbit breeding flourished in the drought conditions. The term 'breeding like rabbits' literally existed. The rabbit population was out of control.

There was no grass around because the rabbits would nibble it off at the roots as soon as it grew. During these desperate times it was decided that we would use poison – strychnine, I guess – to kill some rabbits. We dug up black thistle roots and cut them into inch-length pieces. We put these into 7-pound treacle tins with sugar and poison (and other ingredients that I can no longer remember) and placed it out for the rabbits to eat. I can remember on this one morning finding 580 dead rabbits. They were lying everywhere. We then had the task of heaping them up in a pile for Stewart to skin and bow out. What a sight – a memory I'll never forget!

We never owned a vehicle in those days, so we rarely got to see our relatives or friends. Our living conditions were basic – but I guess what we never had we never missed. There were no neighbours close by; it was a lonely existence. If we needed to use a phone we had to ride to the nearest post office.

There is a saying: 'Rabbit is a poor man's cattle.' I never put rabbit on the menu – Stewart had seen enough rabbits without having to see it served up on his dinner plate at night. Rabbit trapping was our life for over nine years. Our living conditions improved as we moved from one property to another (and my two girls were born). But eventually, in 1959, we finally moved onto better things – our own property and our own cattle! Fifty years later I'm still on this same property and still with dairy cattle and I'm not too proud to say that rabbit trapping was our mere beginnings.

2.

BOY RABBITERS AND FURRY POCKET MONEY

The stories in this chapter are 'Boy's own' tales, many are of childhoods that were so different from those of today, and are so eagerly remembered and re-told that they become favourites. It is obvious that each of these stories rates highly in the author's memory, perhaps because they tell of times and freedoms unavailable to kids of today or perhaps because they hold such a rich sensory load that they take the reader and the teller on a wonderful journey, one that almost makes the rabbit seem a defining influence on the Australian culture and on mateship, inventiveness and the bush experience.

You might want to keep these stories out of your kids' and grandkids' hands – they might feel ripped off at having missed the amazing adventures their dads and granddads got up to, that they have no chance of re-creating or experiencing. When a kid could earn as much as his teacher did in a week, through setting rabbit traps before and after school, there had to be something to what these kids were doing for the economy, let alone for their own sense of business and enterprise, or for the environment.

These experiences are so different from those of the current day that you could hardly call them childhoods. These memories are very much cherished, more for the remembrance of freedom, of a young boy's important place in the world and of the wild passage from boy to man that many might find wanting in more modern times. They are great to reflect on, as they tell just how unique the Australian boyhood was in the times of the rabbit plagues.

Images of young boys with guns bring to mind the horrors of warfare, and the recruiting of the very young to wars and terrorism. Far from those places and these times, boys as young as eight across Australia experienced rites of passage rich in meaning, growth and value. Many will make you wince at the situations young boys found themselves in. You might marvel at their inventiveness and daring as well.

The freedoms of the time, the responsibilities taken on by so many young fellows, on their own or with brothers, mates and cousins, and with or without their dads or uncles; these are stories well worth the asking about and telling. Many of the storytellers would never swap their boyhoods for those of today's kids. After reading these stories, I'll bet you'll agree.

WHAT TO EAT WITH RABBIT – THE WEEDY SHOPPING LIST

RODNEY GALAGHER

My mother often said, 'I brought those boys up on anything that the rabbits wouldn't eat.' It was a most interesting cuisine, when I look back on it. My mother came from the genteel circles of Sydney; a dentist's daughter, but an adventurous type, who went out west to marry a grazier and become the lady of a 'squatter's homestead'. But that soon evaporated in the mid-1930s. She found herself the unpaid shearers' cook. She had to learn very quickly how to make bread, milk a cow and set a rabbit trap. People who survived the Depression, wars and the rabbit plague learned to be very resourceful and to make do, and that included what we ate and what the inventive cook could put on the table.

Mum was a great believer in green vegetables. It was an extraordinary shopping list when I look back on it, even though we were 25 miles from a shop. Firstly, there was pig weed, a succulent plant with a sprawling habit, red-coloured stalks and fleshy green leaves. Boiled and served with a butter sauce, it was a good substitute for beans or spinach.

Then there were stinging nettles. We boys would be sent to gather these pesky little things. Fresh new growth was boiled up as a side vegetable and was a good addition to soups and stews. Very nutritious (or so we were told!). Fat hen was another. I don't recommend it!

Scotch thistle buds: gathering and preparing them was painful, but when you have peeled all the prickles off, the heart of the thistle bud is extraordinarily like a small artichoke. Served with butter sauce or simply steamed with celery salt, they are beautiful.

Asparagus: we were fortunate that much of our property was part of the western goldfields of Victoria. Prospectors' huts often had their own gardens of herbs, flowers, vegetables and fruit trees, long deserted and subsequently gone wild. Asparagus was one of the survivors! When we were out mustering or trapping, we brought home asparagus, growing wild. It was usually eaten raw as a salad vegetable. The rabbits didn't appear to like it.

Prickly pear was another curse, waiting for the introduction of the *Cactoblastis* moth, just as the rabbits were waiting for the introduction of myxomatosis. But in the meantime, can we eat it? Prickly pear has a sweet, purple-coloured fruit, so mother devised a way of singeing the prickles off in the firebox of the fuel stove. They then could be skinned and boiled up. She served prickly pear with rice, prickly pear jam and prickly pear jelly, which we called 'Purple Slime'. (Sorry, Mum!) But she did raise us on everything that the rabbits wouldn't eat, and gave us a set of values to live by. 'Eat what is put in front of you and be grateful.' Thanks, Mum.

TRAINING THE TRAPPERS

HARRY HILL

'Where are we, Dad?'

The man and his two sons stopped. 'There's the Southern Cross, so we're heading south, and those four bumps on the skyline, that's Pine Mountain. The big bump, to the left, that's the Bald Hill.'

We didn't need assurance. We had complete faith in our father's ability to get us to his line of fifty traps that were about a mile from the house. My brother and I were intent on learning. We were Dad's apprentice rabbit trappers. It was 1938, mid-winter, extremely cold, the sky starlit.

'Be careful here. It's that steep bit dropping into that rocky gully. If there's not much water we should be able to step across it.' Five minutes later we ran into a fence. 'Follow the fence, past two strainer posts and when we get to a dogleg there's a fence prop that we can use to get over the fence. The first trap is just a couple of minutes further on.' There was a rabbit in the first trap. 'You can light the lantern now.' Up till then Dad had considered it to be a waste of kerosene to have the lantern alight.

We moved from trap to trap. One a bit to the left, the next one straight ahead, further out to one on a burrow, a right turn to one on a dunghill. Then 50 yards to three traps on a warren. Occasionally, the rattle of a trap chain was a guide for us. Dad didn't need any guiding; he had a map of his trap line in his head. 'The next trap is on a dunghill, just past a kurrajong. It's a bunyip trap and more than likely has a big buck in it.'

Rabbits were removed from traps, had their necks wrung and dropped into one of our shoulder bags. Rather than feelings of pity, sorrow or guilt, each dead rabbit received our approval and thanks. Traps that held rabbits, or had been sprung, were reset. We reset some of the traps with Dad ready to give advice, but only if he thought a trap was going to 'spring' and pelt dirt in our faces.

Halfway along the trap line there would be a stop to skin the rabbits we had caught. Dad took about ten seconds to do the knife work on a rabbit then we pulled the skin off, just like removing a sock. If a rabbit squealed ahead of us we all thought, 'If that one is in a trap we'd better get to it before a fox does.' When we turned for home, if we had twenty skins in our bags we were happy; thirty skins, we were very happy.

We knew the sounds of the night – the throat-clearing of a brush-tailed possum, a mournful mopoke, the cough of a fox, or a dad to answer our 'What's that?'

Dad died before the next winter. He was away shearing and was found dead in his bunk. If he had happened to be thinking of it, his sons' progress as rabbit trappers would have made him pleased.

BUSH-BOILED RABBIT

GARTH DIXON

I was eleven years old in the summer of 1935 and living with my uncle Henry's extended family. It was Depression time and life on the farm was hard. In the hotter months we couldn't kill a sheep because we had no cooler in which to keep mutton. So we lived on rabbit: boiled; stewed; minced; fried; curried; roasted; devilled;

battered – any kind of rabbit Aunty Jane could dream up. Aunty Jane claimed that she could make rabbit taste like chicken.

After several summers I developed a great hatred of rabbit. I often smelt of rabbit, I had skinned and gutted so many. I remember a permanent smell of rabbit under my fingernails. But there was a bright side. I was given the job of shooting the rabbits; only young rabbits and only head shots. Shooting rabbits was the highlight of my life.

It was on one such mission that I disturbed an unexpected resident. About 20 yards away a wrinkled, grizzled man, a bundle of rags, motioned me impatiently towards him. I overcame fear and obeyed. He had a camp of sorts, mainly bags propped up by eucalyptus branches. A small billy can was bubbling over a low fire. In it was half a rabbit, skinned except for the feet, its hind legs projecting into the air. The water only half covered it. The dirty parchment white of the cooking part contrasted sharply with the raw, pinky crimson of the uncooked part. The boiling water was a murky red.

He sat down on a log by the fire. 'Have some dinner,' he commanded. He communicated mainly by grimace, grunt or gesture. Depression and perhaps madness afflicted him; who knows what else. He had found the world too difficult; had been defeated too many times. I was nervous. I wanted to leave quickly but he demanded by animated gesture that I stay. He left me standing, motioned agitatedly when I made any move. I became even more nervous.

Then came dinner: he picked the rabbit out of the billy, tore it apart and gave me one portion, a hind leg. Three-quarters of it was cooked. The remainder was that dirty, pinky crimson. I had to eat it. I was afraid not to. Bush-boiled rabbit with no salt, pepper or sauce, with fur the only addition, was a less than inviting proposition. I took a bite and chewed on it slowly and delicately to postpone having to take a second bite. After a while my host threw his portion into the fire. I took the cue and quickly followed suit. It didn't offend him, he didn't seem to notice. I took my leave without his acknowledgement or protest.

I need not have been afraid of that wreck of a man. I shot my quota and went home to another dose of Aunty Jane's rabbit dressed up as chicken. It didn't taste too bad.

BACK TO BRIAGALONG

MARGARET ROWE

It was 1929. Dad, the late Richard (Dick) Wigmore, was a young man of about eighteen growing up in The Patch, which is a little place in the Dandenong Ranges just out from Melbourne in Victoria. He lived with his parents and five sisters on a small acreage, where they grew berries and other fruit for market.

Jobs were scarce for young lads at that time so Dick and his mate Harry Pride decided to travel to Briagalong in East Gippsland, where Harry's uncle owned a farm. He had told the boys they were welcome to camp on the farm for as long as they wished, to trap rabbits and split posts.

Dick and Harry loaded up a wagon with gear and of course plenty of rabbit traps then, after harnessing up the horse, together with the dog they set off for Briagalong. The journey took several days, the boys camping by the roadside each night. On arrival at Briagalong they located the farm and then set about building themselves a two-room bark hut complete with a fireplace. Dad said that it might have been a bit roughly built, but the hut provided them with warmth and shelter over the duration of their stay.

Next the two lads set their traps. This was quite a task as they would have to go around the traps twice a day, morning and night. Dad told me a few of the nearby farmers lost a bit of wire from their fences occasionally, because the boys had to peg out the skins. Once a week the two lads would take the horse and wagon and the dog into town where they would sell the rabbit skins and stock up on a few supplies.

Dick and Harry also split ironbark posts, which was really hard work. The posts were so hard that the sap had to be grooved out with an axe before they could be split. Harry and Dick enjoyed their time on the farm, although Dick remarked that he could not look at a rabbit for years after and neither could the old dog, rabbit being the main source of protein in their diet for months. A letter from Dick's mother back at The Patch arrived, asking them to come home. Not long after that the two lads packed up and set off for home.

Years later, in 2004, my husband took my father to Briagalong as a surprise so he could see how the little town had fared. Dad was thrilled to be back for the first time since 1929. When I was growing up in The Patch, I can remember Dad taking the rifle down to the bottom paddock. Not long after he would come back with a rabbit for our dinner. My brother and I really enjoyed rabbit either baked or braised by our mother.

FIRST KILL

GAVIN LOCK

There are four hairs on my chin the first time Pop lets me shoot. We are walking up the hill one morning, and he's just finishing bending the arm of the float on a leaking water trough. I am thumbing my whiskers, looking alternately at the rifle we have with us and at the sunlit dew hanging off the spiders' webs that straddle, for entire rows, beheaded stalks of the crop.

Pop notices me, and sets up a small rock on top of a larger one some thirty paces away. 'Let's see if you can't knock him off then,' he says, handing over the rifle. I load a round with the bolt and take aim, locking the butt into my shoulder as I have observed on countless occasions, and look through the telescopic sight. 'That's it, nice and steady now,' Pop encourages. Taking care not to snatch at the trigger, but to squeeze it gently, I am surprised it doesn't fire. I try again, with the same result. I look over at Pop, who raises his eyebrows and I remember: the safety catch. I chastise myself before re-aiming and the rock falls before the weapon sounds. 'Nice shootin', Deadeye Dick,' Pop says. After knocking it over twice more, we continue walking.

I spot a rabbit that is busy licking its front paws at the base of a massive lichen-covered rock, and receive the rifle again. 'Hit him and we'll go out spotlightin' tonight,' Pop says as incentive. Looking through the sight, the rabbit's magnified head is enormous; too large to miss – almost unfair. I fire, hear the bullet zip home and the rabbit slowly keels over onto its side. We walk over to inspect it and find that I have literally blown its brain out of its ear. Both of its eyes hang outside their sockets. 'First kill. Well done,' Pop says, patting me on the shoulder.

He keeps his word, and later that night I prepare to shoot from the open window of the ute. Pop, from the driver's seat, explains the intricacies of aiming: 'Line it up naturally; don't muscle it. Breathe in, you aim low. Breathe out, you aim high. When you're ready, take a breath in and let it out slowly, till you're dead on. Then fire.' It is sound advice, as out of the nine and a half pairs that I go on to shoot, all but two need a solo bullet. Each of the troublesome pair refuses to sit still long enough for me to get a definite first shot, but both succumb to the second.

TEXAS ON A SATURDAY

JIM PURVIS

As a young boy, living on a Texas, Queensland, property, I was involved with the rabbit plague at its worst.

I used to set half-a-dozen traps after school. I would run them after tea with a hurricane light, and before school in the morning. I would probably catch three or four, then gut them, put them on the handlebars of my bike, and take them 3 miles to the Texas Freezing Works (no bitumen roads then). There I would be paid up to sixpence a pair for them. I would then go to school.

Weekends I would set twenty or so traps; I would skin and sell the skins on Saturday. The kids of Texas made good pocket money in that era. The Texas Freezing Works in 1930 was reported as having processed 30,000 rabbits in the first fortnight of operation, and that they would be exporting 3 tons of rabbits daily. Later the rabbits were made into tins of bully beef and camp pie for the soldiers in the war, and the skins for their hats.

My father used to poison them. He would feed boiled wheat, molasses and other secret ingredients to them in a freshly dug trail for two nights, then mix strychnine with the mixture and lay it out on the third night. My brother and I would be up before daylight to help gather the dead rabbits before we went to school. I remember some mornings it was so cold and frosty, we would skin the first two rabbits we came to, turn the skins inside out, and wear them as gloves. We would probably gather up to a hundred from each trail. My father would skin them and stretch the skins to dry on a bow made from number 8 fencing wire.

On Saturdays there would be up to seven skin buyers in Texas. I remember Dad got ten bob a pound once. With about five skins to the pound, this was good money in those days. This was mostly cash money, so pubs and shops did well. There were a lot of mortgages and debts paid off from rabbits. People would get up to 100 rabbits every night from trapping and poisoning. There just didn't seem to be any end to them.

I remember one weekend I had my mare loaded up with about twenty traps and I was setting them when the traps must have pinched the skin on my horse; next thing she took off, pigrooting. Traps went flying everywhere. About two hours later I managed to find most of the traps and caught my horse and continued setting.

Looking back, these were exciting times for us kids. There was also the shooting of the rabbits. I remember once I had my .22 rifle and my brother had Dad's double-barrel shotgun. He sat on a termites' nest, aimed the gun at a couple of rabbits and accidentally pulled both triggers at once. The blast was deafening. The recoil blew him clean off the nest. He was about twelve at the time so he probably had a pretty sore shoulder for a while. I don't think he hit the rabbits either, but he sure gave them a heck of a fright.

Early in the 1950s, myxo was introduced and that was the end of the rabbit plagues as we knew them. The cash flow from rabbits had dried up at Texas.

BLUE'S TALE

RON NEWLING

My father was recalled to the family dairy farm in late 1946. He was on a third share with his sister and their parents. The farm was reasonably large – 310 acres of mixed soils, from beautiful black soil river flat back to gravelly ridge. In those days they relied solely on rainwater. There was no tractor; they milked by hand. My aunt owned a utility; she went to town once per month. Dad took us to town on the alternate fortnight.

Rabbits were a nuisance. I'd say Dad was sick of digging out warrens with a pick and shovel in his spare time. Somehow we acquired traps, and at about the same time the boundaries were netted. I have no idea where the money came from for these or for the Fordson tractor a bit later. I was big enough to carry a corn bag with one end on the ground, so one afternoon, Dad, with my assistance and under the strict supervision of my cattle dog, Blue, set some traps around the gully next to the house. This was my start into rabbiting. Well, it was a profession – I may have been a bit young but who's counting.

Next morning, instead of bailing up the cows at the dairy, Blue – he knew where they were – and I went around the traps. So by the time Dad was finishing up at the dairy he could see that he had a job too: skinning the haul. Every time he came out to the copper for more hot water I'm sure that his chest had swelled a bit more. All I could do was stay down at the chook yard and strop the pocketknife on the side of my dad's hand-me-down, oversized boot; it had to be sharp for the job ahead. 'How many, boy?'

'Nine, Dad.'

Whoosh! He up-ended the bag to start skinning. 'Bloody rabbits!' That's what he said as rabbits went every which way. To this day I am unable to wring a neck.

Soon afterwards I had to go to school, but I still trapped; I now carried a piece of axe handle on a bootlace to despatch many luckless bunnies. After the first day it was me or Blue; if I could not handle it, then, 'Skitch it!' was all the encouragement that was needed. I sold the dried pelts for pocket money. There were no freezers around so the carcasses were left for the crows, because we didn't eat many. All Dad wanted was more feed for the cows.

A CLOCK ON THE HANDLEBARS

BOB GUNN

It was early, the rooster was crowing. A voice called, 'Bobby, get up, it's school today.' I stirred, looking at Mum standing beside me.

'Go on, lovely, don't keep him waiting,' she said. Reluctantly I reached for my shorts and blood-stained shirt. My trapping mate,

Ron, was dressed and, with eyes aglow, said, 'We should get five pair today.'

'Five pair?'

'Yes! Rabbits.' Already in his mind, Ron had de-trapped, gutted and cleaned them ready for the freezing works. At three shillings and sixpence a pair our bank balance would soon be worth fifty quid.

The night before, we had set twenty traps on a neighbouring paddock. Martin, the owner, trusted us to keep clear of his grazing stock and dam and to shut the gates behind us.

I stepped down onto the cool earthen floor, which Dad had built out of anthills and crushed, dried mud. It always smelled earthy when Mum wet it down on a hot, dry day and was so cool on your feet.

Ron was checking the tyres on our old bikes and was looking at me impatiently. 'We won't have to take the traps home today,' he half-shouted. 'We can put them in Martin's old shed, under the Whippet.' I was relieved, as lugging the steel traps was the worst part of rabbiting.

'Are you right?' shouted Ron. I checked my pouch for my sharp pocketknife; with Chicka, our foxy, barking around us, we were ready.

'Bye,' says Mum, gently. 'Watch out for snakes and don't forget to check your clock, as school starts at nine.' Ron had the Westclox Big Ben in a billy can, tied to his handlebars; its loud tick was audible over the noise of the rattling bikes.

Martin's property was a good 3 miles away, a mile past the rickety old wooden bridge that crossed the Balonne River at St George in south-west Queensland, 1942. When Dad and Mum first came to St George, in 1932, they had leased a garden from Mr Horton, a few miles downstream from the old bridge. The river flats were very fertile but prone to flooding in the big river rises.

Life was idyllic; fish were plentiful in the big holes. Dad would tell me about the 70-pound Murray cod he caught when I was home. 'A good sign,' he was heard to say. A lot of his observations were of his early days in Canton, China. He came out to help his storekeeper uncle in Chinchilla. He fell in love with the Australian bush at first sight and lived and died there. In his travels he met and married Jessie, the eldest daughter of James, a Chinese storekeeper, and Elizabeth, a Scottish missionary, in Goondiwindi. Mum was a gentle person and her marriage to Dad was viewed with much apprehension, particularly by her nine siblings. Dad had led a hard shearer's life!

Wool was bringing record prices, graziers and contractors were paying top rates for top workers. Dad was the best shearers' cook in the district but, as in past history, the blood of hard-working men was sucked by the inevitable parasites. Wartime St George was no different; these came in the form of two-up touts, SP bookies, sly-groggers and corrupt coppers.

Horton's garden looked like a good place for Mum and Dad to start a family and Ron and I spent our early childhood on the Ballone. Later on, after a couple of big river floods, we moved into St George proper. A weatherboard lean-to on Riverview Terrace became our new home, modest but comfortable; we also had good neighbours.

Ron was five years my senior and became a father figure when work took Dad to various parts of north-west NSW and south-west Queensland. Money came from these distant outposts in the form of postal orders to be collected at post offices; this was enough to put food on the table and clothes on our back. A little extra for a rainy day never came to fruition.

Rabbits were in plague proportions, becoming a problem to the graziers, eating out pastures and creating burrows where stock and horsemen came to grief. In the early 1940s, Ollie, who was a diesel

Father and son, Nyngan, New South Wales, 1959.

engineer, opened up a freezing works just down the road from us. Because of high wool prices, graziers were holding on to their sheep and not slaughtering them. So it seemed sensible to turn a pest into a commodity, but to send the rabbit carcasses to market they had to be frozen. Rabbit carcasses were bought from the rabbiters, unskinned, but gutted with their kidneys intact. Keeping in mind that the basic wage in the 1940s was around six pounds, a good living could be made by professionals and opportunists by selling rabbits to the works for between three shillings and sixpence and five shillings a pair. This became a good secondary income for all in the wool off-season.

'What will become of us?' Mum voiced aloud her private thoughts.

'We'll be all right, Mum,' her eldest son assured her.

We schoolkids decided to become opportunists with an approach to Mum for a 'lend of a quid' and when asked 'Why?' we answered simply, 'Barney Waters.' Our neighbour had given us first offer of his six rabbit traps for a pound, so nervously, with our green pound note, we jumped the fence to take Barney at his word. Barney's dad said to him, 'Give 'em your setter, as it's no good without the traps.' A setter was a combination tool, a hoe on one end and a hammer head on the other, used by professionals. Our first attempt in Martin's paddock netted us seven rabbits on a Sunday. Over at Ollie's, open seven days a week, three and a half pair got us twenty-two shillings and threepence (one pound, two shillings and three pennies). 'Not a bad investment,' Mum said later.

Our best customer was Mrs Waters, as she would take the half-grown ones and give us an extra sixpence for skinning them. Skins stretched on U-shaped wires to dry were worth eight shillings a pound. 'These are made into diggers' hats,' Ollie told us. We were a little proud of our contribution to the war effort.

Our rabbiting was confined to weekends and holidays as school was most important. If the pests were thick we would venture out weeknights and mornings, sometimes netting us an extra ten pairs a week; hence the Big Ben on the handlebars. A typical weekday sortie was to run the traps, clean and get the rabbits to Ollie's, collect money, rush home, wash under the tap, de-flea each other, have a quick breakfast, get clean clothes, say bye to Mum and dash to school before parade, where we saluted the flag and sang 'God Save the King'.

I would ask my mate Darcy to scratch my back when an evasive flea appeared, or made a quick trip to the toilet where the shorts were dropped to get to places where it was unseemly to be seen scratching. Other entrepreneurs at the school had the same problem; the teachers were very understanding.

The art of catching rabbits in steel jaw traps was simple: find your paddock with lots of warrens and distinguish a fresh hole from an abandoned one. Fresh tracks and dung denotes this. The trap is buried at the entrance to the burrow in a trench that has been made to house the trap, trailing its chain and steel peg, hammer in the peg, set the jaws (carefully) and the trigger plate last. Cover the paper with fine soil until the whole trap is covered. Cover all signs of your presence around the trap; an operation that would take no more than fifteen minutes, depending on soil and terrain conditions.

When running the trap, the timid rodent is generally caught by the foreleg and is extracted and its spine stretched until broken, a 30-second operation. Gutting the rabbit is messy: a slit up the belly from the tail to neck leaving the kidneys intact, and the contents must be buried to alleviate blowflies. Some 'cowboys' threw the gut down a burrow, which caused big fly problems and the rabbits to abandon the burrow and dig a new one.

When we left St George, myxomatosis was not a factor. But it did kill the rabbit industry in later years. I met Ollie again in Goondiwindi in the late 1950s where he had an ice works. We swapped some yarns about rabbiting. The freezing works later became the centre of another industry: the harvesting of kangaroos around St George. The animals of our national emblem were processed for pet food and the restaurant trade.

COLD NIGHTS AND EERIE SOUNDS

BOB RUMING

In 1945, my father had just returned from the war and we lived in a quiet village in the New England region of NSW. Casual work was difficult to obtain so to supplement their income, many people relied on rabbits. Both Mum and Dad trapped rabbits on the farms near the village and I helped Mum by carrying her traps in my billycart.

Rabbits were plentiful and landowners were pleased to have somebody trapping on their land to reduce the rabbit menace. Stocking rates for sheep and cattle were seriously reduced by rabbits competing for grass and their burrowing and scratching increased soil erosion.

I was nine years old when I first set traps on my own. I was given twenty traps and a setter and off I went to my own little patch. I was not strong enough to set a trap with my hands, so I carried a strong stick which I could poke under a log or rock and use as a lever to press down the spring, holding it down with my foot and using my hands to slip the tongue into the plate to hold down the jaws. The slightest mistake would result in the trap being set off so the operation had to be repeated. On more than one occasion I caught myself and had to go home in pain for help to get the trap off my finger. Even today the nails on each of my index fingers carry the evidence of damage done by those steel jaws.

The traps were set after school and then after tea I would go around them and reset any that had caught rabbits or had been set off by foxes. I used a kerosene lamp which lit up a circle about 5 yards in diameter and found my way from one trap to the next by walking in the direction indicated by a scratch I had made in the ground after I set the trap.

I vividly remember those cold winter nights out there on my own. The stillness seemed to amplify the sounds of the night: the mopoke hooting; a fox's eerie bark; a rabbit, recently caught, rattling the trap's chain; and frogs croaking, reminding you that you were near the dam.

In the frosty morning, with warm gloves and a balaclava, I would go around my traps and collect the rabbits. I would average about fifteen from my twenty traps and, added to my night score, I would be disappointed if I didn't average more than one rabbit per trap per night. Traps would be reset on the second night and then moved to a new location.

Mum often helped with the skinning and pegging out of my skins so that I could get to school on time. Skins were worth about a shilling each and I could earn as much as four pounds per week if I worked hard. I was allowed to keep three shillings for pocket money to spend when we went to town, which was about once a month as we did not own a car.

My rabbit-trapping days were over in 1948 when I was sent away to school in Armidale. In school holidays I still chased rabbits, but with a rifle and a box of bullets. It wasn't long after that that myxomatosis wiped out most of the rabbit population in New England and rabbit trapping was no longer a source of supplementary income.

RED DIRT AND RABBIT STEW

RUSSELL KNOLL

My family were market gardeners on the red soil of Silvan in the Dandenong Ranges, a patchwork of hilly farms interspersed with blocks of bush. These were mostly fringed with blackberries, particularly along the creeks, which were dammed for irrigation and lined with scrub and white gums; perfect environs for rabbits.

We eight children, seven boys and one girl, were raised as farm kids, spending hours exploring and hunting in the bush. Rabbits were always a problem, particularly as we were carrot growers. They would eat the tops off the young plants, beginning on the beds closest to the bush and working progressively out into the paddock. Dad was a patient man, much more a farmer than a hunter, but there were times when the rabbit damage crossed a certain line and out would come the old shotgun to blast a few, normally from the seat of the tractor, until the numbers were down and the crop was getting ahead.

My older brothers, more inclined towards hunting, set traps with great success, though the early morning and evening trap rounds, up and down the steep hills, generally dampened their enthusiasm to do it for long.

Following the example of my second oldest brother I took up using the shotgun in my teens. After school during summer months I would walk across the farms and down valleys stalking the known rabbit haunts, trying to outwit them by coming from different angles, downwind, or crawling on my belly to get the shot. The gun had a shortened sawn-off barrel after the end was trumpeted when it went off while my brother was climbing through a fence with the end of the barrel on the ground. This meant that the pellets spread quickly, making it almost impossible to miss at close range.

I remember walking up those hills towards home with the gun in one hand and four or five rabbits in the other. I only kept the ones that weren't mangled, as a shotgun is prone to do, and I had ideas of tanning the skins and making a rabbit coat. Once home, I would skin and gut them in the shed and hang the skins on wires. One summer I had sixty skins, a few black ones among them, hanging from the rafters of my Father's tool shed. I was horrified though when one day I went to examine them to find that they were so weevil-infested that they just crumbled to dust in my hands.

As for the rabbit meat, I would put the gutted rabbits in the farm coolroom where Dad would find them and take them to the house, where he turned them into various blends of rabbit stew. A few years on I trained as an apprentice chef, after which I boned the rabbits out and made schnitzels served with all kinds of fancy sauces, which went down very well with the family.

HOLIDAY RABBITING FOR A CITY KID

RON CARROLL

Rabbits! School holidays! You beauty! In 1942, for a ten-year-old kid transported from life in a then fairly remote western district locality beyond Koroit, to a new life in the inner Melbourne suburb of North Fitzroy, the mention of rabbits was synonymous with heading back to the bush during school holidays and the promise of days spent rabbiting.

Catching the Port Fairy train at Spencer Street, I was placed in the company of some unsuspecting traveller who was asked to keep an eye on me for the long journey to Moyne. This station is now long gone, particularly after the train, stopping at a myriad of tiny localities, failed to reach Warrnambool before the winner of the historic and legendary Melbourne to Warrnambool bike race!

Warned to make sure the windows were all up before entering the Geelong tunnel, to avoid the carriage being filled with choking black smoke and the promise of an eyeful of grit which could turn the adventure of the trip into a red and teary-eyed nightmare, the journey began, to end at Moyne, two stops beyond Koroit.

From Moyne by Grandfather's jinker, we were off to Tarrone, the sheep and cattle station, home to Uncle Tom, a station worker living in the residence some miles from the homestead. Tom not only had to oversee the stock on Tarrone, but had to work on reducing the rabbit population, present in great abundance, among the ferns and rocky outcrops dominating the landscape.

Here the rabbiting adventure began. With eighty to a 100 traps set the night before, the morning began with checking the traps. Four out of five would hold a squealing bunny soon to be released but only to have its neck wrung, be thrown into the potato sack slung over the neck of my station hack, and transported back to the house, there to be gutted and hung over the rail in the cool of the pine trees. Collection took place by the rabbit buyer from Port Fairy and those rabbits would end up at the Melbourne Market and the tables of the local population.

After re-setting the traps and a hearty breakfast it was off with the pack of some twenty mixed-breed dogs eager for the hunt. Tiger, a cross-bred greyhound, was the champion hunter of fleeing rabbits, but in his enthusiasm often returned from the hunt with bruised or bleeding feet from his chase through the rocky outcrops. He wasn't happy when left at home on the next hunt. My other favourite was Lucy, a dappled whippet, whose method of operation was to squat in the rabbit runs and wait for an unsuspecting rabbit dashing in search of safety.

Riding our horses we had to be alert for the squeal of a catch, and quickly reach the successful dog with the caught rabbit, to snatch it with a plain fencing-wire hook before the skin was too damaged, rendering the pelt unsuitable for sale. Rabbiting was great fun for the holidaymaker and a very profitable sideline for Tom.

OF BUNNIES AND BOYS!

RICK HUTTON

Take twenty sixteen-year-old city boys, a crisp still Adaminaby night, one sheep farmer with Land Rover and spotlight, and a Monaro grass paddock. Listen to the grumbling of the boys as they complain: 'Where are we?', 'I'm bloody cold!', 'Why are we out here?' Then the spotlight picks out two red eyes. 'There's one!' says the boss in the Land Rover, 'And another!' 'It's a rabbit!' says a boy, the excitement of seeing the creature numbing his complaints of the cold. 'What'll we do?' says another, like a young pup held hard on a leash. 'Chase it!' says the boss, and like a line of greyhounds from their starting boxes the boys are off, scattering over the grey-toned paddock, mindless of any holes, rocks, or sharp tussock grasses.

More red eyes, more yelps and cries, stepping and weaving left and right, some collide, covering any bangs or bruises with a testosterone-fuelled, laughing bravado that boys only have at sixteen. Some become captains of the battlefield, calling for flankers, decoys, blockers and chasers. Some giggle and squeal at the fun and mayhem of it all, while some stumble and fall and let go with expletives that would shock their mothers and certainly surprise their fathers. And just when the boss and the teacher, having laughed themselves silly at the craziness of it all, are considering calling off the calamity, one determined battler bags a bunny. 'I've got one!' he cries with wondrous simplicity.

His half-surprised call echoes and reverberates through the hunting party. 'He's got one!' they cry. 'Show us! Hold it up! Take it to Sir!' and like white Masai warriors they half-run, half-dance their way along the beam of the spotlight following the anointed leader whose prowess in the battlefield, against the sworn enemy, has positioned him at the tip of the phalanx, the grey furry trophy hanging by the ears from his triumphantly raised hand.

'What will we do with it?' says the champion. 'Cook it for dinner!' says one boy. 'Skin it for a belt!' says another and, as one half-timid voice begins to say, 'Let it go!', the boss' booming voice says, 'Break its neck!' The order having been given and received, the cries of 'Yes, break its neck!' encore through the throng, and the champion cooperates, snapping the rabbit's neck so violently that blood sprays from beneath its fur onto the faces and jackets of the inner circle of tribesmen.

'Yay!' goes up the cry. 'Let's get another one!' and so the chase recommences, with the scanning of the spotlight, the scurrying of the foot soldiers and the occasional flash of red eyes in their gunsights. Fifteen minutes more, with no more captures, no more trophies, an increasing collection of grazes and sprains, and just plain weariness, the battle fizzles and the troops turn for home.

Bunnies and boys are a strange combination but worthy of watching, if only to see how basic nature can be.

'THE LITTLE TRAPPER'

DAVID FRAKES

I can't find it! It's gone! Disappeared! I have searched all the Rotary book stalls, the libraries and school fete book sales. 'Taken off the shelves years ago,' I hear. My favourite book as a child was one of the Golden Books series, *The Little Trapper*, and I am not kidding; I've been searching for it for years – the book that inspired me back in the 1950s to trap rabbits as a young teenager. They were still there, you know; myxo hadn't wiped them all out!

My string of six traps was enough weight to carry on a bicycle to the outskirts of town; enough traps to ensure my family a feed. My skill at reading the ground, to know where to place my trap, the fine art of setting the trap by placing my foot firmly down on the spring then reaching under the jaws with my index finger to set the tongue against the top plate that balanced delicately, then the pressure of the tongue on the top plate finally sets the waiting jaws. Skill was needed to sink the hole, in the same shape as the outline of the set trap with enough room at the spring end away from the jaws to house the chain, and about one inch of the foot-long peg that is driven into the ground to make sure the prey could not escape.

Oh, how the Little Trapper would have been proud of me as I placed the 6-inch square of newspaper over the plate and jaws, sprinkled fine dirt to bury the whole lot, and camouflaged it like the little trapper had done. I can see him now, standing on the book cover in his red jacket, bordered by a gold strip embossed with continuous words 'Golden Book'. It was cold in the mornings when I set out to collect the traps; the sun wouldn't be up when I went to take my bicycle out of the shed; cycling the few miles out of the town, trying to keep my fingers warm and insulated from the already cold handlebars. Thanks to my camouflaging skills, remembering where the traps were was always a challenge, especially if they had not done their job. Most weekends Mum would be pleased with my catch as I only ran my lines on Saturday nights; school saw to that!

Time has gone by now; you can't use traps. Nostalgic grey-power shoppers can buy them one at a time. Freshly blackened to look like new, at inflated prices from the bric-a-brac stalls at the now popular community markets. Or, if you travel over the ranges, it's not uncommon to pick up a string of fifty old rusted traps, still working, at damn near the same price. Can't find that book; must have been a dream. Life's like that.

TWO AND SIX A PAIR

IAN KELLY

It was below freezing, frost whitened the ground as far as the eye could see – which wasn't very far, given the thick fog that enclosed the landscape. Typical winter weather on the farm but the boy had become used to coping with the cold as he went around his traps at six every morning. It was always six because his grandfather was up at 5.30 am every day to milk the cows, so he rose to the clanging of the milk buckets.

He'd set about a dozen traps the evening before, looking for the fresh scrapes that indicated the rabbits were around. Setting a trap was not easy for a slightly built ten-year-old. Mick, the station hand, was as strong as one of the Hereford bulls in the back paddock and could hold the spring with one hand while setting the plate with the other. He could probably have done it with his teeth.

The boy needed to step on the spring, using his meagre weight to hold the trap jaws open. He needed to be sure he kept his weight in place until his fingers were clear; getting caught in the jaws of a steel rabbit trap hurt, even if it wasn't freezing cold.

Finding a fresh scrape, he used a setter to dig out a hollow for the trap and to hammer in the holding stake. The tool was about 18 inches long with a small mattock head on one side and hammer on the other. It was one of only two pieces of equipment needed to set the traps. The other was a newspaper. 'It's for the rabbits to read while they're waiting for you to release them,' he was once told by a relative with tongue firmly in cheek. In fact, the newspaper was torn into small squares, each one placed on the setting plate to prevent the weight of earth from setting off the trap prematurely. It was a good story, though, and one the boy believed for about ten minutes.

The setting tool with mattock and hammer had another use. The squeamish might look away. The accepted way of despatching a rabbit caught in the trap was to wring its neck. The boy, being small and not all that strong, sometimes struggled with this task. A firm whack with the setter usually did just as well.

These were pre-calicivirus days. Myxomatosis was the virus of choice. But 'mixi' rabbits gave themselves away and could not be sold to the local buyer for two and six a pair. It was the eyes, you see. A 'mixi' had gummy eyes – it couldn't be sold, it couldn't be eaten. No matter. The buyer had only one eye and that wasn't very good, so a bit of dust into the mixi's eyes and the bunny passed muster; another two and six in the pocket. The boy has not eaten rabbit since. He was never interested in controlling rabbit numbers either. It was always about the two and six a pair.

... AND THE CREEK SHALL GIVE UP ITS BOUNTY

JOHN FERGUSON

I remember it well, the creek that ran past the homestead on its way to enter the river at the place that was called the Junction, behind the town two miles away. It was a fast-flowing rushing kind of creek when it came down but dry most of the time. As a boy and one of the station children that creek gave us many things. From the trees along its banks, we selected our shanghai forks. From the same tree we found our boondy sticks. From its sandy floor we filled our pockets with shanghai stones. We swam in the temporary waterholes that sometimes remained after the creek had stopped flowing.

We knew most of the trees along its banks; climbed many. We knew the names of the birds, their favourite haunts, their favourite trees and where they had built their nests. We also knew where the rabbits were in their largest numbers, about a mile from the homestead, where the creek curved its way through a large pine forest. More rabbits could be found in this forest than anywhere else along the creek. Why did they favour this pine forest so much? Perhaps the light sandy soil made digging their burrows so much easier or maybe they just liked living among those tall pine trees. When you are a ten-year-old, you wonder about things like that.

In our part of the country, the word 'boondy' is an Aboriginal word for throwing stick. No one ever showed us how to make one; we just knew. Just like the willie wagtail, which knows how to make such a beautiful and complex nest; it just knows. We selected our boondy sticks with great care. It had to taper at one end; the length and weight had to be just right; not too heavy, not too long. We removed the bark with our pocketknives.

From 'boondy-ing' rabbits, as we called it, we moved on to trapping them. We set our traps at night by the light of a kerosene lantern, sometimes aided by a flashlight. Lots of times we went around our traps early in the mornings before riding to school. Oh, those early winter mornings. The frost crunchy, our legs cold, our fingers numb, but when we came upon a rabbit caught in one of our traps, well the cold didn't seem to matter so much any more. We hung our rabbit skins on wires in the old buggy shed; the buggies long gone.

Sometimes a fox skin would appear there, nailed to the wall, shot by an older brother or one of the station hands. A good quality fox skin was worth a pound in the war years, a princely sum of money in those times. From the money I saved mainly from the selling of

A young boy puts a rabbit in a bag, Nyngan area, New South Wales, circa 1958.

rabbit skins, I bought my first rifle, a single shot .22 calibre for six pounds from the local general store. Then I handed over six shillings for fifty rounds of ammunition.

So we had moved from boondy-ing rabbits, to trapping them, then to shooting them. Remembering back, rabbiting in different ways as a boy did teach me a few things, like discipline, rising early in those cold winter mornings to run our traps; saving money to buy my first rifle; to observe what's happening around you; to teach yourself. Did I make use of all these things? I would like to think so.

TWO BOYS AND TOBY GO RABBITING

HARRY POWELL

In the late 1940s, at the age of four, I accompanied my father in his horse and sulky and can still remember the mass of white rabbit tails running up the hills in front of us as we trotted along. In those days, poisoned trails laid with thistle roots mixed with strychnine and vanilla essence were an effective way of controlling rabbits. My job was to cut the scotch thistle roots into small pieces. To this day, I still have to cut thistles, and smelling the roots reminds me of times gone by.

Another effective way was to squirt Lavacide down the burrows after we had blocked all the holes up except for one. I was told many times by my father to 'get out of the friggin' road or you will get gassed'. My eyes often streamed with tears as I waited for a rabbit to bust out.

In the mid-1950s, the little grey Ferguson tractor with a three-tine ripper came along, filling a lot of the large warrens in. Then myxomatosis was introduced, which helped bring the masses under control. During this period I spent most of my time with Mick Jones, who helped Dad, and Mick always had rabbit traps set. My job was to peg Mick's rabbit skins out and for my wages he gave me the coloured skins.

When my little brother, Bill, and I were five and seven years old we would load Old Bill, the horse belonging to Dad's helper, Walter, with traps, and go and set our own traps. We also took Toby, Dad's old dog, with us and he would tell us just by looking if we had a rabbit. If he stopped, it meant we had a rabbit. If he stopped and then went on, it meant we had a leg or a sprung trap and no rabbit. We used to store our skins in a sugar bag under our beds until we could sell them. Quite often we would lose the skin from our fingers either by cutting ourselves while skinning our rabbits or when setting the traps.

As we grew older we spent our spare time shooting rabbits, and for years Bill and I gave each other a packet of .22 bullets for Christmas and birthdays. When I was at boarding school in Sydney I used to trap rabbits in the school grounds for my biology teacher, who used them for our biology experiments. Looking back I feel we were fortunate to grow up in such a great, unrestricted environment at such a young age and learn from our mistakes. Trapping rabbits was a period in my life I've never forgotten.

REELING IN THE EXPERTS

GRAHAM WILSON

As a young lad growing up on the family farm in the New England district of NSW, I spent a lot of time shooting rabbits with my trusty .22 rifle given to me as a Christmas present on my tenth birthday. There was never any shortage of rabbits. In the 1960s, after spending seven years at boarding school, I came home and worked on the farm with my father. He was a tough taskmaster and thought a small pay packet would keep me out of trouble. It forced me to find other ways of making money.

I teamed up with a local mate and we started shooting rabbits at weekends. We had a Bruno .22 rifle, an old Land Rover, a spotlight and a couple of good knives. The rabbits had to be head shot, cleaned and taken to a chiller box in Wallabadah after they had been paired into equal sizes. We got five shillings a pair for big ones down to two shillings for the smaller ones. Our efforts were modest; learning how to present the rabbits in good condition and to haggle for a good price. We soon learned some tricks of the trade. We would stretch the smaller rabbits to make them look longer and match them with a bigger one to get the better price.

Buoyed up by the good prices, our weekends were very prolific and we would have to spend many hours cleaning our tally. With fifteen properties to shoot on, we had no trouble finding our numbers. We soon had a reputation around Wallabadah for the amount of rabbits we could shoot and quite often filled the chiller box (which held about 600), much to the disgust of the local rabbiters who then had to go to Quirindi to get rid of their supply.

One night we had been to a property south of Wallabadah and had had a very lucrative hunt. We had the Land Rover full of rabbits and faced a long night cleaning them. The pub was still open as we came through the town so we called in to have a beer; my mate had a plan to save our time. We were having a drink with a few old rabbiters and started discussing the fastest way to clean a rabbit. Soon all these men were skiting that they were the quickest. Next thing we knew they were all outside at the Land Rover and we had a competition to see who really was the quickest. Each man had to clean five rabbits at a time. After a few re-runs we finally had a winner and also achieved the end result we were looking for in that all our rabbits had been cleaned. I heard on the grapevine a few days later that you couldn't get near the pub for the smell. Needless to say we didn't go near the place for some time.

The price of rabbits started to fall and our enthusiasm started to wane, so ending our rabbit-shooting exploits.

MY DAD THE TRAPPER

DOUG CARNEY

I went rabbiting for the first time in 1948, at age seven. Two uncles were my 'offsiders' and first we drove the rabbits to the corner of a large paddock, where a netting fence funnelled the rabbits into a tunnel. We then walked through an area of thick milk thistles and all of a sudden one of my uncles would stamp his foot down and have a squirming rabbit underneath. It was here that I caught my first rabbit – running it down. How I managed this feat I don't know.

My uncles both had single shot .22 rifles and it seemed that wherever they aimed, a rabbit fell. They were good shots, having grown up on a farm, and both were returned servicemen. Skinning was done on the spot, the carcasses left and the skins kept for sale. Much to my delight I was awarded my first shot and with my uncle's help aimed at a rabbit. Unlike all the others it lived to run another day.

Mum and Dad were married in 1930. Dad was a rabbit trapper and was setting a hundred traps a day, near where Wyangala Dam is today. It was rugged country and Dad said that the scrub was so thick the dogs had to run out on the road to bark. Mum was twenty years old and they lived in a humpy Dad made out of canvas and corrugated iron. She cooked outside in a camp oven. When I asked her what she did all day she said that she helped Dad with the trapping.

Before I was strong enough to set traps I dug out burrows with a mattock and shovel. It was hard work, particularly when you hit clay, which was often. Burrows went deep and had many offshoots that I blocked and returned to later. I continually poked a stick up the burrow until it returned with fur on it. Then I would reach in, find the rabbit's back legs and pull it out.

When Dad thought I was ready, he took me out and showed me how to set traps. We set six traps and caught six rabbits, so Dad's credibility went up. We set at holes in the fence (run throughs), burrows and dung hills. I was shown once and that was it – I was on my own. It was set the trap without getting your fingers caught and check the traps after sundown and before sun-up. Sundown so that you can collect any rabbits (and re-set) and sun-up so that you could beat the crows to the rabbit. If you caught a possum or a cat in the trap you needed to get a forked stick to hold it down or it would tear you to pieces.

Mum enjoyed getting the white meat of the rabbits to supplement our meals and I sold the skins after drying them on a wire frame. Six skins made up a pound and I received not much more than threepence a pound.

GRANDPA SPILLS THE LOAD

STAN LOWE

I grew up on a farm on the Broken River between Shepparton and Benalla, in northern Victoria. I am not sure exactly when this incident took place, but I was born in 1946 so I guess I must have been younger than ten, because I think the myxo had taken hold by 1956.

We had a big problem with rabbits and my father laid a poison trail using baited carrots. In the morning, my grandfather and I took the horse and gig along the trail. He drove and I walked along, throwing rabbits in the gig. The trail wound its way through the farm and then between a fence and the river, which was running a banker. When the gig was full almost to overflowing, the trail was very close to the edge of the river and a part of the bank subsided under the gig wheel. It wasn't enough to throw Grandpa into the river but a large number of rabbits fell from the gig into the swollen stream.

Over the next few days, we waited to hear comments from the neighbours about the number of drowned rabbits floating down the river but they didn't say anything – and we were not game to tell them that we had polluted their water with a couple of hundred poisoned rabbits. I don't know if that was the last time we had to lay a poison trail, but I do remember picking up numbers of sick and dying myxo-infected rabbits. Looking back, the poison would not have been a pleasant death, but the sad swollen eyes of the myxo-infected rabbits was not a pretty sight either. After the myxo swept through, the numbers settled down to a level that meant we could share the farm with the remaining rabbits. In return they provided a change from mutton on the dinner table and the skins gave me a little pocket money now and then.

RABBITING BY RAIL

ROB CALDWELL

My mate Rossy Peters lived on one side of the railway line and I lived on the other. Our parents were comfortable with us riding around town to borrow appropriate rabbiting dogs, going rabbiting for the day and often not returning until after dark. A pushbike could carry up to twelve pairs of rabbits, on the crossbar, handlebars and the long-handled shovel overhanging the back wheel. Of course, with a full load you'd have to be careful that the dangling heads didn't get caught in the spokes. We both learned this by unpleasant practical experience! There were many techniques for reducing this risk, not the least of which was keeping the attitude of the bike such that the heads didn't swing.

We were constantly developing new means of transporting the rabbit haul on our bikes. Rossy's uncle Harold was a fettler on the railway and just down the track a bit from our homes was the shed where the trikes were kept. We used to watch and admire the fettlers on the trikes just as much as we'd watch the steam trains. I would write down all the engine numbers (3215, 3420, 3606, 3801, etc); all different classes of locomotives; the time; day of the week; and date.

There were never any trains on Sundays, and one Sunday while walking past the trike shed, we spotted a short length of thin rope hanging over the gutter. It was the key to the shed. Inside we found a two-seater trike, a four-wheel trolley with a see-saw drive, and a four-wheel flat deck. Over the next few Sundays we tried each one as a form of rabbiting transport. The see-saw drive was the most suitable and a few of the slower dogs must have approved, as they got to ride as well!

The best rabbiting grounds were at Cobbs Hill and the run out was arduous, uphill around Horseshoe Bend and about 4 miles from the shed. Of course the run home with our haul of rabbits was a breeze: all downhill.

Then one Sunday, upon leaving the shed, we noticed a pall of loco smoke topping the crest of Horseshoe Bend. But there were never trains on Sundays! The fast retreat to the shed was the last time we used the fettlers' trolleys for rabbiting!

Rossy's uncle also taught us the basics of shooting rabbits and allowed us to take a .22 single shot to Lithgow with us. My parents didn't approve, and there was a risk of the rifle being spotted as we rode around town past the constable's house to collect the dogs. So we planted the gun underneath a railway bridge, just out of town. The policeman didn't concern us too much. When doing the milk-run, driving the 1948 Bedford ute around town at age eleven to fourteen, his billy can of milk was supplemented with his favourite food: a fresh rabbit!

'JUST THREE RULES, SON'

NEIL PORTER

'Just three rules about shooting rabbits, son.' My father's words from 1972 remain as clear as Dartbrook creek between the 1960s drought and the 1980s floods. I was receiving my father's old .22 calibre, single-shot rifle on my fourteenth birthday. He was given this same rifle when he turned fourteen. He had used it to feed his family on rabbits during the Depression. It had no remaining varnish but as a mark of trust and manhood, was more important to me than a Ferrari to my city mates.

'Rule one, son: a gun is always loaded.' I already knew this one as I had shot myself in the right foot with my air rifle that fired completely randomly due to a worn-out mechanism. I had it resting on my gumboot to keep dirt out of the barrel. Rather than let Dad know I had broken rule one, I worked the pellet out with some long-nosed pliers. No one bothered to ask why I limped for a few days.

'Rule two, son: a closed bolt could kill you. This gun is faulty and even un-cocked can fire if dropped.' He hit the rifle butt on the path and BOOM! He sent a bullet into the sky from my rifle in apparent 'safe' mode. I nervously twitched my right foot. 'Son, I once dropped this very gun leaving two clean holes in my only shirt. You're lucky I lived to spawn you.' My mother nodded approvingly at the excellence of this lesson. 'Lucky rifle that, son.'

'Rule three, son: a great rabbit hunter never misses.' Stalking skill and the brilliant open sights darkened by the soot from a burning match are all you need. 'I'll give you ten bullets before each hunting trip, and then count the rabbits and remaining bullets when you return.' Months passed without the perfect ten. Then I had my chance.

Six rabbits from six bullets. Rabbits attached to my belt like a hula skirt of fur and blood worn by a rabbit-obsessed psychopath. I looked down into the swimming hole from the high, steep bank and saw a rabbit looking up at me from under the water. Several times it swam to the surface for a breath only to drop back down under the water in a slow agonising drown. I raced around the bank and over the rocky rapid. I lifted the rabbit from the water and gently placed it on the clover. I pulled its tiny paws back and forwards till it revived. Its bloody, fallen friends flopping forwards from my belt in macabre support. Big decision time, lad. Seven out of six and one won't even have a bullet hole!

I patted the rabbit for a while before leaving it safe in the shade to recover. I was nearly home when I looked down at the weapon. In the excitement I had closed the bolt before dropping the rifle as I dived into the water. 'Lucky rifle that, son!'

THE HUMBLED SQUIRE (GRANDFATHER'S STORY)

MICHAEL GRABHAM

As a five-year-old I remember the rabbits everywhere. It was nothing to see six or seven in the shade of each draught horse as they ate their chaff. Poisoning and skinning rabbits helped turn this scourge into an income, and so that's what my old dad did. And, like every kid, doing what Dad did was the pinnacle of my life's ambition.

Dad dug up, washed and cut up thistle roots before dusting them with strychnine powder ready to be laid. Many times I would be there watching and pleading with him to let me do a poison run. The lethal potential of strychnine meant poisoning rabbits was Dad's domain, but incessant pestering wore Dad down, and he hatched a plan.

'Right, son,' said Dad one afternoon as he prepared for another poison run. 'You better find yourself some thistle roots if poisoning rabbits is what you want.' I was elated. With pocketknife and an old jam tin with the lid cut out, I scampered off to the nearest patch of thistles and began excavating. Carefully each root was extracted, chopped into lengths and dropped into the jam tin, just as Dad did. With both hands reverently embracing the tin, I lifted my offering of freshly washed thistle roots to Dad, knowing full well there was no chance of me being allowed to handle the poison.

Atop a fruit case I watched as Dad carefully sprinkled the white powder onto the roots, gloating with satisfaction as his hand returned to add just a little more powder to my meagre offering of thistle roots. Then came the instructions: 'Don't spill them, use the spoon, and most importantly, don't touch the powder!' Like a humble squire receiving the royal orb and mace, I respectfully received that rusty jam tin and an old battered spoon. Using his little plough, Dad helped cut a trench around the nearest warren, and watched as I administered the contents of the tin. Little did I know that the awesome powder sprinkled upon my thistle roots was nothing more than Mum's plain flour!

Up before dawn, Dad had done his rounds, collecting the rabbits in his sulky and delivering them back to the house for skinning. On the way past my warren, he threw out a dozen poisoned carcasses, now spoils of my first attempt.

With the first hints of morning approaching, I was up and out into the crisp morning air, across the sandy paddock and down to the rabbit warren. A dozen rigid rabbits lay scattered over the warren. I was ecstatic. Triumphantly I picked up two rabbits in each hand and staggered for home, rabbits bobbing around my little legs. With wide eyes I raced to the shed to find Dad pegging out the skins from his morning round.

'How did you go, boy?' Dad asked with a twinkle in his eye. With effusive adulation I blurted out, 'There's *thousands* of 'em down there!'

A HARD LESSON FOR THE KIDS

JOHN BAIN

My uncle Alec was a soldier settler at Woolsthorpe in Victoria, north of Warrnambool. In the 1950s we made a pilgrimage there almost every school holiday to help out, but the truth be known we were probably in the way more often than not. Our adventure would begin with a train trip from Melbourne, with a pie and sauce and a cup of tea at Camperdown Station refreshment rooms along the way. Met at Warrnambool station, we'd travel out to Woolsthorpe, grab the mail while Alec had a beer or three and on to the farm.

One particular summer the whole entourage, complete with caravan, had taken the journey down. More to keep eleven feral kids apart, the strategy was to load bails of hay onto a trailer, hook it up to the Fergie tractor, bung the kids on and away we'd go out into the paddocks. No doubt such a venture in this day of political correctness would be a health and safety nightmare but we pushed on regardless, kids yelling, dogs barking; it was great.

One day we took off after lunch right out the back and into a paddock of canola, which in those days was called rape, and Alec bought a rifle with him; only a .22 but a gun just the same. His instruction was LAW. In those days to disobey the law was the death penalty, so we all walked behind him as we trudged out across the paddock. Suddenly he said quietly, 'Stop,' and everyone stood motionless, even the dogs. He raised the gun to his shoulder and took aim – at what I had no idea – then there was a loud BANG!

Down the paddock something spun in the air and hit the ground motionless. I was mortified; this was my first experience of death and I kept thinking somehow it would stand up and run off. But the poor little rabbit was dead as a doornail in a split second. Next thing another BANG and another rabbit bit the dust. Some of the younger ones started crying – one even screaming – but he continued on regardless and pretty soon there were rabbits going to ground everywhere. Little did we know then that the rabbits were responsible for the failed canola crop, now not even a decent feed for their sheep.

Among the screams and tears, Alec bellowed, 'Come behind!' and looked to see which of the dogs he was chastising to discover it was cousin Josephine who by now was inconsolable with anguish. Then the rifle was swapped for a shovel as we began to dig out burrows and catch the rabbits in their own back yard so to speak. It was then that I began to comprehend the enormity of the problem; talk about trying to bail out the Queen Mary with a plastic bucket! The place was infested with the damn things and no guesses as to what we did for the rest of the holidays – hunted flamin' rabbits!

Then came myxomatosis. The plague dwindled out and for the next forty years and more rabbits virtually disappeared off the planet but guess what – they're back alive and well and living in every state, by my reckoning. Nowhere near the numbers there used to be, of course – not yet, anyway.

YOU'D NEVER MAKE A THIEF, SON!

CHARLES BEAMISH

I was born in 1943, and reared in the Moonah area of Tasmania. As I grew, my love for the country life and my grandparents was so strong that every school holidays I'd find my way up to them and their Derwent Valley farm. I was a child during the 1940s and early 1950s, when there was such a rabbit plague that my farming uncles spent much of their time trying to control the rabbit numbers. With me tagging along with them so often, I also became pretty good at the hunt.

The sheepdogs on the farm were with us all day every day and they became every bit as good at hunting as the 'hunting dogs' that were brought there from time to time for the purpose. Sheepdogs always knew their place and would not chase rabbits unless you had a gun. It was funny how the dogs knew the difference. When you walked out the door with a gun, they would dance and bark in anticipation. Between my two uncles' dogs, it became a real competition as to whose would catch the most rabbits.

As the rabbit plague worsened the uncles resorted to fumigating. The sheepdogs would all be there to help rush the rabbits into the burrows, and then this poison mist was pumped into the burrows, and their entrances covered in with a spade.

As I was still only a boy, I couldn't help saving some of the little different coloured ones during this herding process. I would take them home with me at the end of the holidays. I would play with them for hours. I would put them in a trailer I'd made out of an old box and some old pram wheels, and pull them around behind my three-wheeler bike, making out I was a stock carrier. The odd one would hop out as we went along, so I'd have to stop and 'load' them back into the trailer, but all in all they were pretty well-behaved 'sheep'.

I remember this very old man, when I was about eight years old, who used to set traps all over the place. I found this big rabbit in one of his traps one day, and thought I would be smart and get a rabbit for our tea. But I got too smart for myself. After I killed the rabbit I cut off his foot and left his foot in the trap. I thought the old man would think the rabbit got away. I took the rabbit home. The next day the man came by our place, and I observed from a distance, the old man laughing with my dad. I felt very worried because I could see he knew I pinched one of his rabbits, but how? I remember all the thoughts going through my mind, '... was he a tracker? Did he track my footprints back home?' My father let me sweat for a day or two and then he said, 'You know, you'd never make a thief, because you left your pocketknife on the ground near the trap!'

When I was about ten or eleven years old, I chased a rabbit up a hole in the bottom of a windswept-looking gum tree. I could see that the hole went up the centre of the tree and came out about 10 feet off the ground. I stuck a little straight limb up the hole to stop the rabbit backtracking, and then took my horse up to the side of the tree and stood up on the horse's back ... and there was the rabbit! I caught him by reaching into the knothole. I felt very proud of myself, taking a big fat rabbit home for tea. When I told my pop how I caught him, he promptly took the wind out of my sails, telling me he should kick my bum, because if the horse had've moved I would've been left hanging by one arm and by the time they found me I would've been dead!

CRACKERS AND COMICS

MARTIN KRIEWALDT

Although rabbits are a curse, I must confess rabbits have been very good to me. As a child and teenager, I made good pocket money trapping them. Thanks to rabbits, I was able to buy essentials like crackers and comics! Later, they provided me with petrol money when I was old enough to own a motorbike. I'll never forget my first hunting expedition. I was about seven or eight years old, living in the small country town of Brinkworth, South Australia. It was 1946 or 1947, and rabbits were plentiful in the nearby scrubs. My uncle had given me about half-a-dozen traps which were past their 'use-by date' but which I could just set, if I really tried hard.

One Friday evening after school, I set off for a likely scrub about a mile away with the six traps slung over my shoulders. I carefully set the traps in various warrens and returned home wondering what would happen. The night passed very slowly. Early next morning, I set off for the scrub expecting to be disappointed. After all, my uncle warned me that the traps were too old to catch rabbits. When I arrived at the scrub, I was dumbstruck. I had caught four large rabbits.

But what should I do with them? Expecting no fruit for my labour, I hadn't bothered to take a bag with me. I didn't know how to kill them and I wasn't going to release them. Somehow I had to get them home to 'rub them into the faces' of my two brothers who had teased me I was wasting my time. Finally, I thought of a solution. Fortunately, I was wearing shoes with laces. I removed

Rabbit skinner, Victoria Market, Melbourne, circa 1970.

them and tied the rabbits into two pairs by their back legs. Triumphantly I carried them home and proudly displayed them to my amazed parents and brothers. Next time, I remembered to take a bag with me! And I will always remember my first hunt!

THEY LAUGH ABOUT IT NOW, BUT ...

MICHAEL SCOTT

A rabbit plague at Stanley, Tasmania, ten years ago saw many, many rabbits in my backyard. My young dog at the time would spend hours sitting by their holes, hoping for one to come out and play. One day one did; my dog only wanted to play but got a bit rough for the little bunny. A call from my three young children (six, eight and ten) to come and get the puppy away from the baby rabbit got my attention. I went outside to find a baby rabbit lying on the grass in a poor state and in obvious pain. I asked the youngest child to go and get me the shovel so I could fix up the rabbit. This is where it all came unstuck. All three of the children thought I meant *fix* the rabbit; that is, pick it up with the shovel and take it inside and perform some lifesaving magic on it, like on TV. I had no idea this is what they thought was going to happen.

I actually meant 'put the rabbit out of its misery with a quick blow from the sharp end of the shovel' which, while they were standing there, I did. All three kids screamed and looked at me like I was a mass murderer then ran inside to tell Mum what I had just done. For two years, if I walked around and picked up a shovel, the kids would look at me and wonder what I was planning to do. It then became a family joke that if someone did something wrong, silly or naughty, one of us would yell out 'get the shovel'. I am sure my children, now that they are older, will tell their children about the day Daddy killed the baby rabbit in front of their very eyes.

EVEN THE CAT DIDN'T LIKE RABBIT

HARRISON ROPER

My mum grew up in the rabbit plague in the early 1960s. It's hard for me to understand what it was really like. However, I do know that when a friend gave me a pet rabbit for my sixth birthday Mum wasn't all that impressed with Sooty. She tells me stories of when she had to go out and poison or trap them. I think it would have been cruel, but I'm a town boy and my dad wasn't trying to make a living off the land.

Granddad had a farm west of Nyngan, NSW, and he used to get Mum to drive the old army jeep as close as she could to the nominated warren. Then they would fill in all bar one hole, down which they would put a pipe that had been attached to the exhaust pipe. Mum would then let the jeep idle for a few minutes to gas the poor little things (she used to pretend she was a famous racing car driver on a pit stop). Then they would fill in that hole as well. This worked quite well, apparently.

It caused great amusement when our city cousins came up for the holidays and Nana decided to give them roast rabbit. It was the first time that Mum had eaten rabbit and she laughs about how she and her cousin were sitting on the enclosed verandah just down from the dining table when they realised that they hated the taste. Quietly Mum scraped off the rabbit onto the floor and called over the trusting pet cat. They finished off the vegies, told Nana how delicious it was and asked if they could leave the table. They took off, not realising that the cat didn't like rabbit either. Nana made them clean it up when they got back in the afternoon. They never had roast rabbit again, though.

In the bigger plague, in the 1930s to 1940s, Granddad and his dad used to trap them and sell the pelts. When there was a glut they only had to take in the tails and they would still get paid for the skin. It's hard for my generation to understand what it was like, so this was a good exercise for me to do. I think I know why Mum didn't mind when Sooty ate the Ratsak and died, and why Granddad still likes to wear his Akubra, even though he retired a couple of years ago.

DAD, ME AND RABBITS

GARRY KNIGHT

My most memorable childhood times were spent with Dad walking the hills around Wangaratta, carrying our trusty ferrets, nets and shovel, and searching out burrows which would back up Dad's declaration that 'there's a few bunnies in there'. Typical of men of his era, Dad was not demonstrative with his affections. It was on our joint rabbiting expeditions that we had our 'quality' time together and I can't recall ever a bad word spoken (except when the ferrets refused to surface from underground). We walked many miles together, as rabbiting needs perseverance. Sometimes we had to walk up just one more hill to fill the quota.

Dad bred top ferrets, but the much-maligned rabbit is not altogether stupid and occasionally out-played us. They have a trick of having a small escape 'pop' hole in an undetected location, from where they explode into the air and escape, much to the bewilderment of the closely pursuing ferret. Sometimes on these occasions the ferrets would give us that look: 'What's wrong with you blokes! How'd you miss that hole?' Dad was as expert as you can be at knowing these rabbit tricks, though, and we generally had the pop holes covered with nets, much to the surprise of the rampant bunny who thought his escape was assured.

Feeling the rumble of the rabbit through the ground as they darted through their holes, hotly pursued by our ferret, is a sense never forgotten. We semi-crouched with anticipation, like a sprinter on the blocks waiting for the starter's gun, ready to lunge to the hole where we reckoned the bunny was heading. My youthful enthusiasm usually meant I was on top of the rabbit before it could untangle itself from our carefully laid net.

Rabbit holes provided homes for some unexpected lodgers, too. Once, after putting the ferret into a small two-hole burrow near a railway line, there was a tremendous ground-shaking rumble, then, whoosh, flying out into the net and pulling the peg out of the ground, was one very angry, growling, scratching possum. Releasing him from the net was a very delicate operation, with fur still flying as he scarpered up a nearby gum tree.

We always kept a few of the best rabbits for our own consumption or gave them to Dad's mates who enjoyed a feed of underground mutton too. What was left over, we sold to the ice works for two dollars a pair. This was when my mum's skills came to the fore. Fried, roasted, braised or stewed in the pressure cooker, no one was late to the dinner table when a feed of rabbit was on the menu.

Dad passed away peacefully in November 2008, aged eighty-eight. Thank you, *Oryctolagus cuniculus*. You enabled a struggling family to eat well (rabbits are low fat, but we didn't know that at the time) and provided the best memories of a father and his son.

THAT SIXPENCE MADE ALL THE DIFFERENCE

DON McSHANE

'Rabbit-oh, rabbit-oh!' the driver called from his horsedrawn cart, fresh rabbits hanging behind the seat, his bell echoing through Hobart's chilly morning streets. Housewives hurried to select the best which were then freshly skun. I often saw the 'rabbit man' and observed one lady who regularly bought a rabbit. Her daughter was in my class. It wasn't long before I was delivering a fresh rabbit to Mrs Waters every Monday.

I grew up on the family farm at Broadmarsh, 21 miles north of Hobart, Tasmania, when the rabbit plague of the 1930s and 1940s was having a significant impact on farm life, devastating crops and necessitating whatever controls there were. The major control was poisoning with strychnine mixed with apple or carrot and sugar. The sweetness of the brew was critical – and Jimmy Riley could make the necessary adjustments by tasting the brew, spitting it out, then adding sugar until it was just right!

It was a daunting task to set into skinning hundreds of rabbits and pegging out the skins. Harry Johnson was the local skin buyer (whose prices always seemed a bit low to me!). Some carcasses were gutted and dried for feeding the dogs even months later. (As strychnine remained in the rabbits' intestines, dogs could safely eat gutted rabbits, whereas they die from simply chewing a bone of an animal poisoned by 1080.)

As a child I did not fully appreciate the problem, but rather saw rabbits as an opportunity for sport – hunting with my dog, Towser, and ferret, Jinny. In 1944, my brother Brian and I began our secondary education at Hobart High School, boarding in North Hobart. We were two shy boys from a tiny country school now confronted by 600 students and overawed by so many classrooms! I initially shared a desk with a town kid who knew nothing about farms or rabbits, and that didn't help. Luckily I met a student whose father, George, kept ferrets and hunted rabbits. I changed desks, and there began a lifelong friendship with Bob Leitch.

Brian and I patronised the shop near the school where Mrs Rice sold homemade 'blue heaven' iceblocks and ginger beer, each for one penny. We had one shilling and threepence a week pocket money but my extra sixpence from Mrs Waters made all the difference! I could occasionally catch the tram home!

On leaving school, rabbiting became a necessary part of my life. I trapped rabbits on the farm and was a regular supplier to Geoff Collins' delicatessen in North Hobart.

Ferreting was sometimes time-consuming and frustrating when the ferret 'laid up' (not coming out of the burrow), probably asleep after a meal of rabbit. But ferrets are prolific breeders and my young 'trained' ferrets fetched ten shillings each at Bridgewater's Paddy's Market.

And so Mrs Waters, Jimmy Riley, Harry Johnson, George and Bob Leitch, Mrs Rice and Geoff Collins all played a part when I was 'rabbiting on' around Hobart more than sixty years ago.

PROUD AS PUNCH

RAY BROWN

I am fifty-three years of age and have hunted for rabbits from time to time since I was a boy, on my uncle's farm in Gippsland, Victoria, or wherever Dad took me. I have trapped, snared, ferreted and shot the lagomorph with both rifle and shotgun, and have cooked them in as many ways. The calicivirus, along with my ageing bones, is slowly winding down this pastime but I still have many fond memories of helping reduce their numbers … who am I kidding, I loved doing it.

As a boy on the farm, Uncle would hand me the old Harrington & Richardson single-barrel 'shotty' and two shot shells and say in his husky deep voice, 'Bring two back, boy.' So off I would wander down through a wooded area to a rather large gully at the back of the property. The rabbits were on the other side so they would see me coming a long way off and scamper underground. If I was lucky to get a shot off on the way, I would take it, but if I missed I had some work to do. I would then cross the gully, circle the warrens downwind, lay down within shotgun range and wait. Lying on my back I would daydream, making shapes out of the clouds and once I even nodded off. By this time, most of the bunnies would now be above ground. Lying on my tummy, I would wait till two or more rabbits were congregating closely together. I would then take aim, close my eyes (taking into consideration that the gun was nearly as big as me) and squeeze the trigger. After the dust and smoke cleared, I would pick up the rabbits and head back to the homestead as proud as punch.

STARTING EARLY

JOHN ROBINSON

At the age of six I had my first single-shot rifle. Each time we went to town I would buy a box of fifty .22 'shorts' and next day go shooting rabbits after school. I could shoot one rabbit with every bullet – and on the way home kill a great number more, sitting in their 'squats'. You would skin them on the spot as it was easier to carry the skins only. By dark you would peg them out to dry. The next time we went to town the skins would be sold to buy more bullets. It would have been far more profitable if we'd just used sticks or traps but that did not come into the equation.

During the war years, when petrol rationing was in place, my father would trap or ferret rabbits and pack them in kerosene boxes, skin on and gutted, and forwards them on rail to my uncle's shop in Melbourne. My uncle would sell them to customers who would pay for them with petrol ration tickets. In this way my father and a couple of neighbours could keep their farms fuelled up, as the usual allowances did not cater for travelling any great distance.

There are many more stories relating to the release of myxo and the very great numbers of dead rabbits that had to be buried daily, just to prevent the stench around the homesteads. Packs of rabbit dogs, that were part of the farm's defences prior, would carry home literally hundreds of rabbits a day, thinking they were doing a great job. Of a night, we would go out 'spotlighting' to net and infect rabbits; as it was a far better way to spread the virus as the rabbits would go straight home to their mates. At times when ferreting, you had to pull some rabbits out of the burrow to make room for the ferrets. We also had a cat trained to do the same job as the ferrets; it was far less likely to kill in the burrow than some ferrets that you would put in one hole and soon start digging to get them out.

THE BUSH LIFE

NOEL HABERECHT

My parents both came from farms, but from the age of five, we lived in Wagga for better education, housing and job opportunities. Dad's recreation was inland river fishing, wild pig shooting, rabbit trapping and the like. Subsisting 'in the bush' through the Depression proved the great advantage of leisure activities in putting food on the table.

There was a public recreation reserve on the Murrumbidgee 20 kilometres downstream, with a sand beach better than the one in town. But we mostly went there at weekends in the cooler months. Dad had made about six drum pots for trapping what we called freshwater lobsters – giant yabbies, covered in spikes. For bait, half a rabbit carcass was tied in the centre with thin wire. The pots were rested on the river bottom on the deep side, tied to tree roots close to the water line. If still relatively intact after a week, the bait would stay as the extra smell helped attract the lobsters.

I'm not sure if there was a plague of rabbits, but they were certainly plentiful on the river flats. I accompanied Dad as he started to set about twenty traps. I asked how he would find them all in the grass next week. The method was simple – merely drag a stick along the ground and mark an arrow in the direction of the last trap set. Then start at the last trap and follow the arrows.

He also carried a pea rifle, and occasionally would stop and shoot a rabbit hiding in the grass. I asked how he could pick up the signs of a crouching rabbit. He raised his hand to point out a likely position. Then suddenly he lurched forwards to a clump just a few paces away and crashed his boot on the neck of the unsuspecting bunny. There was no time to aim a rifle.

We always had a car, even when petrol was rationed to 4 gallons per month. Dad's first car, a Buick, cost him ten pounds. Naturally it was pretty much a wreck, but he got it going for a while. His second car was a Bianci, which he cut down and converted into a flat-top 'ute'. This was so he could carry his small shearing plant around to local farms. This didn't last more than a couple of years before it needed some parts which you couldn't get from Italy during a war.

Then, just as people were putting their cars up on blocks as the war persisted, he managed to get a 1930 Chevrolet six-cylinder roadster with wire wheels for thirty-five pounds. He converted it to a ute with sides and tailgate, and this was our family 'car' for ten years, with my sister and me sitting on cushions in the back and nobody wearing seatbelts, which had yet to be invented.

Everywhere we drove in the Chev, Dad carried on the parcel shelf a pea rifle and a wheat bag. We would often stop on the road, especially at dusk, having spotted a rabbit or two, which would accompany us home in the bag. The bag would also come in handy to pick up spilled wheat at harvest time, which was food for the chooks.

During the 1940s my parents took in one or two high-school boarders from farms within 100 miles. They were treated as family members, had small house chores, and occasionally got a father-like dressing down if needed. On many a Saturday, they were told: 'Hop in, we're going yabbying, or to the river'. If there was a heavy frost, the first thing was to build a huge fire. Too hot to get near and make some toast, we would hook the bread onto the end of a 3-metre long branch, and another person on the other side of the fire would yell out when it browned sufficiently. Hot toast freshly buttered, with the bread still soft in the centre – unbeatable!

Our boarders enjoyed rabbit stews, soups and baked dinners. But they later confessed that during the first rabbit dinner, they were puzzled to see in the gravy little black balls! 'Surely not!' they thought. But there we were, quietly putting them aside. Their anxiety evaporated when they realised they were whole peppercorns!

A REAL LITTLE BUSINESSMAN

BRIAN O'TOOLE

In my early days we lived in Black Rock, Melbourne, in a large house in Bluff Road opposite William Anderson and Sons Bakery, on the corner of Cheltenham Road. I was the fifth child of Jack and Mary O'Toole. Being good Catholics, my dad used the rhythm method of birth control and managed to have thirteen kids before he got it right. My story about rabbits began when a friend named Don Bretherton taught me how to set a trap and, as it was wartime (about 1943), I would have been nine years old or thereabouts. My collection of traps soon grew until I had about ten. I found the best place to set them was along the seventeenth hole of the Royal Melbourne Golf Course, where there were lots of holes in the wire-netting fence. There was no shortage of rabbits and I was soon feeding the whole family as well as having another little business as I found people loved underground mutton and would pay two shillings a pair. Also there was a market for the skins. Everybody was poor at that time but I was doing okay. Together with my caddying at the Royal Melbourne and finding lost balls and selling them, I was a real little businessman.

An interesting sideline came one Christmas when I took my traps with me for the school holidays to the old family home at

Dunnstown near Ballarat. This was a family ritual for the boys and we would go to either there or Camperdown or Colac, where my mum's relations lived. My uncle Jim grew potatoes and kept a few cows. After they were milked in the morning he would just turn them out on the road to graze. My job was to go out about 4.00 pm, locate them and bring them home. This procedure had its problems, as one of his best cows was hit by a train and another fell down a well, ending his supply of beautiful spring water.

Rabbits were everywhere up there and we were soon enjoying baked rabbit, and rabbit stew as well. They became another item for Uncle Jim to barter, as was the quaint system of the Irish in those days. A highlight for me was when I trapped the fox that had been stealing his chickens. I was the curly-haired boy after that! Sunday

Burrumbuttock Public School students catch their first two rabbits with ferrets and nets, harking back to the boyhoods of their dads and granddads.

was his day of rest and we would head off to church about 7.00 am, walk 3 miles to get there, hear Mass, talk for about one hour outside and then have to pass three pubs to get home, which was usually lunchtime. Thursday was another big day, as Uncle Jim would hitch his old grey horse to his pride and joy, which was this beautiful black buggy, and trot the 10 miles into Ballarat for supplies. I really enjoyed Thursdays. Another day to remember was one St Patrick's Day when my dad took me into Ballarat and to Lake Wendourie, where it was wall-to-wall Irish, and everywhere kids were dancing.

A GHOULISH ROUND

DENIS DOHERTY

In the 1950s, when I was eight, I spent several months at my relatives' places in South Australia, on a farm at Tooligie on the Eyre Peninsula and at Burra. On the farm at Tooligie there were rabbits everywhere. 'Anything you can do to keep the numbers down will be appreciated,' said my uncle. This city boy then put all his uncle's rabbit traps to work.

Within easy distance of the farmhouse were numerous warrens, and soon all the traps were set and ready to go at the entrances of burrows. Each morning in a ghoulish round I collected the still alive and squirming rabbits; usually around twenty. I had to give them a rabbit chop or kill them in other ways. Later, I was instructed on the gentle art of skinning rabbits. In no time at all I was able get the skin moving down the back legs and soon the rabbit and his skin were separated. The skins were dried along the wires of the fences near the farmhouse; a testament to the mayhem committed on the rabbit population of the Eyre Peninsula.

The apex of my joy was to accompany my older brothers, cousins, uncles and other adults on spotlighting activity. The rabbit would freeze in the spotlights and I would even be given a shot at it with a .22. How grown-up to be able to shoot at rabbits with a real gun, and I was only eight. All this was done at night from the back of a ute; with numerous people shooting at the rabbits there were endless arguments over who hit the rabbit. The rabbits screamed when we hit them and on one occasion we must have hit a nerve as a rabbit convulsed into a 6-foot leap. However, nobody ever called me 'Deadeye Den', so I mustn't have been a good shot.

Before I returned to suburban life there was one more chance to persecute the rabbits of South Australia. Mum's extended family also had an outpost in Burra, in another part of South Australia. We stayed at my uncle Jack's place there for several weeks; he also had .22 guns. Near the Burra place was a small mountain that had been cut very carefully in half by tin miners many years earlier. The cliffs created were a natural habitat for rabbits; it gave them protection from predators and easy digging for their burrows.

It was a boy's dream to shoot at those rabbits from the top of the cliffs. While I discharged many rounds at the rabbits and raised a lot of dust near the rabbits, I cannot recall ever hitting one. After a shot, all the rabbits would disappear down holes and then I would wait patiently for them to reappear. It didn't take long for them to come out and look around and the whole process would begin again.

MY STORY

NORMAN BAXTER

Norman was the oldest storyteller in the ABC Radio 'Rabbiting On' competition.

My brother and I, with the rest of the brothers and sisters, used to go to school at Garthowen. We were taught by William Foster. He taught thirty-two pupils at the Garthowen school. We went rabbiting after school and had to go around the traps in the morning before school. But in 1928, at fourteen, my brother and I left school and went catching the rabbits. We camped in a tent and lay on the ground, with a blanket under us and one over in the winter time; it was very cold. The price for the rabbits then was sixpence a pair. We went rabbiting in the winter from March till August, which was when the old doe rabbit had her kittens. We then had to wait for these small ones to grow up. We would start trapping again the March of the coming year. Other times, we'd do a bit of hay-making with a pitch fork; eight shillings a day and you had to work ten hours to get that!

There was no dole for the single man. My father got a dole ticket for nine of us and that had to do us for the week. We lived five miles from Attunga and seven miles from Tamworth, so we never saw much of Tamworth; we had very little transport. I had a push bike that I bought for three pounds.

Going back to about 1932 and the Great Depression, things were very tough but we saw it through with the rabbits. The disease that killed the rabbit cleaned them out on some farms, but the old rabbit came back. How we lived, you would not like to live like that again. So, at ninety-four years of age, born at Tamworth, in the days of the horse and sulky, no motor cars, or very few of them, I can go back to wagon and bullock teams, carting magnesite to the railway station, from Garthowen to Attunga.

So, this is some of the story. I hope you find it interesting. The rabbits kept us going. This is my story.

3.

QUEENS OF RABBIT RESOURCEFULNESS

Many of us might expect the Australian rabbit story to be mostly a 'Boy's own' adventure and in many stories that is the case. But the surprising element is the many and varied stories from girls, mums, aunts, wives and grandmas about women and the enterprising ways they were very much a part of the rabbit story. Rabbit plagues during wartime and Depression were often the catalyst for women and girls to become more involved with rabbits, on their own or helping out their husbands, families or dads; often with no choice but to pitch in with this difficult task. There are numerous reasons why women and girls were so involved in the 'Great Australian Rabbit Story'. They tell you why in these pages.

Rabbit plagues were so massive that everyone had to be involved; rabbits were in the billions prior to the release and spread of myxomatosis in the 1950s, according to estimates from scientists, rabbit trappers and other people of the time. Rabbit drives became community events and the tools of those drives included kitchen utensils, trays, pots and pans; anything that could make a racket.

In wartime, women and their kids were left to deal with rabbits, as well as the farming and jobs, as so many men went off to join the fight for 'King and Country'. But the rabbits kept breeding. One trapper wrote that he was dissuaded from joining up, as rabbiting and farming were deemed just as important. Rabbits were a cheap or free meal for families in Depression and wartime as well. Hence women's stories of recipes and preparing rabbits – whether caught themselves or by family, or delivered by the rabbitoh – are represented here. The women trappers talk, too, about tramping the hills in their rabbit pursuits, invariably fitted in around other commitments.

Women and girls have always had a critical role in many aspects of running a farm. In the past, when more people lived on small-holdings or acreage, or simply had backyards that backed onto the bush; before the suburban dream, the fenced-in quarter-acre block, became ubiquitous, women and girls were much more connected to the growing (or catching) and preparation of food.

Many of the stories are about the trials of trying to keep a small patch of flowers or vegetables – or a larger garden or farm – going in the face of the relentless pressure from rabbits. Young love features, and we discover how rabbits enabled families to buy both necessities and luxuries. There is even a bold question from a teenager, a neighbour, asked in an Austin family sitting room many years ago. These stories from women and girls are central to the Rabbit Story; some are the most heartbreaking of the collection. All show the enterprise, heart and stamina that the Australian girl and woman have in spades when faced with challenges like the rabbit. Lots to learn here!

A THOUGHTLESS WHIM

MRS CLAIRE McKENRY

My story is from a different point of view, of how a thoughtless whim has devastated a whole country. Back in the 1940s (I am now over eighty) I was invited to visit a Mr Austin who lived nearby in a two-storey homestead. It was typical of the homes built by the early squatters of the western district of Victoria, usually with sweeping lawns and English trees surrounding them. However this one was surrounded by suburban houses and busy roads on two sides. Mr Austin was sitting alone in a dark room, furnished with a heavy dark-brown suite and a huge fireplace. Some remaining large old trees shaded the building, and some windows still viewed Corio Bay from Western Beach.

After polite chatter, I broached the problem of the rabbit plague brought about by his family importing a few in 1859, to become the worst pest in Australia by 1900!

Austin replied that such an idea seemed quite reasonable at the time, as the squatters of those days had workmen to work the farms and, 'a fellow wanted some hunting'. He went on to say that such meets were great entertainment and the means of seeing neighbours for a shoot and riding. In England rabbits weren't much trouble, although they were originally introduced from France. 'Besides,' he said, 'the ladies loved such a get-together to exchange news and put on delightful parties.'

No more said about rabbit plagues – and no more invitations to teenage neighbours!

THE RABBIT KILLER

MRS MARIA MURPHY

The older folk still talk about it today. If you ask them about the rabbit plague of the 1940s they'll tell you how it turned a gentle, seventy-year-old grandmother, whom everyone knew had never harmed a fly, into the most efficient rabbit-killer of them all.

She took the rifle down from the wardrobe. She'd never killed anything before, but the awful ache inside her steeled her to it. She took the box of bullets and a warm coat out into the early morning mist that hung over the land like a silver shroud and went in search of Robbie's killers.

She passed the sorry remnants of her vegetable garden and what remained of her flowerbeds as she walked through the orchard with its ringbarked trees and denuded vines to the open paddocks beyond. She saw them almost immediately – her Robbie's murderers – and an icy coldness gripped her heart.

She saw him riding the bay pony as she lifted the rifle; saw the pony buckle, and the sound of the .22 bullet leaving the barrel in the crisp, early morning silence became the sound of the little bay's leg snapping as it crashed to the ground – sending Robbie hurtling over its head.

She knew the bullet had found its mark when she saw her quarry jerk and convulse from the impact, and she instantly lined up another target. She'd defended them once. She'd felt sorry for them, with their soft brown eyes and gentle ways, and had thought the slaughter of them a sin. But they'd destroyed her pity. They wanted too much; took too much, and had just kept *coming* – more and more of them – until there was not a patch of ground left for anyone or anything else. Okay, Robbie might have been thought careless, cantering the pony across the paddocks, but they were *his* paddocks, for Christ's sake! If *they* hadn't made so many holes the pony might not have put his foot in one.

They found her, as the sun inched its way towards midday, sitting by Robbie's grave with the rifle in her lap and the empty bullet box beside her, and they marvelled at the sight of it. It wasn't that she was there – or that she had the rifle – it was the fact that she had shot over sixty rabbits. The place was crawling with them, fair enough, but even the best marksman in the district would be flat out getting that many before lunchtime!

MUM'S STORY

BELINDA DUFALL

I grew up in the early 1940s on a dairy farm in the bush between Mount Barker and Denmark. We had no electricity and no fridge and, as we usually only went to Mount Barker to shop once a week, we ate what was available on the farm. Something that we had plenty of was rabbits!

My dad shot or trapped them and my mum cooked them. We had rabbit stew, rabbit casserole, roast rabbit, braised rabbit and crumbed rabbit. My mum's speciality was her absolutely delicious rabbit and bacon rolls. They were made by mincing rabbit meat and bacon, adding chopped onion and parsley, rolling up in homemade puff pastry then cooking in our small wood stove. They were much sought after at local functions.

My dad also tanned the skins so that they could be used for mats. My pride and joy was a rabbit-skin coat. My dad had worked on the back of the skin to make it soft and pliable. Mum made the coat and lined it with red silk. Everyone admired it. When I was about seven years old we travelled to Perth on the train to see the sights. The highlight of our trip was visiting the Perth Zoo. In those days people got dressed in their best clothes to go on a visit, so naturally I wore my beautiful rabbit-skin coat.

Everything was going well until we were standing in front of the lion and tiger cages. I had always wanted to see the big cats, but my joy was short-lived. As soon as they saw me they began growling and roaring so much that the keeper came to see what was happening. Apparently they thought that I (in my beautiful coat) was their next meal! The keepers suggested that we should move away as we were upsetting the animals. I was so disappointed. Even though it happened a very long time ago, it has always been one of the most vivid memories of my childhood.

I STILL SMELL RABBIT!

LINETTE TREASURE

I grew up among the pervasive stink of rabbit: buck rabbits, milky does, their warm guts and their carcasses. I was born in country dominated by rabbits, both enemy and livelihood. From letters of the time are the words: 'Mum's sister and husband trapped three thousand this week'; 'Dad's sister shoots fourteen for dog feed': 'It would be a great idea to have a plug of dynamite, as it is nothing to see fifteen rabbits in a space of 40 square feet.'

When I was three I had a pet rabbit, Blacky, spared because he was different. On frosty mornings I would creep out and take him back to my cot where he would burrow down to warm my feet with his soft fur. I learned his favourite grasses and I loved Blacky. I cried and cried when the cat clawed out his eye and killed him.

My aunty Rita supported her family trapping rabbits. She lugged heavy steel traps around the hills, night and morning checking the lines. Sometimes I went with her, learning to see faint tracks through grass and spiderwebs, learning the best spots: beneath the netting fence, on a pill bed or an entrance to a warren.

I grew accustomed to the squeal of trapped rabbits, the swift twist of their necks being broken, smelling their limp, gutted bodies. As kids we dug out rabbits with the old dog scratching excitedly beside us. But we baulked at killing, so took them home and, despite Mum's disapproval, left the bumping bag in the bath for Dad.

My father's people were cattlemen fighting the rabbit with trappers, poisoning, shooting, digging out and dozing. They built netting fences and carried out poisoning blitzes with free feeds of carrot then added strychnine. I remember the horror of one dark night, waking and following the lamplight outside to see one of our favourite dogs convulsing and vomiting as it was force-fed salt and bluestone. This dog had slipped its leather muzzle and eaten poisoned rabbit.

When I was seven I went to school at Dargo, in Gippsland, staying with Mum's people, who were trappers. They ate rabbit, stewed or curried, and money was earned from the skins and then from the gutted carcasses. Every week I travelled with the rabbit man in his truck with the rows of rabbit pairs slung across poles in the back. I left home in darkness for the slow trip picking carcasses left out and covered with hessian. I carried the smell of rabbit, but I doubt that the kids at school smelled any different.

In the 1950s, myxomatosis came. Dad enthusiastically took part in its release. But at Dargo there was concern that the virus would bring calamity. The world did change with myxo. Many people lost income, and millions of dead rabbits created a dreadful stink across the nation. But the earth healed, grass grew, and bush creatures thrived. For decades the rabbit was beaten, but I now can smell it once again, growing stronger.

MUM, ME, THE RABBITS AND THE GREY 28 FERGIE

LYNDLEY CHOPPING

The rabbits were overrunning the farm at Ouse, so along with trapping, ripping the warrens and fumigating, we took to poisoning them with 1080. Mum was supervisor of growing the carrots used for bait (a hard taskmaster when it came to watering, hoeing and weeding the damn things). After feeding the carrots through a carrot cutter, they were put into sacks, and carried on the three-point linkage carry-all on the rear of the little grey Fergie. Its carrying capacity was eight bags of carrots (400 kilograms), but only on the flat road, even with wheel weights on the front wheels!

When going up hills, the front wheels were prone to coming off the ground until the rear of the carry-all touched the ground, stopping the Fergie from rearing any further. Mum, who was on the carry-all feeding out the cut-up 'free feed' carrots, would call out, 'Lyndley, stop it, put it down!' If I couldn't, I used the steering brakes, then we would stop, turn around and back up that bit of a bank. There were always three free feeds (five to six hours each time) as well as the poison feed for each paddock or run, so there was a lot of travelling. Mr Agnew from Oatlands did invent a trailing poison cart which would cut up and feed out the carrots; mechanisation came at last.

One day when free feeding the rabbit furrow at lunchtime out in the back paddock (of course, where else), when I put my hand on the rear tyre as I swung down off the tractor I felt something soft under my hand and thought, 'Oh, no, I hope that isn't the inner tube,' but oh, yes it was.

Well, the thing to do was to 'have that cup of tea and a sandwich', while Mum and I decided to put some soft green wattle bark over the protruding inner tube, between the bar grips of the tyre; we then wrapped strips of sacking around that. With the tyre like a big bandage, we proceeded to bump and limp our way homeward. We finished that furrow and made it home again.

As well as having ferrets for putting down the burrows, we had a pack of twenty-four hunting dogs, and weren't they licorice allsorts. Some were greyhounds, failed track-racers. They were excellent in the open country and paddocks and would gather up the running rabbits in their stride, while the whippets were not far behind. The hounds were better in the tussocks, scrub and wattles for catching the rabbits in squats or digging out short burrows. Then there were the errant, wayward sheepdogs – collies, smithfields, kelpies – who had turned hunting dogs as well. After skinning the rabbits, the carcasses were used as dog food and the skins hung over a rabbit wire to dry. Sometimes this had 300 to 400 strung out for 50 to 70 yards. Thank goodness when myxomatosis came along. Damn rabbits!

A TASTE OF THINGS TO COME

GLENYS THOMPSON

It was mid-January 2007 and our family business was in the process of moving from a small family farm at Jetsonville to a larger farm business at West Scottsdale, at the foot of the Sideling Range near Scottsdale, Tasmania.

The day was hot; the first two to arrive at the farmhouse were me and my son. We arrived in two vehicles; mine a station wagon with a few things, and my son in his four-wheel drive with his belongings, which included his firearms, bar fridge, collection of knives and a few clothes.

We opened the house to inspect our lot and think about where the furniture would go and who would have which bedroom. We proceeded to look around and speculate on a few things when my son said, 'I'll have that room.' He entered the room, looked out of the window and there was a rabbit sitting right outside the window under the tree. He, being a keen hunter, head-shot the rabbit, cleaned it and put it in the kitchen sink.

The scene was set: a totally empty farmhouse, two people waiting for their belongings to arrive and a kitchen sink full of rabbit, ready for cooking! A flash of thoughts entered my mind: yes you can live off the land. My son was thinking, again, of his next meal – and what an opening to a new life on this property!

SPOTLIGHTING WITH DAD

PAULINE TANASKOVIC

Rabbits were in plague proportions, and paddocks in part rendered useless because of rabbit warrens, on my parents' farm in Charlton, on Eyre Peninsula, South Australia, where I, primary-schooled in Adelaide, spent my holidays during 1942 to 1949.

In 1944, at age seven, I accompanied the farm labourer on a rabbit eradication expedition. He set about pushing tube shapes made from chicken wire and closed at one end into the beginning of all but one rabbit hole in a warren, leaving most of the tube outside on the ground. Into the one remaining hole he directed a ferret from a box he carried. He then pushed another wire tube into that hole too. I recall waiting for what seemed a long time in hot sun with nothing happening, certainly no mass exodus of rabbits or ferret. Later I learned that rogue ferrets, or those not well trained, would sometimes stay in the burrows, only emerging after they had had a good feed of bunny, which I suspect was the case on that expedition!

The most successful method of catching rabbits were long-handled, oversized butterfly-type nets that were wielded by the men standing in the back of Dad's small farm truck while spotlighting;

just scooping up rabbits en masse as they were caught in the beam of the spotlight.

Aged eight, after much pestering, Dad let me go spotlighting also, but only if I stood in the back with the dogs and a couple of his mates, getting in and out on my own. He said there was no room in the cabin with him, his mate who directed the spotlight and the guns. Because I didn't know what I was in for, I was not dissuaded. What an experience! I hung on to the rail at the back of the cabin like grim death while the vehicle twisted and turned, jarring every bone in my body, as Dad raced over rough open space in pursuit of game. Excited dogs ran backwards and forwards behind my legs as we belted along – jumping in and out of the truck as game was cornered by the spotlight, shot, and the bodies thrown into the back with me. When each net of rabbits was scooped up, the men quickly broke their necks. Arriving home, the back of the truck was thick with rabbits, and several bloodied kangaroos, all around my legs – all dogs' food. Farmers didn't like eating 'underground mutton', as they called rabbits, and would only stoop to eat this meat if times were bad. I never asked to go spotlighting again.

RABBIT GENES

DELIA BRODRICK

Nineteen seventy-two. I was twelve, so too young to have seen the historic rabbit plagues. Yet in that year, thanks to those early plagues, I learned more about rabbits and genes than I wanted to and, consequently, suddenly grew up. Firstly, for my birthday I got Snowy, a soft, fluffy pet rabbit that I adored. Secondly, at school, we read about Thomas Austin's twenty-four imported wild rabbits, the culling of two million offspring annually and how the survivors continued to breed like … rabbits; how high they jumped and how deep they burrowed. We saw photos of the rabbit-proof fence, of swarthy trappers with dogs, and of dead rabbits. We watched archival films showing hundreds of mad rabbits crazily running everywhere over desolate land. They were terrible! Wild rabbits. Not pets.

The men looked like my grandpa as a young man and were wearing hats like Grandpa's. The teacher, Mr Anderson, asked if anyone in our families lived through the Great Depression and, if so, to invite them to visit the class. I invited Grandpa. I was naive.

'Nineteen thirty-three,' he recalled. 'Hardly any work but I was lucky; I was a rabbit trapper.' (*RABBIT TRAPPER!*) 'We used them for everything,' he said. 'Food, money, debts; even luck. You wouldn't believe how many there were. Swarming; like flies at a barbie.' (*I regretted inviting Grandpa. I felt sick.*) 'We ate 'em. The dogs and chooks did too, and we used their skins. That's how I met my wife,' Grandpa said, tapping his old hat. (*Ate them? Wife? Skins?*) Grandpa dug into his pocket and pulled out a rabbit's foot. 'This,' he rabbited on, 'is a lucky rabbit's foot. I used to trap 'em, skin 'em and take 'em to the butcher or home. The skins went to this pretty girl I had my eye on. A fur-cutter, she was. She cleaned and cut skins then sold 'em to the skin sales.' (*I shared genes with this man!*) 'I asked her to go out with me. She agreed, so I kept a foot from one of the rabbits. It must have been lucky because, you know what,' he winked, 'she married me.' (*Snowy was at home alone with a woman who cut rabbit skins!*)

Paranoia set in. I couldn't get home quickly enough. Thankfully, Snowy was still alive. I ignored them at dinner. Mum had made her chicken pie, always guaranteed to make my day better. 'Fantastic, thanks, Mum!'

My brother was hysterical. Snorting, gagging. Strewth, I shared his genes too. No, I was adopted. That was it. 'Thanks, Grandpa! It's not chicken, neither!' I was in the dunny for ages, finger down my throat.

Two thousand and eight. I am older and a vegetarian. Snowy lived to a ripe old rabbit age, safe from my grandpa's hands. My daughter is a chef. She is known for her rabbit pie. Grandpa taught her to cook. She's expert at skinning and cleaning them too. It's her genes.

THE STONY RISES OF GNARPURT STATION

GWENDOLINE HYNES WITH SIBLINGS NOEL HYNES AND IRENE MEEK

While talking to siblings Noel and Irene about Gnarpurt Station, south-east of Lismore, Victoria, I asked, 'Were there really millions of rabbits on the Stony Rises?'

'Probably more!' exclaimed 66-year-old Noel Hynes. 'I was five when Dad worked as a rabbiter with two other men, Mr Dunstan and Mr Perry. The station consisted of a stately bluestone homestead, seven houses, shearers' quarters, slaughter house, church, school, sheds and a stable. Our family lived in a house close to Mr and Mrs Dunstan. Mr Perry lived in the shearers' quarters. We attended the local State School 4616, with our older sister Beverley. The school was built by station owner Sir Chester Manifold and given to the Education Department. Rabbit drives were then organised to raise money to furnish and equip the school. I still have a book, *The Mighty Hunter*, awarded to me in grade one, and a slightly rusted green tin cannon, given by the Mother's Club from that school.'

Noel talked more about the rabbit drives which he said created great social activity, with men, women and children walking miles, banging jam tins with sticks, and driving thousands of terrified, squealing rabbits into a wire netting funnel formation through to a holding pen. The rabbits had their necks wrung and were gutted leaving the liver intact to determine its freshness. Their legs were interlocked in pairs, tied and hung in portable refrigeration units, to be sold in the city for human consumption. Each family took cut lunches, billies of cold tea and water in hessian bags to have while resting on stones during these busy spring days. Daily, they also sent ferrets down warrens to hunt out rabbits, set steel traps at night and used greyhounds to hunt the rabbits. Each of the three men was paid individually by the buyer, Mr Frank O'Beirne, for their rabbit skins.

'I remember standing excitedly with Mum peering down the long dirt road, waiting for Dad to arrive with our first car, a yellow Ford Anglia brought with money from skins,' said Irene Meek. 'Our stylish grandmother had a fur rabbit-skin coat and beret.'

Noel doesn't remember his grandmother's outfit, but recalls a fluffy orange rabbit that his father had stuffed for him.

Noel continued. 'A teacher, Miss McLennon, queried Mum as to why Irene excelled at counting. "Well! That's because she helps her father count the rabbit skins." The teacher didn't understand, until being taken into the shed that was filled with thousands of skins, hanging to dry or stacked in groups of 100 pairs. "Goodness gracious," she said, hurrying off to get her Brownie camera.'

Gnarpurt Station ran several thousand sheep, along with some cattle. 'Dad was eventually made overseer of the property,' said Irene.

Our parents have passed on, and rest peacefully at the well-tended cemetery at Lismore, with an occasional rabbit or two scurrying around during warm spring days. Our younger sister, Carol, born in 1956, escaped the experience of millions of rabbits on the Station.

QUIETLY HELPING DAD

BARBARA PATTERSON

'Stop,' I whispered in my father's ear. 'I can see two together!' My father slammed on the brakes. The year was 1956; I was twelve years old. The Mallee had seen record rainfall and rabbits were everywhere.

We had a property appropriately called The Birdcage. It was on the Lalbert Creek and its many crabholes had filled with water, indeed the whole paddock had been submerged in the peak of the floods. The Birdcage was uncleared and suitable for grazing sheep only. That is what attracted my father to buying the property in the first place. After the ground dried out enough, my father would take my two younger brothers and myself, after school, to The Birdcage to shoot rabbits. Our car was an FE Holden and we each had a rifle resting on the door, the barrel pointing through the open window. We would quietly say 'Stop' when we spotted a rabbit, then take aim and fire. Quietness was essential as any noise would frighten the rabbits. The rifle shot would get them all running too, but we tried to all have a rabbit in our sights at the one time.

The rabbits had plenty of places to hide; lush grass grew after the rain and there was dead timber all over the ground – negotiating it must have been chaotic for my father. Sometimes we would get stuck in a hole or on a log and the three of us would have to push.

Both my brothers had shot two rabbits with the one bullet and I was excited when I lined up two together one day. However, the excitement proved too much; I moved the rifle and missed both!

We would generally shoot forty or fifty pairs of rabbits in a day. Then came the hardest part; we would sit on a log and gut them: take their intestines out. They would be put into pairs and put on bags in the boot of the car. The innards would have been great food for crows.

We transported the rabbits to a portable cooler which was stationed at Lalbert. At this time most towns had rabbit coolers. I liked going into the cooler – up the steps, through the heavy door and into the coldest place I had ever been in. The cooler was filled with rows and rows of paired rabbits. We were paid one shilling and threepence per pair.

We were part of a huge operation helping to clear the countryside of the rabbit menace. It was an exciting time for one twelve-year-old girl.

SECOND THOUGHTS

ELIZABETH MARTIN

My relationship with rabbits goes a long way back. The family lore tells of my grandpa and his brother Tom living off them in the Depression before he was married and had his own litter of seven children, starting with my dad in 1936. They built a hut in Blackwood, Victoria, that is still there today and protected by the National Trust. From that log hut they hunted rabbits. My grandpa was a good cook and knew how to roast rabbits on an open fire and bake rabbit pie with vegetables and gravy.

My mum occasionally served one up in winter in the 1970s. She coated the torn-apart pieces with bacon strips and a crust made of mixed herbs, bread and onions, and poured milk over the lot. Then she baked it, covered, in the oven. This is a childhood meal I remember with a smile, and a watery mouth. My husband, though, remembers rabbit meals with distaste: poor man's food, and served too often in his family.

I also remember rabbits plaguing the land. I dated a man fifteen years ago whose German grandparents had immigrated to a farm in Edenhope in western Victoria. Rabbits were pests, and we were encouraged to go out and shoot a few. I was very reluctant. My first concern was for my own safety as guns are things to be feared. I also felt uncomfortable deliberately setting off at dusk to kill something. The rabbits were everywhere. They infested the dusty land. We saw them in silhouette up ahead, and the earth beneath our feet was honeycombed with rabbit burrows.

Despite my reluctance, it was exhilarating. I was entranced by the soft light that glowed over the wheat, the long shadows lying on the ground and the whisper of warm wind in the air. There was the adrenaline rush of stalking them, slowly creeping up and advancing one small step at a time, the slow aim of my boyfriend with the sleek rifle, then the snap and echo and the drumming scattering of hundreds of paws.

He missed. So we advanced some more. Around the next bend there was another group nibbling on the stumpy dried grass; some sitting up, ears erect, like flat cut-outs from a carnival sideshow. Again he slowly aimed, fired, and this time one silhouette went down with a spray of dirt and a high-pitched scream.

We ran. The bullet had hit its hind legs, and it was dragging itself away from us. By the time we reached it, me sobbing, the rabbit had crawled into a thick bunch of bracken, squealing like a kitten, unable to be retrieved. We could hear it struggling, trying frantically to get to safety. We couldn't reach it to put it out of its misery.

Sadly, we wandered back to the farm house, watching the sea of rabbits now fearlessly bounding in front of us. Shooting a rabbit seemed suddenly cruel and pointless when faced with hundreds of them decimating the land. They were a plague that couldn't be stopped.

That night we ate chicken.

A CLEVER LITTLE GIRL

LYN CHAMPION

My memories of the rabbit plague in Australia relate to growing up on a property west of Muswellbrook in the Upper Hunter of NSW. My father regularly laid a poison trail for rabbits. I recall as a little girl sitting on the back veranda helping to cut up thistle roots which my father would then soak in poison before laying a trail for the rabbits. He would also give me some of the roots to lay a trail in the house paddock. Each morning my father would be up very early to check the trail and bring in the dead rabbits. When I got up I would check my trail. I was always so excited that I always caught the coloured rabbits, while my father only caught ordinary grey ones.

It was like discovering the truth about Santa Claus when one morning I was up earlier than usual to see my father placing all the coloured rabbits from his trail on my trail. Naturally, my father was not giving me, a child, poisoned baits. However, he gave me a lot of pleasure for a long time, thinking I was so clever 'catching all the coloured rabbits, while Daddy only caught the grey ones!' My contribution to the eradication of rabbits would obviously have been negligible, but I certainly remember the devastation that they caused, and the many hours of hard work put into attempting to control them.

SPOTLIGHTING

LEE SHELDEN

It's Saturday night in Thorpdale, Victoria, and she's just one of the lads, heading off in the ute with a couple of rifles and a bottle or two of sweet cider. She's fifteen and tense with excitement, shivering in the biting cold Gippsland air and wishing she could be part of that great unknown world 'out there'. She has persuaded her nineteen-year-old brother to let her go spotlighting with him and his mates, the Myrteza brothers. The boys are full of bravado. Someone brags about catching rabbits with his bare hands by dazzling a group of them in the spotlight, then running in diminishing circles around them until he can grab one. There are still plenty of rabbits in the Gippsland hills, even though myxo has significantly reduced their numbers.

The comfortable daytime world of the potato farms with their neat patchwork of ploughed paddocks and basic houses now seems vaguely menacing. Cypress windbreaks cast strange shadows on a black and grey landscape. The night is full of possibilities.

Being the only girl, she spends most of the evening in the cab, but when she has a go at the rifle, the boys humour her clumsiness and, even with Joe Myrteza steadying her arm, all she manages to do is send the bunnies running in all directions. But she's exhilarated, her cheeks rosy with the cold and the rush of fresh night air as they cruise along the road, panning the spotlight in great arcs across the paddocks.

Tonight she's learning a lot more than how to hold a rifle and wield a spotlight. While on the other side of the world teenagers are smoking pot and listening to Jimi Hendrix at Woodstock, she's smoking her first cigarette and tuning in to 2SM Sydney on the car radio. She basks in the wild, sexy sounds of Hendrix, Cream, Led Zeppelin. She's carried a long way away from an unhappy family in an ordinary little farmhouse and parents who disapprove of most of the really interesting things that life in the 1960s has to offer. Then, while the others are busy skinning and cleaning rabbits, Joe – strong, quiet, gentle Joe – kisses her and she feels like life is really beginning.

Soon her brother will be called up and head off to Pucka for army training. He doesn't end up in Vietnam like so many other young Australian men at the time, but his world still changes dramatically. She will finish high school with her mind always on the exciting world just beyond her reach – encouraged by radical teachers who invite their students to tea, to sit on the floor listening to protest music and discussing politics, feminism and the sexual revolution. Yet when she goes to college in the city she will spend a lot of time sitting under a gum tree in the park, gazing up at the sky and longing to be back in that dark country night, spotlighting.

'WATCH THE HOLE'

JULIE BRAILEY

When our family used to go rabbiting in the 1960s and 1970s we would camp out in various places in the southern highlands and rabbit all weekend. 'Watch the hole,' my dad used to say. You would see us, heads to the ground to hear the rabbits coming up from underground. One memorable time was while rabbiting at Crookwell, when Dad had some live rabbits to take back to a dog trainer. Our family of five spent the night in a park all sleeping together in the back of an old Valiant Regal station wagon. Ferrets got the front floor. The live rabbits were in a hessian bag under the car. It must have been very cold that night, as when dad got the rabbits out from under the car in the morning, they were all frozen stiff. It is one pastime that children of today would never do.

ALL THINGS WILD

PAULA VERA

Well, where do I start? How far back can I remember having feral rabbits in my life? Was it at the dinner table, or the Esky full in the back of the Cortina, or our hunting dogs retrieving relentlessly, or is it the photo of me as a cute three-year-old with blonde curls, down on my knees in the garage in the middle of the night in my pink nightie wowing at the great haul that Dad and the uncles brought home?

Being a first-generation Aussie from Italian parents who came out in the early 1950s, a huge part of my life was – and still partly is – the hunting, preparation and eating of all things from the wild. I once caught a very young cute feral rabbit as a young teenager, and was desperate to bring it home as a pet. Mums always know in advance that it's them who take care of the little creatures. Sure, I looked at it now and then, watched it grow into a young adult, but a pet it wasn't.

This happened at that stage of my life when I stayed up late, worked hard during the week at high school having fun and slept in on the Sundays when we weren't out hunting or being dragged to

Sunday Mass. This particular Sunday, I got away with staying in bed till lunchtime, when my dear gentle loving Mamma called me to come to lunch. I sat dozily at the table (I can remember this as if it was yesterday, but unbelievably it was thirty years ago!) trying to focus and be appreciative of the beautiful roast that she had put on for us. But then something clicked; I think it was the size of the rabbit pieces. Again, eating rabbit, duck, quail and the like was an everyday event, but the young succulent pieces called out, 'Don't eat me, don't eat me.'

Jean and Ken Crawford and their children, the Hardham youngsters, and Phillip Gilmour, with their rabbit catch at Jidbinbilla near Canberra, 1959.

I looked at Ma. 'Well, what did you think I was going to do with it?' was her comment, as she munched away on my sweet fluffy rabbit. I love her dearly, I trust her body and soul with the grandchildren, but never again with a pet. Even to this day, there is no greater gift to my parent than a frozen homegrown young rooster, wild rabbit, hare or a wood duck or two.

THE GROUP FELL SILENT

DENISE EBERLE

When our two boys were aged four and seven we took them on an outdoor adventure to our friends' property. They were thoroughly enjoying the outdoor experience as the property was next to the Burdekin River near Charters Towers in northern Queensland. We set up camp near the river.

As it was the Easter long weekend we had four days to enjoy the area and company of our fellow campers. The others were younger than us with no children but we all got along well and the boys had a great time, fishing, riding motorbikes, shooting tins – all of the activities little boys love to do but never get the opportunity when they live in the city. Having spent a couple of days doing all the activities and just enjoying the beautiful surrounds, we decided to visit our friends at their property on the Saturday afternoon. We ended up staying that night and enjoyed a lovely barbecue meal.

The older men in the group decided that they would go for a drive over to the cleared paddock to see if there were any rabbits, which had been causing the farmers a lot of problems by eating their crops and crippling any of the stock who were unfortunate enough to walk into the many rabbit holes, which were everywhere. We all decided to go for the drive as it was a beautiful moonlit night. Sure enough, we saw rabbits everywhere in the spotlights.

The two utes pulled up in the centre of the paddock. The men got out and took their rifles from the back of the vehicles. All of a sudden a small voice from the back of our ute said, 'Please don't shoot the Easter Bunny!' Every adult in the group fell silent. We had all been having such a lovely evening we had forgotten that it was Easter and the Easter Bunny was due in the morning.

The men communed silently with each other and put their rifles away. We ended up just driving around looking at all the rabbits in the spotlight, much to the delight of the children. Bump, bump, bump over the holes we went. The next morning the boys woke to find the Easter Bunny had called during the night and left them a small parcel of eggs at the end of their swags.

That evening at the campsite we enjoyed a lovely meal of roast meat that had been skewered onto sticks and cooked over the coals. The children loved the food and often asked why we never had this lovely meat at home. We told them that it was Burdekin chicken and it was a delicacy. We never had the heart to tell them that they were eating rabbit. If my sons read this story they will find out but I am sure they will now understand. Times were tough then.

HARMONIUM FRIGHT AND FLIGHT

MARY FINLAYSON

My mother-in-law, who played the harmonium (organ) for forty years, tells this story. She retired aged ninety-two.

'Kilcoy Church in Scots' Corner was built in 1882 on a hillside surrounded by paddocks. In early days, services were held once a month. During the rabbit plague, rabbits built a warren under the wooden church. When the next service began with music from the harmonium, a rumble came from below the floor and a cloud of fine dust filled the church. The view from the windows could not be believed. Confused rabbits, going in all directions across the paddocks!'

RUN, RABBIT, RUN

AUDREY HOFFMAN

'Mum, if we don't catch any bunnies today, what will we have for tea?'

'Lamb's fry.'

Our faces fell. Without hesitation we went off with our shovels and sugar bags, dragging them awkwardly to the quarries where there were mazes of burrows waiting. These were the 1940s in western Victoria and not only were rabbits a pest, but they were dangerous.

On the day after a dreadful fire my uncle took me with him as he gathered rescued burnt stock and checked fences. Being a problem seven-year-old, I didn't heed instructions to stay in the truck cabin, but jumped out and ran around until my left leg lodged in a burning rabbit burrow. Stupid rabbits! Their fault, not mine!

Those years were challenging times, recovering from the war and the 1944 bushfires. But we youngsters had a great life rolling tanks up and down paddocks and building cubby houses. Some of our best fun was had when our school Parents' Association held rabbit drives to raise funds.

Dad's big, bulky, khaki ex-army truck carried lots of us to a place in the Stony Rises littered with rabbits – big, fat, tender bunnies devouring the sweet grasses of this volcanic country. We all knew what to do: line up across one boundary, close together, to walk across the paddock making lots of noise, wielding sticks to bring the rabbits out of their warrens.

Scurrying out, they could but go one way, off helter-skelter in front of us. The bunnies were surrounded by netting fences. We giggled, laughed, yelped and screamed. Rabbits scurried away; we were not only having fun but also trying to eradicate them for the benefit of our farmer fathers as well as making pounds, shillings and pence for school funds.

We had other forms of entertainment too. One of the school parents, Arnie, held movie nights in his big tin shed. We loved the reel-to-reel 8-millimetre films he hired, and the supper was special. One night we were shown a film of one of our rabbit drives. While this was entertaining in itself, the best was to come when the film was run backwards. Rabbits backed down from where they were strung across the back of a ute, their guts flipping back into the slits down their chests, their legs gathering momentum as they ran backwards, and bottoms-first, back into their burrows with us hilariously backwardly retreating. After that, every time our family sat down to rabbit and bacon stew, I wondered if the stew might become 'alive' and rabbits bolt backwards out the door, home to the Stony Rises.

PESKY FLIES AND MANGY RABBITS

MISS LAUREN WOOD

Living near a park reserve in Devonport, Tasmania, we would often see wild rabbits in plague proportions in summer. In the mid-1980s, just as flies would be pesky due to an influx of sheep boats that docked off the coast, so would mangy rabbits. The rabbits weren't the cute bunny flop-eared type that you associate with the Easter Bunny, but scatty, large, wild and unattractive. One afternoon in the summer holidays I lay basking in the sun on a towel. Out of the corner of my eye I saw a wild beast and screamed. Mum who was napping upstairs, flew down the stairs and armed herself with Dad's fishing net and a pair of gardening gloves. These rabbits weren't to be messed with! We didn't harm the alien creature, as we felt no animal deserves to be killed, but let him go in some scrubby bushland.

SKINS LEGACY

CAROL HILL

'Rabbits: they were everywhere, thousands of them,' so said my father, and he should know, because his father, my grandfather, made his living out of skins. Sheep skins, possum skins, but mostly rabbit skins – probably millions of them. If old Ernest John Sidebottom knew anything, it was about rabbit skins. A bit of a pioneer in northern Tasmania was old E.J.; a man not afraid to take chances. He went bankrupt twice. But somehow he always seemed to bounce back. I didn't know it when I was growing up in Mary Street, East Launceston, in the big old house that had been owned by E.J. and passed down to my father, that the lifestyle I was enjoying – the big grounds, the coolness in summer under the weeping willow tree, the rambling home that always seemed so safe in a thunderstorm – was all because of those blasted rabbits; maybe millions of them. Australia might have ridden on the sheep's back, but the Sidebottom family rode on the rabbit skins!

'THUMP, THUMP, THUMP'

HELEN BENNETT

Being born and bred in the Mallee, I have never known our environment to be short of rabbits, thriving in good seasons and surviving in the poorer ones. No matter how extreme the weather conditions, the rabbit endures them all. Although myxomatosis and the calicivirus have helped in reducing population numbers dramatically, followed by the ripping of burrows and poisoning campaigns, the rabbit still carries on breeding regardless of our relentless crusade against their existence.

Researching my family history took me one day to our local cemetery. A lonely, fenced-off reserve at the top of a rise on the outskirts of our little town, it was situated a few hundred metres from the road within a local farmer's paddock. I stopped my car at the closed paddock gate, opened it, drove through and continued up the incline to the cemetery gate. With my two-year-old daughter asleep in her car seat, a cool, partly cloudy day meant I could leave her resting with the windows down while I, armed with pen and paper, walked to the cemetery gate prepared to record information from the headstones. When I opened the gate, rabbits disappeared down their burrows within the cemetery grounds. Vermin I saw almost on a daily basis. It's not something that attracts my attention so I didn't take much notice.

I went about my task and was almost done when I was jotting down information from a concrete-covered grave. It was where I had sighted the rabbits vanishing when I arrived. The opening of their burrow sheltered beside the grave and wound down into the earth. I stood beside the grave and suddenly felt a thump … thump … thump … through the soles of my feet. Knowing damn well it was only the rabbits underneath, it did not prevent me from starting to walk – then accelerate quickly to a run – back to the gate, hastily closing it and not hesitating to return to the driver's seat of my car. Only then, with my heart beating at a furious pace, was I able to recuperate from my experience. I laughed at myself, glanced at my daughter still snoozing in her car seat, and returned home feeling a little rattled from the incident.

Many times since I have returned to the cemetery, but that one occasion remains the only 'spooky' event I have had the displeasure of experiencing there. The rabbit remains and probably always will, ongoing; making the most of its existence, continuing to survive the harshness of our landscape. I will never forget my 'scary' rabbit encounter and still laugh when I recall one of my first visits to the Waitchie Cemetery.

A CASUAL DISDAIN

PAMELA THOMPSON

A visit from a city cousin – much worse, a girl – was the Richardson boys' worst nightmare. However, when I arrived in Charlton, Victoria, to stay for the holidays, my tomboy appearance seemed to allay some of their fears of being stuck with less than appealing girl's games. The boys were going rabbiting on Curnow's Hill and I was invited! During the morning I learned to set traps and camouflage them as we went from one burrow entrance to another. We chatted easily and I was accepted as one of the 'boys'. Later in the day the traps were collected, along with two rabbits.

I can only imagine now the utter horror when I insisted on saving the rabbits! The boys, used to quickly dispatching the catch and skinning them ready for the pot, were totally at a loss to deal with my compassion. Their parents insisted that, as a visitor, my rescue efforts should be allowed and any attempt to thwart them would incur punishment. I put iceblock stick splints on the rabbits' injured legs, binding them with a professionalism usually only achieved by a medical practitioner. I did not see the boys again for the rest of the week as I lovingly tended my patients.

On each subsequent school holiday visit to Charlton, I was treated with a casual disdain, and never again invited to go rabbiting. I guess I will never know what happened to the two bunnies when I left. Perhaps they only had a short but confusing delay between the trap and the pot. As adults, the boys constantly reminded me about the incident, but I think in time I was forgiven.

STILL CATCHING RABBITS IN MY SEVENTIES

MELBA AUSTEN

As a young child I was taught to catch, skin and clean rabbits by my older brothers and sister on our property at Blaxland Creek in the Clarence Valley. A kerosene hurricane lantern was used for a light to go round the traps. Of a morning, as we brought the cows in to milk, the rabbits would be collected. Times were hard in the 1930s and we had no boots so we would warm our feet where the cow was lying down in the frost. We sold the skins in the wintertime when the rabbits had good thick fur on them. The skins were sent to Armidale on the mail service car. The best price we received was one pound for a pound of skins in weight. This money was such a help to the family in hard times. The rabbits would be skinned and the skins put on wires to dry out. We also ate a lot of rabbit. In the 1950s and 1960s, on a property at Chambigne, we were issued with the myxomatosis virus and with neighbours caught some rabbits at night with nets on long poles by spotlight and injected them with the virus. That worked well. I did a lot of trapping over the years to keep them down. We also used a poison called Pindone. The Rural Land Board issued raw carrots and I used to take them around the warrens on a motorbike and feed them for three nights, then put out carrots with the Pindone on them. This also worked well. We also had a Land Board man come with a gas gun which started a fire but luckily we had taken some bushes with us and could put it out. That was not a real successful venture.

Now in my late seventies, I still have to catch the odd rabbit that comes into my vegetable garden. I skin and clean them for the dog or, if it's a good clean young rabbit, I give it to a lady who likes to eat them. I have eaten many of them in the past, but could not eat them now.

DEAD OR ALIVE

FLO, FROM CLUNES COMMUNITY CONVERSATIONS

In the early 1960s Ken, my husband and a builder, was called away to do some work. I was pregnant at the time. To supplement our income Ken bought a portable freezer. He had advertised in the local paper, 'Rabbits wanted – dead or alive'. When he was about to leave I asked, 'What happens if someone comes with a live rabbit?' He told me, 'Just stretch its neck.' I decided to let the live ones go. We didn't make our fortune!

FIVE BOB A PAIR

CELESTE ROSSETTO

Although I grew up in country Victoria with poor parents, I never realised we were poor. In order to make a little money we used to go rabbiting as we had been fed on stories by Dad of how rabbits were a staple for Australian families in the Depression. My brothers and I looked upon rabbiting as an adventure – something to do on the weekend to keep out of Mum's hair, avoid chores and make some money. In those days we could be out all day and never worry about any catastrophe that might occur. We were more worried that our freedom would be curtailed.

We would load up my old pushbike with the mattock, the nets and the ferrets. I had a sneaking suspicion that this was for the convenience of my brothers because I was the youngest and a girl at that. Or maybe it was that my bike had a basket on the front handlebars. We'd call up the dog and we were off! We would pedal to a farm a few miles out of town to our 'possie' that always proved successful. The ride out increased our excitement. We jumped off the bikes and quickly unloaded all the paraphernalia, making sure our lunches were in a safe place and out of the sun. We'd march into the paddock, tack our nets over the burrows' exits and then send the ferret down. This was a risk because ferrets sometimes fail to come out of the burrow, so there was always trepidation mingled with the excitement. The dog's tail was always an indication that the rabbits were on the move. My brother would issue orders for me to get ready and then a ball of grey-brown fur and muscle would tangle with the net and I would grab it and wring its neck, then wait for another. This procedure was repeated until mid-afternoon, because by that time we would have enough rabbits to sell.

My eldest brother skinned and gutted the rabbits. He would stretch the skins over the old wire stretches. When my squeamish city cousin came to visit, he'd happily chase her around the backyard threatening to cover her in rabbit guts. What a laugh for me, but terror for her – something I could never understand, as it was only blood and guts! Didn't she realise that they couldn't hurt you? You could always wash the blood off.

We lived on the Hume Highway and Sunday nights ensured a steady stream of cars reluctantly making their way back to the city for work the next day. These weekend escapees were our ticket to riches. Mum made sure the rabbits were clean enough for sale and then we'd drag out our hastily scrawled sign that read: 'Rabbits for sale – five bob a pair'. We always sold out, which gave us wealth and a sense of achievement, but most of all, good memories.

FROM BIRTH TO THE GRAVE

GRETA BALSILLIE

Rabbits have pestered me since birth and will follow me to the grave. It all began in 1944 when they were in plague numbers. For a start, my mother's name was Austin, but thankfully not related to Thomas Austin of Barwon Park, who released these ferals in 1859.

Early memories are of rabbits eating everything my hard-working father planted; grape vines and fruit trees were all chewed. So we made individual wire-netting cages, which was hard work for a seven-year-old girl. The furry ferals quickly learned to climb up the wire to eat the juicy foliage.

We got our revenge by trapping and shooting the beasties and eating them stewed, baked, curried, whatever; all delicious. Many families in the early 1900s survived on what was called underground mutton. In 1906, around 92,000 rabbit carcasses were exported and the industry employed thousands of people. We know it takes twenty-seven rabbit pelts to make an Akubra hat!

The myxomatosis virus was starting to spread widely in 1951 – the same year as my rugby league team South Sydney (named the 'Rabbitohs' because they raised funds from rabbit sales) won the premiership. By 1953 the virus had destroyed eighty per cent of the rabbit population in the eastern states. It must have affected South Sydney, as their prowess in rugby league also faded.

In drought-stricken central Victoria the rabbits still eat anything and everything; even memorial flowers placed in the cemeteries. They burrow under monuments, foul lawn grave plaques with their droppings. My own 'fate worse than death' is the thought of being dug up by a rabbit! (I'm going to be cremated.)

Must go and cook dinner. Rabbit pie sounds good. 'Go, Rabbitohs!'

MUM AND FOUR TACKERS GO HUNTING

MAREE HERON

My memories of the rabbit plague are from when I was a toddler. At that wee age, it didn't mean a lot to me or my brothers and sister. We lived in the hydro village of Bronte Park, situated in the cold, inhospitable central highlands of Tasmania. It was at the time of construction of the hydro power system. Canals and pipelines had to be built, man-made lakes, all to get water to and from the power stations and generate power for the growing Tasmanian industrial and public use. Many postwar immigrants were brought to Australia from Europe to assist with this construction work. They lived in single men's camps, little wooden boxes of one room and an entrance veranda. They were usually situated on the edge of the main villages. Fresh food was difficult to get as Bronte Park is over 100 miles from Hobart, and good, formed roads were few and far between, and delivery transport even worse.

So Mum and Dad, with four little mouths to feed, grew vegetables at my grandparents' farm at Elderslie, collected every weekend. During the week they hunted game – roo and rabbits – and caught a few mountain trout, but why so much? Remembering about the roo hunting is easy. I still can hear Dad complaining about me letting his best hunting dog off for a run, never to be seen again. Rabbit hunting was Mum's job, to get a bit of extra cash and probably to keep her sanity. She contracted to build a fence around the cattle/sheep grazing area and the growing hydro village. I was never certain at the time why, every day, Dad would head off to his day job as a transport driver; sometimes driving an ambulance, delivering babies on the road on the way to the Ouse Hospital.

Mum would take us out on the fence line; four little tackers: Micky, Regina, Butch and me. My little brother, in a pram as easy transport, was controlled during the day with a child harness and a long rope attached to a large gum tree, even bigger now. It must have been his wandering habits; they have grown like the tree.

Along the fence Mum was building, she set traps at night and cleared them in the morning. The captured were skun and dressed. Skins pegged out on little wire hoops. Mum made mention of 300 bunnies a day. These products of the plague were sold to the camp kitchen as part of the insatiable feed requirements of the hard working labourers. So looking back, I understand and appreciate the work my parents did; not just to feed us little people but the multitudes.

At my last visit to Bronte Park, still some bunnies there, the big tree standing tall (no rope burns) and the fence, like my mother, showing their age and wear from the tests of time.

The lessons we learned: food collection; farm skills; money conversion, and understanding and appreciation of other new and interesting ways to cook, taught to us by the immigrants. We have a love-hate relationship with bunnies. Hate them in our paddocks and garden; love them in a roasting pot and we always wear an Akubra hat.

A WEDDING WAITS FOR RABBITS

BRONWEN HAYES

Everyone was talking about the wedding being called off, all because of the rabbits. I was a city girl who'd been swept off her feet by a handsome soldier. Bert and I met just after the war when they shipped him back to Fremantle. The evening he proposed, I was wearing a blue dress. Bert said my eyes were shining as bright as the Aussie sky. There was so much hope in the air. We could hardly help falling in love. My parents thought it a young girl's foolishness and forbid us to marry for a year. I'm sure they imagined it was a passing phase. They didn't believe I could be happy as a farmer's wife. So while Bert returned to the family farm, I stayed in Perth. He wrote me letters – he had beautiful handwriting. There were so many letters! He wrote about the farm, the stock, the machinery, the shearers, the dogs. He told me about his favourite place by the riverbed. Bert poured his heart out in those letters: planning our future and telling me his dreams for the place.

Then the letters stopped. I knew something was wrong. I remember thinking he'd met someone else. A local girl. A girl better suited to farm life. So it was probably jealousy that spurred me to get on a train and head bush. I got there just before nightfall and knew right away what had happened. I could see the paddocks moving like water. But there was no water. It was rabbits. They were everywhere. When I walked into the kitchen, Bert jumped from his chair, threw his arms around me and burst into tears. 'I didn't know how to tell you. There's not a skerrick of grass left on the place. I can't even show you the river or we'll both end up with twisted ankles.' I held onto him and told him it would be all right, but it was hard to believe.

The next day, I watched teams of men working. Ploughing up warrens, pouring smoke down burrows, setting traps, laying poison – they tried everything. It was a war against rabbits and the locals weren't winning. The place looked terrible. When Bert and I rode into town, I could hear people whispering about us. They knew the state of things. Bert didn't look to have much to offer a new bride. Just before I headed back to Perth, Bert gave me a gift. I remember what he wrote on the note – a 'going away outfit for dearest Maisie'. He'd sewn me up a rabbit-fur coat. What do you think of that? To me, that said everything about Bert; he was an optimist, even in the hardest times. He reckoned you could always find a rainbow if you looked hard enough. I was so proud to become his wife. I wore the coat on our honeymoon. I've still got a photograph if you want to see it. I had that coat for years.

BUNNY

SHARON HESSE

When I was a little girl, say about ten years old, my father decided that we needed to 'go to the country' for a visit. At the time we lived in Revesby, Sydney, and did not know much beyond our suburb boundaries. My father grew up in the country and described himself as a 'country boy', and used to tell stories about the millions of rabbits and how they used to cook 'underground mutton'. Mind you, he went to the big smoke when he was nineteen! Anyway, Dad took Mum, my two older brothers and me to see an old bachelor friend of his from the old days. Uncle Tom (not really an uncle but you used to call old men that) lived by himself in an old shanty on a property outside Stuart Town, central NSW.

Boy, was I excited! Along the way we saw heaps of rabbits and they were so cute. I really wanted one to keep. When we arrived at Uncle Tom's, I asked my mother, 'If I catch a bunny, can I keep it?' Mum thought that there was no way I could catch a wild rabbit and said, 'Yes dear, you may.' Uncle Tom took us for a walk around the dry, barren, eroded property for a look-see. As I was exploring the eroded cut-outs I saw a bunny just sitting there waiting for me to pick it up and love it forever. Gently, I crept up to the bunny. It sat really still and allowed me to pick it up and cuddle it. Love for both of us. I whispered in its ear that I would take care of it and love it forever. I took bunny over to where Mum and Dad were with Uncle Tom. My excitement was overwhelming. 'Look Mum, I caught a rabbit, and you said that I could keep it.' I went to Uncle Tom, who was sitting down, to show him my new pet. He grunted, took the bunny and WHACK, hit its head on a rock!

Well, can you imagine my horror which turned to hysteria. I sobbed, 'The bunny loved me and Mum said I could keep it.' I was in my mother's arms, sobbing as she tried to comfort me by saying that Uncle Tom didn't mean to upset me, but he wasn't used to little girls and besides the rabbit had myxo! Myxo? Who cares? I just wanted my bunny back. I didn't understand the meaning of myxomatosis but was sure that I could have fixed bunny up! That was the start of my nursing career.

THE BEST SEVEN-YEAR-OLD DOZER CLEANER IN THE NORTH-WEST

ROBYN NUGENT

The black party-line phone had been ringing nonstop. The bank manager wanted to know what Dad would do. The fuel depot manager wanted his money. I only heard Dad's end of the conversation but I worked it out. Things were bad, Mum was crying.

'If the farmers can't pay, then I can't pay.'

'We need to sink dams now while it's dry.'

'The farmers will pay when they get the money, but that's not now.'

'Can't you hold a man a bit longer?'

'The season will turn.'

'Sorry, Bill, that it has come to this. It'll take a good flood to break this drought but we'll get going again.'

I watched from the kitchen window as Dad gave the men their final wages. They signed the old, worn exercise book that somehow smelled of diesel. The book, which I was never allowed to touch, was the record of their wages and held an envelope of tax stamps.

Finally it was all done and the men paid their wages. 'Come on, Bub, we'll clean the dozer down. You can help me knock the dirt off her,' he'd said to me. This was fun. There was always a sixpence for me if I worked hard. I was glad the men were all gone. They usually cleaned up but today it was my job to help. My heart raced with excitement. It didn't matter if I almost choked from the dust. The big clods of earth fell from the dozer blade. The tracks were heavy with clods. I hit these with the shovel. As a seven-year-old girl I was the best dozer cleaner in the north-west.

'You're not taking the child rabbiting. She's too young for that. It would be different if she was a boy, but not girls, Jack,' Mum said. It was on again: Mum trying to stop me going with Dad. She thought everything was dangerous. I wasn't scared. Dad always knew the best about everything. I knew about rabbits. They were a big pest. Dad said they were destroying the country. This was a plague, and ruination for Australia.

The sun's last rays were still hot and angry as we made our way in the truck to One Tree Hill. As we arrived, darkness was falling. 'Bub, you have to carry the Tilley lamp. Be careful and keep it straight.' The lamp exploded into light as he lit it. The traps rattled as we walked along. Dad stooped to set the traps, walking until they were all set. 'We'll be careful tomorrow when we come back, but no fear, the traps will all have rabbits in this plague.' The next night, there they were. I was still on the job with the Tilley lamp and the rabbits went into a wheat bag. I was paid sixpence for my job. I was making good money out of this plague. After that we had fricasseed subterranean chicken most nights.

TWO RABBITS AND A GREEN TAFFETA DRESS

PAM LORD

I remember one really terrible dust storm when the rabbits and drought were bad. The dust blew all day and all night. During the day it was pitch dark: you would think it was the middle of the night. We had the lights on all day. In the morning it would be no use going out with the broom. You had to get a shovel first and shovel it all off and then sweep it with a broom.

We did things to make life more pleasant, like planting vegetable gardens and trees, with wire netting around because of the rabbits. We started planting trees almost the very first day I got here, rushing to put tree guards on, to protect them from the rabbits. One night we had just four tree guards left to make. We decided we would risk it and do the guards in the morning, but the rabbits ate those four trees. You really couldn't leave anything unguarded, even though we didn't have many rabbits around the homestead. We would check the fences every night to make sure rabbits weren't getting in.

Rabbits were just part of life. We used to occasionally go shooting a rabbit. I don't like killing things much. We have always dressed up for dinner every night; not way out things, but we just do, at the end of the day. But one night I had on a green taffeta dress. We had an elderly governess here, teaching the children; we got quite a few rabbits that day and I was carrying two on the way home. The poor governess; I don't think she ever got over it, seeing me come up over the rim of the dam, green taffeta dress and two rabbits!

Rabbit meat was beautiful when we used to season and roast them. Once, when we were doing some building and had some builders here, we had a man who helped us in the garden. He offered to cook for them if I would do the desserts. They used to get him to roast rabbits for morning tea!

It seemed terrible to think we were giving rabbits myxomatosis, but if you went out in the paddock and saw little lambs that didn't have green feed because the rabbits had eaten it all, it puts a different light on it. The calicivirus really was so quick. There would be a lovely fat rabbit, and we didn't know we had the virus here and then we saw lovely fat rabbits dead! They must have died very quickly and they cannot have suffered. I have loved this place every day; there has never been a day that I could ever wish I was anywhere else.

4.

POCKMARKED PADDOCKS AND BUSH BATTLES

The tale of frustrated farmer turned hunter versus the rascally rabbit is a well-known one, with a long tradition, including cartoons. In these, the hunter tries hard to get even with 'screwy' rabbits; but always rabbits outwit them. A simple and humorous storyline – or so we thought. In our leisure time, we've laughed and followed the tribulations of the hunter chasing that intelligent creature, that lazy, constantly chewing, smart-aleck of a pest animal. The hunter always at it, shooting off rounds from his rifle to no avail, week in, week out. The farmer or hunter and the rabbit are constant enemies, the rabbit always gets away.

The reality for farmers and landholders in many regions, mostly rural, across Australia has been, with the exception of two significant episodes, a constant and debilitating problem, with rabbits able to bounce back from whatever the farmer or scientists try.

Just over 150 years ago a landholder, Thomas Austin of Barwon Park, Winchelsea, near Geelong, imported wild European rabbits, just twenty-four of them. He was later to receive an award from the Victorian Acclimatisation Society. His rural mansion was once host to the Duke of Edinburgh, who, while visiting, was able to shoot the game Thomas Austin had imported especially for sport. But within a very short time – around eleven years – rabbits had already become such a pest that a processing plant was established in a nearby town to handle the rabbits being killed in the region. A legacy of that time are the beautiful dry stone walls – now a tourist drawcard – running across the region, which were supposed to stop the rabbits, but failed.

But times have dramatically changed. We have now had almost three decades of Landcare, which started in the same region as rabbits were released in Victoria. Landholders now have a greater awareness of the impact of rabbits on the environment as well as on productivity, so have double the incentive to manage rabbits. Stories within this section are from landholders who have been at the receiving end of the damage from rabbits on their properties and who have been at different times desperate, jubilant, wary and concerned at rabbit densities. These stories tell of the impacts, the heartaches, the losses and the unending battles waged.

Rabbits, released in 1859, successfully spread out and appeared in much of the southern and central parts of Australia between 1900 and 1920. By 2009, farmers in the Atherton Tablelands in Far North Queensland could spotlight rabbits in the same area as bandicoots. They are very concerned about the pest reaching an area still bio-diverse, and previously thought too wet for rabbits.

As we now know, the rabbit is a highly adaptive and resilient animal, just the type that will potentially flourish with climate change. Landholders are the first to tell you that. Most landholders would be surprised to know that as little as one rabbit per hectare can prevent new plants sprouting. They are also becoming aware that vigilance and other controls are crucial while waiting for updated virus releases to follow the last release of a new rabbit virus (which was calicivirus, in 1995). In the meantime, cleaning up areas where rabbits are breeding, destroying warrens and other control methods are essential to keep the rabbit under that critical one animal per hectare level. Our environment and our farms need this, and looking at the costs of rabbits, we cannot afford *not* to take control seriously, wherever rabbits breed.

MYXO – THE GREATEST EVENT IN AGRICULTURE

DON WRIGHT

My earliest memories of the rabbit plague are of the early 1930s, of the van collecting the carcasses around the Toongi district in NSW and delivering them to the freezing works in Dubbo. Our property, Springwood, had three full-time rabbiters on 3500 acres. The rabbits were trapped, disembowelled and hung in pairs on a pole in the shade, covered by a hessian bag to keep the flies off. Most farms had rabbit 'drives'. Our best effort was over 5000 in a 50-acre paddock in 1946. I rode around the boundary, checking the fences twice a week.

We had a pack of 'rabbit dogs' of many breeds and crossbreeds: greyhound, whippet, beagles and fox terriers for going up the hollow logs and under rocks. The star of the pack was Wally who always brought the rabbit back to us. The dogs always had to be well-fed to deter them from eating the rabbits. They were kept in a large enclosure with a lot of kennels.

The rabbits sometimes dug under fences or echidnas made holes, and trees and branches fell on the fences. I carried 12-inch rabbit-proof netting, pliers and a shovel on my horse. We only had two neighbours who checked the fences and five who didn't. I do wonder how many Australian farmers made a good living prior to 1950 when myxomatosis was introduced. It was, by far, the greatest event to happen in Australian agriculture. The rabbits disappeared very quickly; the carrying capacity of Springwood increased from about half a sheep per acre (plus a few cattle) in 1950 when Dad died, to between three and four sheep per acre in 1974, when Mum died.

This vast improvement was achieved by spreading superphosphate and growing subterranean clover and lucerne on the suitable country, made possible by the eradication of rabbits. The effect of droughts prior to 1951 were greatly magnified by rabbits once they reached plague proportions. The contrast between properties kept free of rabbits and those that weren't was beyond belief. In January 1947 a severe storm flooded the Dilladerry creek running through Springwood. Three of us picked up and killed 463 rabbits we found sitting on logs and rushes in the floodwater.

RABBITING ON IN NORTH-WEST TASMANIA

JIM OAKES

It was in 1952 that I arrived in north-west Tassie as a seventeen-year-old migrant from the United Kingdom to start work on a dairy farm. In just the first week after arriving it became very evident exactly what a devastating effect the rabbit plague was having on the farming community. Hundreds of acres of what should have been green pasture were just bare dirt eaten out by rabbits; huge warrens, home to hundreds of rabbits, scarred the landscape, and farmers were fighting a losing battle to keep them under control. With ideal feeding conditions, one pair of rabbits could turn into 184 rabbits in just eighteen months.

Any of my spare time on the farm was spent helping Mick, one of many trappers in the district trying to keep the rabbit population under control. Mick and I would load up a horse with traps then move to set up a trap line, usually along a fence bordering bush or a creek, setting traps just a few paces apart. In places the rabbits were so numerous that we could hear the traps springing that we had set only minutes before. The same trap line could be used for up to four or five days before being moved on to a new location. When the rabbits were retrieved they were gutted, paired then carted by horse to the farm gate where they were hung over a horizontal pole. They were then covered with hessian to later be picked up by trucks from the local processing factory, International Canners of Ulverstone. Trappers were paid one shilling and sixpence a pair for their rabbits.

On leaving the farm in 1955, I obtained employment at International Canners and worked for a time on the rabbit processing line, which was in its last stages of operation. Myxomatosis had been introduced into Tasmania in 1953 and the rabbit supply was fast dwindling. In the early 1950s, over 25,000 boxes of frozen rabbits a year were produced by the local factory. Each box contained three dozen rabbits, making a total of nearly a million rabbits a year. These were exported mainly to the UK where food shortages still existed following the Second World War. Rabbit skins were hung on wire frames and dried in large ventilated sheds to later be baled and sold to the felt trade, where they were used mainly in the making of hats. Exporting frozen rabbits had first started in South Australia, and between 1914 and 1924 a total of 160 million rabbits were exported and 700 million skins were processed.

Numerous methods were used to overcome the rabbit problem in Australia: trapping; shooting; poisoning; fumigating; ferreting and using dozers to destroy the rabbit warrens. Despite all these attempts, the rabbit had survived in increasing numbers for the past

100 years. It was the introduction of myxomatosis and the calicivirus that finally brought the rabbit population under control. Or has it? Looking around north-west Tassie today, one might begin to think otherwise!

RABBITS, RABBITS, EVERYWHERE!

JILLIAN WIGG

I was eight when my family moved from a dry wheat area to higher-rainfall sheep country. The new property had 4000 acres with only 500 cleared! A bulldozer was brought in to work for two years, clearing most of the bush. Big trees knocked down and pushed into windrows. What a mistake!

Rabbits were rapidly multiplying and moving westwards. When they arrived at this new area, everything was ready and waiting for them. They did not even have to burrow into the ground to make their homes! All they had to do was move into a heap of timber – and multiply; something that rabbits perform very rapidly. There was shelter and protection in all directions.

Dogs were the answer. The sheepdog was enthusiastic, but could not run fast enough. A kangaroo dog was acquired. Something like a greyhound; long, lean, fast – and dumb. It could catch the rabbits, but what next? When chasing one rabbit and another crossed their path, he was confused! The sheepdog came to the rescue. They worked as a team. Kangaroo dog would run, catch the rabbit, then stand looking stupid with a rabbit in his mouth until kelpie arrived. Rabbit was dropped, kelpie would give one 'crunch', and the pair moved on to the next victim. A daunting process, considering one only had to walk outside the house to see the hillside get up and move before one's eyes. The rabbits knew there was no need to hurry.

Before school and after, rabbits ruled our spare time. Either they had to go or we had to go! As the timber became dry enough, windrows were burnt from one end to the other. Then everyone available was set to pick up sticks and stoke fires until all cover was burnt. My brothers and I spent many weekends 'picking up sticks'. We set traps in burrows and then killed the day's catch. The rabbits were cooked for feeding the hard-working dogs.

Our next attempt at eradication involved the engine from an old shearing plant set to drive a fan, which drove a burner to make smoke that was pumped into the holes. Then all accessible warrens were ripped.

Then there was poison. Our faithful working horse was put into the old cart to go around the windrows as poisoned wheat was dropped in a trail near the rabbits' homes. A few days later the cart would return to pick up dead rabbits, which were later thrown on to a burning heap of timber. That worked for a while.

The last effort was the 'rabbit drives'. A length of wire netting placed near a corner of a paddock – all available hands called in again and, with as much noise as we could make, the rabbits driven into the corner, the wire pulled shut around behind. Then someone had the task of killing the seething mass; today science has come to our aid.

A BEAUTIFULLY SCROLLED CHEQUE

JOHN LAZZAROTTO

In 1948, my parents, my sister and I came to Cobram, Victoria, where Mum and Dad purchased 160 acres of sand hills. They came from a much larger town, Wangaratta, where they were vegetable growers. A roll of wire netting was purchased. It was partially buried in the ground about 6 inches deep, so the rabbits wouldn't burrow under it, and the job of growing started.

The rabbits came in their hundreds. A trap line was laid around the netting line. My mother would walk around this line every morning and bring the rabbits home, where she would skin them. Skins were left to dry then packed in a small bale and sent to Melbourne for auction. I can remember how exciting it was when a beautifully scrolled cheque arrived from Dalgety's, imprinted with bullock and ram heads and ears of wheat.

Some of the carcasses would be placed in a copper and boiled up for the chooks. This went on for a few years but didn't put a dent in their numbers. The next step was strychnine. Pears were purchased from a local packing shed. Dad went out with a horse and a single furrow plough and made a furrow line over the hills. Pears were chopped up and laid in the furrows without any poison for about four to five days. The big day came and the strychnine was added. Next morning: hundreds of dead rabbits. Most of these were picked up with a horse and sled.

A grey Fergie and more netting was purchased and fumigation started. A flexible hose was joined to the exhaust of the tractor and the other end placed down a rabbit hole. We kids would stand around and wait for smoke to appear. Holes were quickly blocked up, and I remember Dad saying this would be the end of them. But they still came. Ground was worked up, and fruit trees planted, soon to be ringbarked by rabbits. So Dad made up a brew of cow manure and lime, about a 50:50 solution, and smeared it heavily on trunks. This did work.

I think back now and am sure that most of Mum and Dad's time was spent trying to combat those little furry creatures. They did not win until myxo appeared on the scene. I recently spoke to one of our old property neighbours, who told me that there was still the odd rabbit around. So who won? By the way, we were all professional rabbit eaters: roasted; casseroled; steamed; and fried.

OUR PLAN WORKED

DAVID MURDOCH

In the years 1950 to 1951 the rabbit really took over most properties in the Holbrook district in NSW. My brother and I worked on a plan of our 6000-acre property to secure each paddock. A large number of the internal netting fences had rotted off at ground level. Twelve-inch netting, better known as 'foot netting', was still in very short supply after the war. We had to demolish some of these fences and cut our own foot netting on our saw bench. We built a U frame around the saw blade and ran the circular saw backwards at a much lower speed than normal.

We secured some coils of 42 inch netting and cut these into 14-inch strips as well. When we completed fencing a paddock of 300 or 400 acres we dug thistle roots up and cut them into pieces. Then we soaked about 1000 of them in a 7-pound tin with lid plus decoy, and several spoons of sugar. Next morning we put the contents of the tin on gauze screens to dry. At about 3.00 pm we set off on a poison cart, which made a little trench in the ground, dropping a bait every 6 or 8 feet. Next morning we would start off about 5.00 am and pick up the dead rabbits. Our best day was about 860, but we averaged nearer 450 per day.

After poisoning for about four days straight, we then proceeded to poison each burrow with Lavacide, then filled in the burrows. There were four of us in the team, and every day one member would check the previous day's work. When we finished this operation, the Ferguson tractor would be used to rip the burrows and destroy any harbour.

Many landholders made the mistake of just trying to rip the burrows without doing the previous two operations, which ended up a mess and still had no control. We had completely eradicated the rabbits on our property by 1951. Myxomatosis was introduced soon after, which was a great relief for careless landholders who only half-completed the job in the first instance. I have a feeling CSIRO need to quickly come up with a virus, because we are heading for a plague, particularly with so many national parks to provide breeding grounds for rabbits to quickly multiply.

RABBITS CAN'T READ

BARRY HADLOW

It was a very big heavy gate in the rabbit-proof fence. It had been hit and damaged from both sides by drays side-swiping it and trucks that didn't stop in time. It was an honest gate, but no longer straight. The gate was just wide enough for the horses and carts to pass through and had been patched with odd pieces of netting and wire, and even galvanised tin to cover big holes. There was a big strainer post on either side. The gate swung from one post, and the other had a heavy chain and hook to keep it fastened safely. There were big painted signs on either side of the gate highlighted with reflectors:

Rabbit-proof fence
CLOSE THIS GATE
By Order

Where the gate had been opened and closed over the years, there was a deep groove in the gravel road surface. Timbers were placed under the gate where it closed to make sure it was rabbit proof. The fence ran off either side as far as you could see, getting lost from sight in the bush. We dragged the gate open and then asked Dad, 'Couldn't we leave the gate open, just for an hour? It is so heavy. It drags on the dirt and the final lift up onto the timber base nearly bursts our foo-

foo valves. We will shut it on the way home.' Dad would have nothing of this and insisted that the gate be shut, securely, now!

As kids, we knew very little of the tsunami-like scourge the rabbits were causing in the wheat belt of Western Australia. Our farm was to the east of the fence so we had seen plenty of rabbits but they were not an enemy to us kids, they were just rabbits, something the dogs liked to chase. So we shut the gate and were on our way.

Then what should we see, a rabbit as large as life sitting on a freshly dug burrow. 'Dad, look over there, there is a rabbit on this side of the fence! What are you going to do, Dad?' Dad shook his head and said words which will not be repeated here. As he drove on, his hands squeezed the steering wheel even harder and we heard him muttering, 'Blasted mongrel rabbits; some dopey coot has left that gate open, I'll bet you.'

Whether someone left the gate open or a tree had fallen over the fence, it mattered little now, for the rabbit had a free run right through to the west coast. It took a while for travellers to realise there was no point in shutting the rabbit-proof fence gate any more; the rabbit plague had moved on. The old gate posts and remnants of the fence remain to this day as a lasting monument to man's attempt to stop the rabbit, but they also remain a tribute to the rabbit's ability to go anywhere they desire. As I said, 'Rabbits can't read!'

WILTIN'

MARJ WOOD

Our first farm, which we bought in 1966 for 8000 pounds, was set in South Gippsland's green and rolling hills in Victoria. The farm was called Wilton (named after somewhere in England) but we thought it was called Wilton because everything on it, except the blackberries (as big as houses), ragwort, tussocks, bracken (paddocks covered with them) and rabbits (swarming everywhere), was wiltin'. At the time it was the only farm we could afford, and from the air it would have been clearly visible as a great splodge on the landscape surrounded by beautiful, clean, dairy farms. Upmarket accommodation for all the rabbits was provided by the masses of blackberries, ragwort, tussocks and bracken; I bet all our neighbours hated Wilton.

We set to cleaning up Wilton so that it no longer brought shame to the district. It was hard work and, as we had no money, we had to do everything ourselves. When we got rid of the blackberries a lot of the fences fell down (the blackberries were the only things holding the fences up), when we pulled down a fence near the house our outside toilet fell down (the fence was what was holding the toilet up) and there were various other daily disasters. As Bill ploughed up the paddocks and burnt the blackberries, the rabbits' homes were destroyed and they were forced to relocate. In the evenings millions of rabbits came out to play (and to dine on neighbouring green pastures). There were so many of them, Bill and his gun were fighting a losing battle. He shot them, trapped them, poisoned them, demolished their residences and went spotlighting for them with our dog Skipper.

Skipper loved spotlighting even more than cow work; when they were setting off to go spotlighting his whole body would be wagging with excitement and he would be wearing his 'You stay home and do the dishes my good woman, this is work for men' look.

Lots of us on Wilton were grateful for the rabbits. We ate the un-mangled rabbits curried, stewed, baked, in salads, omelettes and in Rabbit Surprise (whatever was to hand in the pantry and fridge thrown into the frypan with rabbit pieces was called Rabbit Surprise; it was a surprise that it tasted okay when it didn't look all that flash). Skipper ate the rabbits (skinned) that weren't fit for human consumption and the pigs dined on rabbits that had been boiled for ages in an old copper and then mixed with pollard; they ate this with obvious enjoyment and gusto.

Gradually the battle against weeds and vermin was won, and after eight years our farm no longer looked wiltin'. I'm pretty sure we didn't eat all the rabbits inhabiting the property, but they were gone. As they disappeared, our pastures bloomed and at dusk the paddocks no longer moved. Other farms followed and we made jolly sure no rabbits enjoyed our hospitality. And after Wilton we didn't eat another rabbit, ever.

COLD TURKEY

BARRY HADLOW

Waging war on the rabbits was every farmer's preoccupation. Trapping, shooting and poisoning were the weapons of war. Dad was a regular poisoner of rabbits.

One evening he started his trail of poison baits about 200 metres from the farmhouse. He was a careful man and knew that none of his livestock would be tempted to pick up the bait. However, he had forgotten all about Mum's prize turkeys. Mum kept vigil over these plump young birds, totting up in her head their value on the Christmas market.

Unfortunately, Dad was not thinking of turkeys as he went merrily on his way around the paddocks, completely oblivious to the fact that the turkeys were following along behind the poison cart gobbling up the baits as fast as the machine was punching them out.

Dad arrived home after dark wondering what all the fuss was about; Mum looking daggers and yelling, 'You ought to be more blooming careful where you lay that blooming poison. Look at all these beautiful birds, deader than dead!' Dad was very remorseful about knocking so many turkeys over with his baits, but even in all the uproar he was thinking, 'Can't waste good tucker, surely the neighbours would like a bit of fresh turkey meat.' Mum, already terribly upset said, 'What are you thinking! They have been poisoned and they are dead from that poison. You can't give them to people to eat, they will die too!' Dad said, 'I don't think so. If we take out the turkeys' crops straight away then the rest of the bird should be okay.'

Dad had that kind of quiet authority about him. So we whipped the crops out of the turkeys and bled them. It was interesting then to hear Dad on the telephone ringing up the neighbours. 'G'day there, how're you going? Wondering if you would like a couple of turkeys to eat? Yes, they are nice young birds.'

You could almost hear the person on the other end wondering why they were the chosen recipients of a couple of nice young turkeys and what may have been behind Dad's generosity. Under his breath Dad was heard to mumble something about they are dying quicker than what we can eat them but they are okay. I guess the neighbours believed Dad because he was a member of the Road Board, also the president of the local football club. We kept a couple of the biggest turkeys for our own pot and gave all the other birds to the neighbours. I am glad to report nobody in the general vicinity died in the next few months so Dad must have been right. One of our closest neighbours even remarked the next Sunday, at the tennis, how really nice those turkeys had been to eat – much tastier than the rabbits they were used to. But I also remember becoming very nervous if the topic of turkeys and rabbits were used in the same sentence over the next few months.

THE RABBIT PLAGUE – A HAPPY MEMORY FROM CHILDHOOD

LIZ HANRAHAN

After some fifty years, I returned with my grandson Aidan to the 'Hill Paddock' to reminisce about experiences of my childhood. The Hill Paddock was part of our family farm, on Claude Waldron's

Road at Middle Creek, near Beaufort in Victoria. The landscape reminded me of a moonscape. The rocky outcrop along the ridge of the hill was rugged and still; the trees, a skeleton of their former grandeur; while the lush green ferns, once protection for wildlife, were gone. Drought conditions were visible. There wasn't a rabbit in sight.

Memories flooded back as I explained to Aidan the enormity of the rabbit population that once made the Hill Paddock home, and the fun we had as children, scouring the rocks for rabbit holes and waiting for the thumps as the ferrets hunted the rabbits out into the nets. The Hill Paddock was alive with these furry creatures, which I adored as pets, but came to realise the damage they caused in plague proportions.

My family bred merino sheep then, and the struggle to maintain grasslands became a war of survival between sheep and rabbits; wool was our main source of income. A day on the Hill began with packing lunches and hauling the canvas water bag from the well, where it kept cool.

The first task was netting off the rocks to contain the worst of the plague. Larger paddocks were netted into smaller holdings, to give some order in a hopefully successful operation. Poison (1080) on carrots was used in an early attempt to kill rabbits, but was discontinued when birds began dying. Ferreting, fumigating and ripping warrens, too, were all part of the extinction plan. Myxomatosis, which caused unsightly swollen eyes and eventually death, gave relief for a time, but unfortunately rabbits developed resistance and numbers again swelled.

The rabbit drive remains a vivid memory. One Sunday we gathered at O'Loughlin's farm for the rabbit drive. There was much excitement as this was a new adventure for the Franc kids. Families armed themselves with anything that made a noise. As we marched across the paddock, rabbits appeared from everywhere, their little white tails bobbing up and down like ping-pong balls riding the high seas. At the end of the paddock was a high netting fence on three sides, where the rabbits amassed. So intense was the mass that they stacked one on top of the other, until some escaped over the fence. Hundreds of rabbits were killed and trucked to Sutton's cool store and sold. Funds raised went to maintaining the local hall.

After the release of calicivirus, the rabbit population dwindled and Dad was able to focus again on farming, but on reflection, the plague was not all bad news as it provided quality family time, fun and a source of income for us, and cheap nutritious food for struggling families. Food! Not for me. Myxomatosis totally quashed my appetite for rabbit, and for Aidan, rabbit meat is foreign. His experience remains with Oscar, his pet rabbit. This story is written as a memorial to my sister Marie, who was part of these adventures, but died on 10 September 2008, a victim of suicide.

DÉJÀ VU

DENNIS AARTSEN

Oh, the melodic call of the magpie. I can't help smiling at the black and white bird as it sings to the smoke-stained sky. As I stroll by to check the hose fittings on the water tank, the wallabies hardly flinch. They enjoy nibbling off the fresh shoots in our island of green. This is bushfire season so I continue around the house paddock, just checking that all the containers are full of water, and buckets are at the ready. Squawking cockatoos push aloft as I round the shed to look across the forested hills. Those plumes of smoke are thicker now and appear to be closer together. It's hard to gauge if they're actually closer to me or not, but shit, it's already over 30 degrees and it's not even ten o'clock. The breeze is strengthening but it's still going towards the smoke at this stage.

A small mob of grey kangaroos present an iconic scene as a flock of grass parrots rise from the paddock in a twittering cloud. The smoky air isn't too bad. You can smell the eucalyptus but it's more like sitting around the campfire; you know, when you put some gum leaves on for smoke to chase the insects away.

What's that? Aargh! Just those bloody rabbits; I've ripped that warren twice in the past couple of years but just can't finish them off for some reason. I'll have another go next time I've got the rippers on.

I'll just check the bushfire shelter on the way back inside. I only built it after a couple of years of nagging; that we lived in a bushfire prone area, yada, yada, yada. I kept finding excuses to postpone the job, until one day I had what some people call a 'eureka' moment and built a bushfire shelter with water-filled walls. I'm quite pleased with it, actually.

Over lunch is a good time to listen to the bushfire updates. It's becoming a real 'blow-up' day and the latest reports are warning everyone to be vigilant. It suddenly starts to get dark. A huge boiling column of smoke is quickly blacking out the sky. A curtain of burning embers is falling like a spectacular fireworks display. Hundreds of small spot fires are advancing across the paddocks. I'm almost hypnotised by the speed of this approaching hell.

'Everyone, do your jobs,' I yell as the door slams behind me.

Two days later I'm standing in a moonscape. Much of the ground is now bare, scorched earth, and all the fences are gone; only blackened tree trunks hint at the once precious forest. Not a sound. No twittering of the grass parrots. No squawk of the cockatoo. Not even the satisfying sound of the wallabies' teeth munching on the green shoots. Nothing.

I hear the heavy thump of a falling tree off to my left, but a movement out in the ashen paddock catches my attention. A rabbit has emerged from its burrow. It sits on its haunches and preens before digging a small hollow in the earth and defecating.

BRINGING OUT THE OLD SKILLS AGAIN

CHRISTOPHER PETERS

By the time I was born in the mid-1960s, the rabbit scourge was well and truly over. But growing up on the land with parents who had been through the worst of it, it came up again and again, such was the impact on their early lives.

The stories: checking the lines of traps around the hills at night with hurricane lanterns. Making baits using scotch thistle roots laced with some strychnine concoction. Bathing the ferrets on Sundays and having to dig them out of burrows when they failed to come out. Having to sell land where the rabbits could not be controlled. They would never eat rabbit again, having had so much of it when they were young.

There were also constant reminders on the property I grew up on. The pile of rusting traps in the corner of a shed. The U-shaped wires hanging from a rafter that were used to dry out the skins. The forgotten glass vials of some very toxic substance packed in straw in a wooden box; I knocked it over once, exploring the contents of an old slab shed, and nearly gassed myself. The washouts on the side of the hill that we were not allowed to ride our horses through.

There were always a few rabbits still around, but one season, when I was in my early teens, there was a bit of an outbreak on one of the hills and a number of warrens became very active. I think out of fascination with the stories, I asked my father to show me how to trap. After so many years the skills came back to him without effort. Some traps were selected from the rusting pile, cleaned up a bit and 'tuned up' by filing the notch that holds the plate onto the little flap, so that it would hold, but release with the flick of the wrist of the hand holding the spring of the trap. The head of an old tool for digging in the traps and hammering in the pegs was found and a new handle fitted. Squares of newspaper were torn up – they had to be just the right dimensions to cover the plate and jaws of the trap.

Dad and I then went trapping one afternoon after the cows had been milked. He showed me how to find fresh scratch marks in which to lay the traps, dig them out to the right dimensions, hammer in the peg, set the trap and handle it so as not to lose a finger if it went off accidentally, lay the paper over it and sprinkle the soil back over the trap. We laid about fifteen traps. Before we had finished we could hear traps going off already and the squeals of the trapped rabbits, which we went back and removed straightaway, snapping their necks as Dad showed me.

I caught over twenty rabbits in a few days, but it then rained and the myxo returned to decimate the remaining small colony. While it was an inhumane task that I am in no hurry to do again, it gave me an appreciation of what my parents had been though and a greater understanding of the stories of their past.

RABBIT PLAGUE RECOLLECTIONS

KEVIN SALAU

My earliest recollections, as a five-year-old in 1938 on our property in south-west NSW, are of the paddocks literally moving with the rabbits in plague proportions. To eliminate them was as important in the daily routine as breeding sheep. My parents together set 200 traps in a horse and jinker, put the rabbits into hessian bags (no refrigeration of course) and took them to the town freezer 20 miles away, for the great sum of sixpence per pair.

Rabbits bred in thick lignum bush. We hunted them out of the bushes and into hollow logs which Dad would cut open, catching them as they tried to escape. The 'back country' was also a breeding ground, but in the dry, the rabbits moved to the river flats for a drink.

As we grew older, we kids walked through the bush; rabbits in such numbers we could shoot hundreds. Better ones went to the freezer; others were skinned, skins pegged out to dry and finally baled in wool packs. These were sold to the Wool Stores along with the wool. One year my brother and I walked along the riverbank in the evening, shooting, as we walked, 250 pairs, which bought him his first Holden ute. Around 1946, we laid carrot and apple baits soaked in strychnine supplied by the Wool Stores. The baits were laid in a trail through the burrows; it was a terrible job the next day to pick up the dead carcasses. We always had thirty dogs: greyhounds and sheepdogs, taking ten at a time for the chase, but they became bored with the monotony and lost interest.

Dad had a kerosene tractor and mouldboard plough, and spent many hours ploughing out the burrows. Our job was to hunt the rabbits back into the holes, with the dogs chasing them as well. Landowners who could afford it put up wire fences, but kangaroos and emus kept knocking them down and this proved to be unsuccessful. Properties were simply overrun by the huge numbers eating out all the feed. We cut down apple bush for sheep feed, but they had to get to it before the vermin.

In dry paddocks, ground tanks or dams were the only water. Fencing these off and lifting and dropping the fence trapped hundreds of rabbits inside. In better seasons the Murrumbidgee River flooded, leaving islands in the floodwater. An old wooden boat took us from island to island shooting the marooned rabbits. It was a great day's fun, along with getting rid of the wretched things and making pocket money at two and six a pair.

Many men became professional trappers and shooters to make a living. Jack McCraith had portable chillers, leaving them at outlying stations; often two transport loads went to Melbourne each week. After the war, ammunition was scarce. The bullets supplied to us by the freezer owner came from Czechoslovakia, wrapped in newspaper; not good quality, but 'no questions asked'.

In his later years my father still had a long-standing hate for rabbits, setting fires in hollow logs, ploughing fresh burrows – his own private war. Finally myxomatosis took effect and wiped out the rabbits for many years.

THE GREAT RABBIT PLAGUE

PHILLIP SHOOBERT

Back in the 1950s there was a huge rabbit plague. I was working as a station hand on a property between Coonamble and Gulargambone in NSW, and the rabbits were in their thousands. In 1953, it was extremely dry and drought was finally declared. All the sheep were sent away on agistment; it was now our job to clean up the rabbits.

Rabbits don't normally drink water when there is plenty of green feed around, but there wasn't any, so they needed to drink. They could come into the dams and troughs of a night to drink, flocking like a mob of sheep to water, so I decided to set up traps. I got some rabbit-proof netting and put fences around the dams and troughs, leaving about half-a-dozen holes big enough for rabbits to get in. On these holes I made little funnels about a foot long out of the same netting.

When the rabbits went in and had a drink, they would follow the netting around trying to get back out and jumping over the little funnels. For weeks on end we used to catch between 2000 and 3000 rabbits a night. We would kill them, load them onto an old army Blitz and take them away and burn them because they were in very poor condition due to starvation.

The owner of the neighbouring property decided to have a rabbit drive. We built a yard on the boundary fence with a wing shaped like a

V leading into it. Several men, including myself, rounded up as many rabbits as we could, making a noise by banging drums. These rabbits were in a bit better condition, so we sold them. We got 2000 pairs of rabbits and the money raised was donated to the Warren Hospital.

I remember coming home from town one night and our house yard was full of rabbits. The garden tap was dripping and there was a puddle of water about a foot wide. The rabbits had found it. I put a fence around the tap next morning and the following day I got 600 rabbits out of it.

Of a nighttime the rabbits used to climb up the gauze on the doors. They could smell the food inside. Every tree around the house and various trees around the paddocks were ringbarked as far up as a rabbit could eat. Naturally, the trees died. You could ride around the paddocks, and any leaning trees you could look up at, there'd be rabbits up in the branches. It was nothing to be riding along and have a rabbit fall out of a tree on you.

But then the myxo hit them. It was a disease that was introduced to control the spread of rabbits, carried and spread by mosquitoes. It almost completely wiped out the rabbit population. Today in the same area you'd probably be lucky to catch enough rabbits to make a stew.

THE BEST AND WORST ...

ALAN MCCONACHIE

'I remember as though it were yesterday.' And, 'It was the best of times and the worst of times.' A childhood growing up in Scotland with Stevenson and Dickens hadn't prepared me for rabbits! Everywhere rabbits!

Our 200-acre dairy farm in South Gippsland, Victoria, had its fair share of kangaroos; never short of any in the top paddock, but everywhere there were rabbits. Acres of burrow pockmarked landscapes on the sandy rises above the valley floor, where at dusk hordes of the pests spread out to feed on the grassy flats in a moving, shimmering, brown mirage-like blanket. Only it wasn't a mirage!

It was a never-ending battle: them or us. There was little enough pasture for the dairy herd; the kangaroos didn't venture too far from the bush, but the rabbits! We trapped them, shot them, ferreted for them, poisoned them, dug up and ripped their burrows to little avail.

Before school I went round my rabbit traps that I had set the previous evening. I never failed to get a few, which I hung in the 'bag' by the roadside. These bags were hessian-covered horizontal poles by the road; familiar sights in the district. The telltale dip in the bag, where the Rabbit Man had placed the money, always caused me an expectant thrill when I came off the school bus.

Best-ever price: five bob a pair, big money for a thirteen-year-old in the 1950s! I saved enough to buy an ex-Army gun-sight to attach to the .22 rifle. The sight's accuracy enabled me to shoot rabbits through the head. It was common to aim at one, but so numerous were the pests that sometimes two or more would fall over!

Weekends were spent ferreting, with the neighbour's son. We rode a pony to the burrows then used it to transport the rabbits home. Best ever was fourteen pairs. The pony didn't think much of this smelly constraint draped over its back, judging by the nip I received on my behind.

Poisoning entailed sealing off a selection of burrows by blocking their entrances and checking where they were by burning a handful of sulphur at a burrow's mouth. The dense smoke produced showed all the exits. A liquid poison that became a gas was then poured into this burrow system.

Poisoning required laying baits with a poison cart, originally a horse-drawn vehicle that scratched a furrow into which baits were mechanically dropped from a hopper. The baits were generally chopped carrots and after a few nights of free feeds they were laced with strychnine. Best ever: 300 poisoned on one night, and it took a bit of digging to make holes deep enough to bury them. Could we say we controlled the rabbit numbers? Perhaps a little, but then, almost overnight, they were gone! Myxomatosis was magic! 'It was the best of times …'

BLACK MOUNTAIN BURROWS

WAYNE WATTS

My rabbit story goes back to the 1960s on a property called Black Mountain, Parkville, near Scone in NSW. My father, Noel Watts, who worked on Black Mountain for thirty-eight years, had the job of helping to start the myxomatosis virus there.

As the property was fairly steep, horses were the only way of accessing the areas we had to reach to perform this duty. I used to go with Dad on horseback and he would set some rabbit traps in a particular area of burrows. Early the next morning we would ride back and Dad would give the rabbits we caught an injection of myxomatosis. He would then dress the rabbit's injured leg with Stockholm tar and release it back down the burrow, hopefully to infect other rabbits.

Other times when I went with Dad to poison rabbit burrows, I remember he took a bottle of deadly poison (called Lavacide) and a small mattock on the side of his saddle. We would ride out in the paddocks and, whenever we came across a burrow, I would hold the horses upwind, while Dad (holding his breath – no face mask in those days) would pour some Lavacide on a small stick or dry cow dung, throw it down the hole and quickly dig it in. I remember at times Dad dry-retching when he was a bit slow.

SOMETHING BETTER HAD TO BE FOUND

CHERYL RYAN

I grew up on the south coast of NSW, on a dairy farm that started out as a large property with a lot of dense bush and, in some areas, a type of coastal rainforest. Within this bush area there were some wonderful examples of the diversity of Australian fauna and flora. However, my parents, in the wisdom of their generation, set out with the sole intention of clearing the majority of this bushland area to cultivate it into rich pasture for the cattle.

Some of this land was river flats, but much of it was small, undulating hills. This land was then divided into fenced paddocks, which were often separated by the creek and the tidal river. These waterways would often flood in times of heavy rain and the water would spread over the river-flat paddocks and, in turn, leave behind piles of logs and associated rubbish, known locally as 'flood rubbish'. This was also wonderful habitat for families of rabbits, as they didn't have to burrow to make a comfortable family home in which to raise their ever-increasing numbers of offspring.

As all children of that time made wonderful free labour, I was in the milking shed each evening when dusk arrived and you could see the wonderful colours of the setting sun. But the best view from the north-facing building we were in was the ridge that had recently been cleared and sown with green pasture. Upon this ridge the whole hillside came alive as all the rabbits came out of their homes for their afternoon nibbles and frolicking play. To see this area of a few acres come alive with such a moving mass of wildlife was amazing – and to think this happened each afternoon at dusk. Although the sight was amazing, for the family who had spent many weeks cultivating and preparing the pasture for planting of expensive grass seed, this was just like watching your money get eaten up by the plague of rabbits.

Some minor control of the pest was done by the younger children trapping them and learning to shoot them; they made wonderful target practice. But the breeding of the rabbits far outnumbered our poor efforts. Everyone agreed something better had to be done. On hearing of the mixi virus, high hopes were held that the numbers of rabbits would decrease, but this was only effective to a small degree. Something better had to be found.

I don't know where the knowledge came from, as I arrived home from boarding school once and found it was already in full swing. With one man operating the tractor with a ripper behind it, the warrens were dug up, each of the burrows was exposed and a type of gas was poked down them with a long stick. Then all the holes in that warren area were covered over and the area levelled with the tractor. This enabled anyone checking the warren area to know if any rabbits left out of the burrow had attempted to dig in, or of others that may have dug out.

Although it took many years and many man-hours, the rabbit problem was minimised from the plagues that had inhabited many areas of the farm. The rabbits became visible as the scrub was cleared and improved pasture was sown, thus making them even easier to spot in the cleared areas.

PLAYING POSSUM: WHO'S THE BUNNY NOW?

RUSSELL KNOLL

Growing up on a farm, we had various pens for our poultry. One of these was made from an old corrugated iron tank turned upside down with a wire netting door built into the side. This had remained unused for some time.

My brothers and I often went exploring in the bush adjoining our property. We would cut sticks from young black wattles and use these

Experimental fencing against rabbits, Nekarboo Station, New South Wales, circa 1895.

to slash paths through the blackberries and scrub. Working in line, one behind the other, the first would slash a narrow path. The next in line would make the path slightly wider and flatter and so on till, after four or five had added their bit of labour, we left a wide, easily passable trail behind us. In this way we would slash our way into thickets and blackberry patches to get to the places one could not normally go.

One time, we slashed our way into a thicket where ringtail possums had built their nests. The noise and commotion caused a young possum to abandon its nest and run for cover. Making chase, we managed to capture it by throwing a jumper over it then wrapping it up. Taking our catch home, we put it into a box while we prepared a cage for it to live in. We used the old tank pen, arranging a dead gum limb inside with a tree home made from a converted potato box. Adding water, fruit and vegetables, we released the possum into its new home.

Not long afterwards we caught a young rabbit. Rabbits were a problem on our market garden, particularly because they ate the tops off carrot crops and stripped the bark off the trunks of young chestnut trees. Young rabbits, still naive about potential dangers, often hop around during the day and are not too difficult to catch. We decided to put the rabbit in with the possum with another converted potato box home on the ground.

They'd been together for some time when one day we went in to check how they were doing. We looked into the box on the ground but there was no rabbit. Searching behind everything on the floor we still found no rabbit, nor any evidence of escape. Checking in the possum's home in the tree, we were astonished to find both rabbit and possum together. Though the trunk was quite steep the rabbit had managed to run up the tree to be with the possum.

Not long afterwards, this partnership between possum and rabbit was to cause us even more astonishment. This time when we went to check on them, we found no rabbit or possum in the tree or ground house. Searching around the floor, we found a burrow in the hard dirt floor going down, out and up. Both rabbit and possum had used this tunnel to escape. We felt quite outwitted by this unusual partnership, while also admiring their ingenuity.

PART OF EVERYDAY LIFE

DON BIRD

Rabbits were a part of everyday life until I was seventeen, when the myxomatosis virus arrived. From as early as I can remember it was almost a daily chore; if we weren't trapping them we were poisoning them or netting waterholes to catch them when they came in to drink.

We were always destroying warrens, which they promptly dug again. Later I used to fumigate the warrens with a charcoal fumigator, after getting the dogs to chase as many as possible down the warrens first.

But best of all, it was almost our only recreation and entertainment. From as early as I can remember, we always had about three dogs which we used to catch rabbits; we seemed to work as a team. The dogs used to catch the rabbits and hand them over to us, and we took them home. We used to skin them and sell the skins; it was a good money-spinner for us. Apart from the fact that we almost lived on rabbit, so did the chooks and pigs. My father used to cook up a brew in half a 200-litre drum which looked good enough to eat as well and, judging by the pigs and chooks, it was pretty good and something to look forwards to.

When I was about ten years old I was given a ferret, which added a new dimension to the whole world of catching rabbits. If I had visitors it was easy to entertain them; just get the ferret out and you would have to see it to believe it just how excited both the visitors and the dogs used to get. We were always skinning rabbits, so we always had the smell of rabbit on our hands. We called this 'BOBO' which stood for 'bloody 'orrible bunny odour'.

On the economic side of things, from the time you put a crop in until you harvested it, the rabbits were eating it. We had a paddock of 40 acres which had bush on three sides, and some years we only harvested 10 acres because the bunnies got the rest. This was despite the fact that I used to have about fifty traps set around it most nights. I used to get an average of forty rabbits a night. I do know of at least one farm where they looked at the crop and decided it would be ready for harvest the next week, but when they arrived with the machines the rabbits had done the job for them.

The February floods of 1955 changed everything for the rabbits. I was still trying to think what to do with the huge warrens along the creek bank when the flood came. The flood destroyed the warrens – and the rabbits in them – and all the water led to a mosquito plague which spread myxomatosis. When I was ploughing that year, there were rabbits everywhere. When I came to seed the same land, there were dead rabbits everywhere. Although the numbers have built up a few times since, they have never got anywhere near the numbers that we used to have.

PATHOS

RODNEY GALAGHER

At 4.00 am the train stopped at an unmanned station on the Mudgee line in NSW. It was the beginning of the August school holidays in 1949. My father was waiting at the station to meet me and ride to our house about 4 miles away. A fire and a billy of tea warmed the frosty morning. We started for home, Dad on his black horse and me on a pony with my rucksack across my knees. After the usual pleasantries, Dad was very quiet. He had problems on his mind.

As the first rays of daylight brightened the sky, I became aware of the reasons why: several natural disasters had converged to make life on the land very hard indeed. Wool prices, which had been high after the war, had declined, Prickly pear and Bathurst burr had spread at an alarming rate on all arable land, and the rabbits were at the height of plague proportions.

I had come home in the midst of a major rabbit eradication programme, by poisoning. Firstly, baits had to be prepared. Scotch thistle roots, like little white carrots, were dug, washed, cut into pieces and placed in kero tins with about an equal quantity of oats and water, and brought to the boil until the oats were swollen, then molasses was added. This was the bait.

Barney the draughthorse was harnessed to a single furrow plough and a furrow dug in a big semicircle around the paddock. One of the men followed, scattering the bait along the trail. Next morning an eager inspection revealed that the bait had been taken by the rabbits. That evening the bait trail was renewed, but this time laced with strychnine!

Before dawn, we were all awake, full of anticipation. The cold, frosty air and the first rays of light revealed the carnage. The river flat was strewn with bodies glistening with frost on their white bellies. I felt like cheering, but there was a strange silence. Death, even of a plague of rabbits, brings a feeling of pathos.

Now the work began. They had to be skinned. The rabbits were picked up, gathered into heaps. Pocketknives, carefully sharpened the night before, were put to use. Just as there are 'gun' shearers in the shearing shed, there is fierce competition in skinning rabbits. Someone would say, 'I skun more than you!' How many thousand rabbits were skinned and the skins stretched on wire bows and hung out on fences to dry? I will never know. After a splash in the rocky waterhole to clean up, weary but satisfied, we went home for tea. Mum produced a large shepherd's pie out of the fuel stove, golden brown on top and smelling of onions and thyme and, of course, rabbit. 'For what we are about to receive, may the Lord make us truly grateful.' Ah, RABBIT!

THE HUBCAP TRIAL

BOB MOFFAT

It was spring or summer of 1980, towards the end of a fairly major drought across much of inland NSW, and I was on a property called Irymple in central-western NSW, between Cobar and Hillston. The ground tank (aka a dam with contour drains leading to it) near the homestead had recently gone dry. Dead and dying kangaroos were a common sight; rabbits were abundant, as were their predators: foxes, cats and wedge-tailed eagles. When I say rabbits were abundant, I am not kidding; the CSIRO Division of Wildlife were conducting research on aspects of rabbit biology at the time in that area and I vaguely recall they had a circuitous transect of about 30 kilometres and had spotlight counts from the back of a slow-moving four-wheel-drive vehicle of something like 11,000 rabbits along this transect in one night – a hell of a lot of rabbits!

One afternoon after work, I was relaxing on the veranda of the old farmhouse with a cool ale while staring out over the landscape. Being a bit of a birdwatcher, I decided to put some water out to see what bird species might come in for a drink. I found an old hubcap, filled it with water and placed it under a gnarly old almond tree in the paling-fenced yard, an area in full view from my drinking site, me with my binoculars handy.

Pretty soon the resident apostle birds chanted through and had a quick drink, typically chattering away and making a fuss but it wasn't long before the rabbits cottoned on and surrounded the hubcap, managing to nudge the apostle birds aside. Eight thirsty rabbits sat side by side in a ring around that water-filled hubcap with another ring of thirty or forty surrounding the drinkers waiting for a spot at the temporary water supply. Around these were another hundred or so thirsty bunnies.

As I watched the scene through my well-worn binoculars I noticed a spotted bowerbird; not being a common bird of the area, it was exciting to see this arid-land mimic of other birds and mechanical sounds arrive in the almond tree. This bowerbird obviously had a thirst to quench as it was interested in the hubcap and its precious contents; after watching the ring of rabbits for a while it imitated the hissing snarls and screams of a feral cat – the rabbits immediately scattered, the bowerbird plopped to the ground and hopped to the hubcap for its afternoon drink before departing and leaving the last drops to the returning rabbits.

Irymple is now part of the Yathong Nature Reserve, an extensive reserve sampling a range of inland plant communities and their dependent fauna. I expect there are few, if any, rabbits now at Yathong, with the calicivirus having severely depleted the rabbit population, and the Irymple bowerbirds save their cat calls for other competitors.

RABBIT STORIES FROM SOUTH WONWONDAH

JIM HEARD

When my forbears came to South Wonwondah, an early grazing property south of Horsham, in the Wimmera region of Victoria in the early 1920s, rabbits were a problem. Rabbit Inspectors were regular callers to report on rabbit numbers. Sometimes district meetings were called to discuss how the rabbit problem could be attacked.

In the early 1930s, one inspector came through the district pushing the sale of a rabbit fumigating machine. Very few farmers had spare cash as the Depression set in. Those who didn't buy, so the story goes, were served with a notice 'for not destroying rabbits'. Most of the district farmers were summonsed to appear at the Horsham Court to answer this charge. The Heard brothers, Tom and Harry, were to appear, but their case was not heard by lunch break. A group of local farmers walked down to Perrings Cafe to eat. Harry ordered 'fricassee chicken' but found a rabbit's shoulder blade while eating it!

When I returned from schooling in Geelong, in the early 1950s, the rabbit problem was again acute. South Wonwondah farm was divided north–south by the Norton Creek, which was the boundary between two Inspectors' areas. On the west of the creek it was the

Natimuk Inspector's territory, on the east was Horsham Inspector's jurisdiction. We had to keep two Inspectors happy.

As a youngster, I thought it rather humorous that the Natimuk Inspector's name was 'Hughie Fox'. There were some sandy rises on South Wonwondah, and the rabbits loved to burrow there. One long ridge was particularly favoured, and Mr Fox was always onto us to 'plough in the burrows'. This looked like a long job with a single-furrow road plough. There were no three point linkage tractors or hydraulic controls, so two men were required, tractor driver and ploughman, to walk behind to control the plough. The boss decided this was too slow, so he said to use a five-furrow disc plough, with a power lift mechanism. A trip rope was pulled as the plough moved along, causing a crank to lift the plough. It worked well on firm ground, but once the sand was disturbed the lift wheel would drag, so the crank wouldn't work. This caused the tractor to bog in the loose sand. This meant unhooking the plough to extricate the tractor, so a long chain could be used to pull the plough to firm ground. Mr Fox came along as we were working. He said the job would be useless in destroying the burrows. However, we had no other choice, so we worked the whole ridge. There has hardly ever been a rabbit burrow on that ridge in the following fifty years of my farming career. The soil had been so disturbed, that the 'scent of rabbit' had been dissipated.

In 1953, the boss bought twenty wheat bags of carrots to use in a poisoning campaign. For the next two weeks or so, five or six men and boys sat around the woolshed dicing carrots. We used up the whole twenty bags of carrots and buried 4500 poisoned rabbits. Of course, a certain number of rabbits died in their burrows. Blowflies could be seen flying down the burrows for days afterwards. As seven rabbits were said to eat the same amount as one sheep, we considered that we saved a large amount of grass with this campaign.

MEMORIES OF A RABBIT PLAGUE

GARTH DIXON

Mine is a sad story. It was the summer of 1932, Depression time; I was eight years old. The bank had got the family farm and I was staying with my uncle Henry on his farm in the central west of NSW.

The talk around the dinner table was gloomy, mostly about how rabbits were reaching plague proportions, and farmers had been unable to afford the labour and the fencing materials to keep them in check. 'Time to get out the poison cart,' said Uncle Henry. My uncle Henry knew a lot about rabbits. He talked often and feelingly of the great rabbit plague of 1902, when the rabbits first erupted; the most terrible year of his life. He told how the rabbits ate the grass, then scratched up the roots and ate them, then ringbarked small trees; how the sheep all died. The rabbits became 'too weak to get out of your way'; 'We hit 'em with sticks'; 'The dogs stopped killing 'em'.

Total war was declared and a 'scorched earth' policy adopted. All the log fences Henry had so laboriously constructed were burned. Anything that harboured rabbits was dug up, gelignited, cyanided, trapped or netted out. But the rabbits came back each year.

The Government weighed in, paying a bounty for 'stray' cats from the cities and towns. Thousands were dumped in the western district of NSW. Judging by the volume of protests, one suspects that most of the unfortunates were household pets. Only the very fittest survived, not on rabbit, but on the native fauna. Their descendants are still out there.

Back to 1932: I recall rabbits so numerous that a hillside, criss-crossed by hundreds of bobbing white tails, seemed to move. I saw sheep struggling helplessly on, moving their heads from side to side like automatons, searching blindly for the little the rabbits had left. I remember also the piles of 'dead wool' which we kids later collected and sold for a few pence.

I watched the men get out the poison cart and make thousands of baits. The cart was like a small plough making a single furrow, or trail. It was horse-drawn, operated by two men – one controlling the horse and the other dropping baits about a yard apart into the trail.

The bait was pollard (chicken feed) mixed with phosphorus. The poison was hideously cruel. It killed by burning out the bellies of its victims, taking up to three weeks to do so. The fresh pollard was irresistible, equally to rabbits and to most of our native birds, animals and even reptiles. After a poisoning, a hush lay over the land and the stench of rotting carcasses lingered long in the air. The ghastly process was repeated year after year. In my bed on the western veranda in the still night, I was roused from a half-asleep state by a rabbit squealing, piercingly, insistently. The cry was coming from the poisoned fields. I was moved to tears.

RABBITS, RABBITS EVERYWHERE, AND NOT A CROP TO REAP

RON PROVIS

It is said the rabbit was brought to Australia as food for the foxes, which were brought to Australia to enable the red-coated gentlemen to carry on their sport, the jolly old 'tally-ho'. Unfortunately, Australian conditions did not prove satisfactory for fox hunting, but due to the mild winters it was just what the doctor ordered for the rabbit and fox. The fox varied its diet by turning its attention to the local fauna. There was always sufficient grass and edible vegetation for the rabbit, and due to its phenomenal breeding capability, it soon multiplied to plague proportions. There were not many places in Australia where rabbits could not be found, eating crops and pasture, driving some off the land. Much native vegetation was either destroyed or reduced in size and numbers.

No farm was without a rabbit dog or two – not that they reduced the rabbit population by much, but it became customary to have one, even if it was only for the kids to take for a run and stir a few rabbits up. Rabbits became a part of life on the land; one learned to a certain extent to live with them, controlling them where possible. Trapping and poisoning were the only ways before the days of the bulldozer and ripper. In the hill country where we lived, with its creeks suitable for rabbit cover, I have seen the old house cat bring home a rabbit for its kittens.

How I remember those days: kids racing around, the dogs chasing every rabbit in sight. As they seldom – if ever – caught one, I think even the rabbits enjoyed it, having the safety of their holes if things got too 'hot'. Rabbit skins brought in a little pocket money for an energetic child who would set a few traps, and look after them.

Over many years I have trapped, skun and carcassed hundreds of rabbits, with over 100 traps out at a time. The traps were made of steel and I thought nothing of it, but now that I am an old man I shudder to think of the agony for the animal caught in these. Before the days of bulldozers and rippers many different methods were used to control the rabbit. A two-wheeled, horse-drawn contraption designed to drop poison bait at intervals was common. There was a machine designed to blow cyanide down the rabbit warren. This was worked by hand – a most boring job, I found. My father soon got bored as well. 'Fill the hole in, son,' he would say, 'it must have gone through by now.' I had a certain amount of doubt about that, but no inclination to dispute. There was a liquid gas called Lavacide which one put a certain amount of, by a long spoon, down the rabbit hole, then filled it in. Some tried blowing up the warrens – sometimes with unlooked-for results, such as a man I saw with singed hair who claimed, 'It's a mug's game.'

Rabbit terms became part of Australian vocabulary, like: 'He kept rabbiting on' (a long talk with little sense to it); 'He became the bunny' (some unfortunate who was shouldered with the blame); 'He is a bit of a rabbit' (someone with unorthodox views).

Then we got myxomatosis, which worked like magic. On hills I had seen crawling with rabbits it became difficult to find even one to feed the dog. Australia will never be free of rabbits, but I hope never again will they be seen in the numbers I have seen. There is no doubt myxomatosis gave Australia hundreds of millions in extra production, despite the fact it was criticised when introduced. Even with the more modern methods for rabbit eradication that we have today, without myxomatosis, the rabbit would still remain supreme, with millions of little mouths chewing away at Australia's rural production.

THIS DREADFUL PEST

BETH HOWARD

In the 1930s and 1940s, my father owned a large farm north of Gilgandra in the central west of NSW. My sisters and I were children born into the Great Depression but we had no idea of the difficulties and deprivation of that time. Though farmers suffered, they were probably better off than people in the towns and cities – we had sheep to kill and the pesky rabbits were a good source of meat. My father and his workman spent days ripping rabbit warrens with the tractor and plough. The rabbits ate every blade of grass and all the young cypress pine trees that emerged from the ground after rain.

We children and all our young neighbours and school friends didn't mind the rabbits. We didn't know any better; they were part of our young lives on the farm but we had no idea how devastating they were to our land – they must have held farming and agriculture back for years. We had many canine creatures in those days; every farmer had a pack of dogs. The dogs gave the children great entertainment. My father purchased two large greyhounds which were tolerant of children and which had pleasant smiling faces; we were greatly impressed by their tremendous bursts of speed when chasing rabbits.

I have sometimes wondered what we would have done as children without the sport those plague animals provided. We spent glorious weekends on horseback, dogs in tow, carrying axes across the pommels of our saddles, chasing rabbits up logs. There was a good deal of fallen timber and the rabbits used this as harbour from the predatory humans bent on their destruction. Off we would ride, carrying the axes to cut holes in the logs. How expectant the dogs were when we trapped a rabbit, eyes glued to the end of the log, bodies tense and alert.

These were fun days for the children: no TV, no video games, no mobile phones, only fresh air and sunshine and the joy of youth. Most children set traps each night, and we made a fair bit of pocket money from selling the skins. All the farmers owned a poison cart; pollard and phosphorus were fed out in the trails, the next day was spent picking up dead rabbits, piling them in heaps and burning them.

When my husband and I were married in 1951 we were still putting out poison baits; I think they were shredded carrots mixed with strychnine. In the same year, the CSIRO brought out the wonderful myxomatosis virus. We drove to Coonabarabran to get infected rabbits to release onto the farm. Miraculously, we saw the rabbits vanish; the grass grew and the cypress pines came up in abundance. We are fearful again, though, that, after long years of drought, rabbits are again breeding prolifically and seem to have become immune to myxomatosis, no question. We are praying the scientists will again come up with a new way to wipe out this dreadful pest.

RABBIT-FREE FARM

ROBERT DONNET

In 1950, our family moved to a farm on the Yarrandale Road, between Tooraweenah and Gulargambone, NSW. It only had two netted boundaries, the northern and eastern, which allowed the rabbits a free run between farms. The week we moved in, Mrs Lesley, a friend of Mum's, gave her a collection of flowering succulents for her new garden. I remember as a youngster helping with the planting. Mum dug and raked a bed, about 4 foot square, and planted about ten of the plants, and we watered them in one October afternoon. This is my earliest memory of gardening.

Imagine our horror next morning when my brother and I went to look at the new garden, to find there was not one plant left. The rabbits had eaten them, roots and all. Not one left! When we asked Mum what had happened, she said the rabbits had eaten them. 'What are we going to do?' we asked.

'There is nothing we can do,' was her answer. But our dad had fought the Germans and the Japanese and won, and these small furry wretches would be beaten as well.

Before moving to the farm, he had a 600-acre block which he was trapping for skins, but, as the rabbits started to beat him, he decided to try poison. Thistle root was the go, but we had no thistles. I remember standing on the back of our Ford Blitz lorry helping Dad and Mum pick budda pea leaves and putting them into 44 gallon drums. These were then sprinkled on a trail, but this did not work. Then a family friend, Mr Bob Smith, said he was having success with oats and strychnine and so the new war began. It was about this time we moved up to the farm.

On a trip into Gilgandra a new set of discs were bought for our ten-disc Sundercut plough, but only one was put on the back box, and away Dad went, trail cutting. The first trail was cut around the house; two 'free feeds' two nights apart – and then BANG, the strychnine. That night he got 347 rabbits which he picked up in the wheelbarrow (which we still have). They were then skinned and stretched onto wire bows which were stuck in the ground to hold them up so the skin could dry out. This was also an art: the bow had to be run straight down the backbone so the skin was evenly divided in half, then you tied the back legs together which stretched the bottom of the skin, the neck being at the top of the bow. The better presented your skin was, the more money you received. At the peak, skins were making one pound per pound of skins; this certainly helped to offset the price of the poison.

The oats were boiled in half a 44 gallon drum. In those days forty-fours were very plentiful as all petrol, kerosene and diesel came in drums. The drum was stood upright on three bricks and a fire lit around it at dinnertime. Boiling about 6 gallons of dry oats made about 10 gallons of wet oats. At afternoon tea, the oats were tipped into a strainer to drain, this strainer was also a drum – one-third of a 44 drum with holes punched into the bottom. Once the oats had drained they were put into buckets and the trail was run. The strychnine was mixed in the strainer with a paddle about the size of a cricket bat, made from a four by three-quarter board. The poison was bought from the chemist and had to be signed for. I vaguely remember a price of around twenty-seven shillings and sixpence for a 2-ounce tin. Thus came the saying 'as dear as poison'. The last trail I remember was January 1952 and the rabbits were dead on the trail maybe 18 inches apart.

Dad also netted in the only two dams on the place and funnels were put inside for the rabbits to enter, but not return. This helped to get those sly rabbits who did not take the poison. The burrows were ploughed in and the few logs we had were split open to deter any rabbit from an easy home. If we saw a scratch, a trap was set. This went on until possibly 1954 when, with the help of myxo, we saw no more rabbits. This farm is still rabbit-free to this day.

While this was going on the other boundaries were netted, as netting became available. After the war all steel products were in short supply, so you had to wait some months for your order to be filled. In those early years, the rabbits were an industry. There were many families at Tooraweenah and Gulargambone who made a fair living out of trapping for the chiller. On Mt Tennandra there were six rabbiters working, each taking in excess of 100 pairs a night. It is said that Mr Jack Balderson caught a rabbit in every trap he set. He used to say he was born with a trap on his back. I can still remember seeing him crawling out in the pouring rain, on a black soil road, with a load of rabbits on his old wooden-spoked Dodge ute; this was 1950.

Riverstone Meat Works had placed chillers all over New South Wales and into South Australia to take advantage of this bountiful supply of meat. Mr Pop Anforth ran the chiller at Gulargambone from 1950 until it closed about 1961. He had a fixed chiller. When there was a wave of rabbits on, Riverstone would bring in a mobile chiller to cope with the extra business. His son Sid organised a contract carrier from Blackheath who ran five trucks daily to Sydney, drawing rabbits from chillers in our district. Each truck held 3500 pairs of rabbits. At the peak of the plague the Gulargambone chiller was taking 2500 pairs daily. In 1950 a pair of rabbits was worth ninepence. These truck drivers formed a close bond which still holds to this day. One of these same drivers is spending his Christmas break this year with the Anforth family in Gilgandra, such is the mateship.

As I look back, they were good years. People were keen to work and things moved ahead. I've never been much of a trapper, but have done my fair share of poisoning, firstly with 1080 at Purlewaugh in the Coonabarabran Pastures Protection Board and now at Burragate in the Bega Rural Lands Protection Board, using Pindone. And so the fight continues. We've come a long way with our methods, both in safety and application, but for me the thrill of seeing a strychnine trail will never be erased from my memory.

TEXIE AND ME

BETTYE SCHULTZ

When I was a child on our Wimmera, Victoria, property in the early 1940s, years of drought were commonplace. Sometimes it seemed the only animals to thrive were the rabbits – and thrive they certainly did. Two areas of our farm appealed to them the most: a large sandhill and a larger timber paddock. The sandhill was riddled with numerous burrows and the timbered area contained many hollow logs that provided hiding and shelter for the rabbits.

We had a lovely, lively kelpie sheepdog that enjoyed nothing more than joining me on a Saturday morning as I galloped off on one of my ponies to go rabbit hunting. I would arm myself with nothing more than a 2 metre length of sturdy fencing wire. Texie my dog had his natural digging abilities and very sharp teeth.

All entrances to the dozens of burrows in the sandhill had first to be inspected by Texie with his strong sense of smell as he ran from one to the other before sensing the presence of some likely prey. So with some vocal encouragement from me, he would set to, digging vigorously into a particular burrow and continuing for several metres until finally succeeding in capturing at least one adult rabbit and maybe a nest of bunnies as well – much snapping of teeth and their lives were no more!

As for the ones hiding in the depths of hollow logs, their fate, too, was often sealed. I could direct my length of wire into the log, gently poke one end into the mass of fur around the rabbit's head, turn the wire slowly till it gripped a mass of this fur and gradually draw the poor doomed animal out of the log and into Texie's waiting jaws! One sharp bite to the head was usually all that was needed for death to occur.

With lengths of string I tied my kill to the saddle – sometimes as many as seven or eight – and I recall having to ignore the bloodied bodies flapping against my trousered legs. Then I headed for home to remove their skins while the carcasses were still warm. My father and brothers had taught me how to do this and how to stretch them over U-shaped wire frames to dry. Months later I was able to collect as much as a shilling each for my labours!

Strange as it may seem today, my feelings then were of real gratification at the extermination of just these few animals that we regarded as vermin. None of the members of my family ever remotely considered eating the flesh of a rabbit. Quite plainly, we regarded rabbits as dog food!

GRAND PLANS FOR TULIPS

CHRIS HAWLEY

Bouncey, bouncey, bouncey, there goes cute little Peter Cottontail. Peter Cottontail, with his razor-sharp teeth and a voracious appetite. Cute? My …!

We really should have taken better notice of the telltale signs around the property. You know: rabbit poo more noticeable than the blades of grass; rabbit holes every fifty steps: and, of course, the ringbarked saplings on the property. But we were going back to our roots – farm life.

We smelled that fresh air ('aah'); and not a neighbour in sight! My father had taught me well. It was a high rainfall area – 30 to 40 inches on the old scale – with an all-weather spring oozing forth from the small gully. A clean, fresh all-year water supply. Perfect!

We did see the surrounding pine forest and the multitudes of blackberries, but hey, State Forests controls its own pests, don't they? We weren't exactly blind to the tell-tale signs of fresh soil scrapings and those little aniseed balls (signs of destruction), but we'd get on top of that, wouldn't we?

Not bloody likely, mate!!!

Grand plans of a tulip farm, back-breaking planting in freezing conditions, babying our little treasures. Squeals of pleasure and absolute delight as our first season of blooms opened up to display their glory. Oh what joy! We were spurred on! We planted beech trees, flowering cherries, flowering peaches, flowering plums. We planted thousands of dollars worth in the hope of creating an open-garden dynasty for generations to come. And we did. The generations that came did enjoy our bounty. They just weren't the two-legged type.

Spring has sprung! The drought hit, and hit hard. The neighbours said they hadn't seen things this bad since 1939. The rabbits were out in military force. My 'dearly beloved' thought he had found the solution, especially when he found out the high price for a gun licence. 'We'll burn the bastards – hot cross bunnies!' He didn't count on the vapour hanging around and delaying the ignition, did he? Singed eyebrows, scorched clothing and a charcoal face. He assured me he had a Plan B.

Now our Garden of Eden is looking like Mungo National Park. We had three dogs loose at night to ward off the rabbits, but even they became sick of rabbit – literally! Fat bellies and the satisfied look of a chocoholic who has eaten their fill. They could no longer summon up the urge to chase and kill, let alone stomach another rabbit dinner. We knew they had reached their fill when all three started to heave and heave and heave. I have never imagined my luxurious rabbit-skin lounge-floor rug would be decorated with bones, blood and canine saliva. Observing that, our guests from the city were suddenly sick from rabbit too! We still haven't named the property yet; perhaps Fallen Arches? The Ruins? Folly Farm? Friends said we should name it after my husband, as it seemed the most suitable name: Warren.

GRANDFATHER'S RABBIT TALE

ELISE SVANBERG

'Well, you've got two choices,' I remember the government man saying to my father. 'Either you stick around and pray things get better, or walk.' Walk? Walk off the land we had farmed for generations? Our blood, sweat and tears were in those paddocks. And there had been plenty of those lately. *Just then I hated those Austins. Those Pommy migrants who had rabbits sent over from England just so Thomas Austin could go shooting.*

If we wanted rabbits to shoot, then we had 35,000 of them on our property alone, and that was 3000 kilometres from where Austin let them go near Geelong in 1859. They were on our property even before the rabbit-proof fence was finished, which made Dad hopping mad. We had crops and pasture ruined, erosion problems and as kids we couldn't run across the paddocks without twisting an ankle in hidden burrows.

My dad had tried every trick he knew, and all the government knew as well: trapping, ripping burrows, fumigating, 1080 and, from the 1950s, myxomatosis – and we ate them. This was before the calicivirus in 1996. It was a grisly business and nothing seemed to work for long. The rabbits kept coming back. You had to have a sense of humour. Once a bunny got caught in my dad's gumboot; he didn't kill it but kept it as a pet. We had so many rabbits that one part of the farm was called the 'Peter Rabbit Block'.

But now it had come to this. Dad had had enough. We could handle all that God gave us – drought, floods, bushfires – but rabbits were too much. A 'gutful' as my dad would say.

Dad had to choose. It was his farm, and his dad's and granddad's before him. It was his pride and joy. Every paddock had special memories; his reason for being revolved around this land.

Even though he asked us – my mum, two brothers and me – we all knew it was his decision. He had battled rabbit plagues for years, wasting time, money and energy. Time better spent mending fences broken by kangaroos and emus; money, for summer feed and superphosphate; and energy, for playing with us kids.

Dad knew about fighting. He was brought back from the Middle East by John Curtin to help defend Australia from the advancing Japanese. His dad was born on the farm. He helped my great-grandfather to windrow, plough and plant the first crops in the days of telephone party-lines and generators. Now everyone in the district was affected by the rabbit menace. It wasn't for his sake but ours when Dad made that decision. We walked. We didn't leave with bitterness. We moved on to where pastures were greener; another chapter in our life. Rabbits had beaten my dad when the Germans and the Japanese could not.

We've all got reasons to be thankful. However I won't be thanking the rabbits and I won't be supporting Geelong either. But I LOVE Akubra hats!

CHILDHOOD MEMORIES OF RABBITS

MARGRET HAWES

During the later part of the 1940s our family lived on a property in northern NSW. At this time rabbits were in plague proportions, and one of my father's jobs was to reduce their numbers and improve the general condition of the land. Reducing the number of rabbits was no mean task. Early each morning we checked the traps that had been set the day before, and collected the rabbits that had been poisoned with a mix of arsenic, molasses and oats. My memory of this time is of cold mornings and how much I loved my fleecy top which kept me warm.

Dad, my brothers, a workman and I would work our way through up to 500 or so rabbits each day. Even as a small child I took great pride in being able to skin them, particularly when I managed to get the skins off without cutting into the flesh. If, for some reason, some of the rabbits were not dead, a quick wring of the neck would soon put them out of their misery. However, being so small, this practice presented me with a problem as I lacked the necessary strength. Instead I would stand on their feet and pull them up by the neck; sadly not always the quickest death for them.

The skins were put on to pieces of bent wire and hung up to dry in a shed; the smell will remain with me forever. Some of the trapped rabbits were used as dog food while the remainder was buried in a quarry near the cow shed. Hopefully Mum had not cooked rabbit for lunch.

On other occasions we would work at digging out the warrens. First we would close off most of the burrows, leaving the last few open. Dad would then instruct us to sit on the remaining open holes while he gassed the trapped rabbits. I hated it when they would scratch on your bum trying to get out, but Lord help us if we got up and let them escape. I doubt this practice would meet today's occupational health and safety standards.

Dad also put up a rabbit-proof fence around the homestead to protect the garden and vegetable patch from the rabbits. You can guess how popular we were when it was discovered that my brothers and I had caught and kept some kittens under the house as pets.

While numbers were dramatically reduced, there were still many left. When the property was on the market we worked out that if we went around the property on a given route on the motorbike and/or on horseback beating drums with sticks, Dad could then come behind with the prospective buyer, the noise having scared most of the rabbits back into their burrows. This would create the impression of a relatively rabbit-free place!

TWENTY THOUSAND RABBITS TRAPPED IN THREE NIGHTS

JOHN LORD

After the breaking of the 1945 drought I was camping at a dam here on Thackaringa, far west NSW, and you could see rabbits coming in for water. You could see the dust about 2 miles away. Some of the scientists said rabbits won't travel more than 600 yards, but these were walking a mile. We had a mob of about half-a-dozen professional trappers down there; they fenced the dam off and caught 20,000 rabbits in about three nights. That is what you had to do to try to control the rabbits. But it was probably too late when they had got to those sort of numbers.

In 1950, myxomatosis came through and made a big impact on the rabbits. The numbers dramatically collapsed. We have kept our stocking rates static at fifteen sheep per acre; we haven't carried any more sheep ever since those times. A lot of people grizzle about the rabbits, but they were a good source of food. Before refrigeration, we used to live in camps all the time, and we would have a fresh supply of meat. I'd roast them and put an onion in the rib cage. A gentlemen we had here fencing said to me that he'd never been short of a quid, as the rabbits carried him over the lean times. But I say there is only one good rabbit, and that is a dead rabbit.

5.

FOUR-LEGGED RECRUITS: DOGS, FERRETS AND CATS

There is something about the relationship between people and their companion animals that fascinates us. But in this case, the working relationship between human and animal shows a true partnership, and often a delightful and sometimes hilarious romp through Australian landscapes and times.

On reflection, we are amazed that we allowed cats and dogs to be rounded up in cities, placed in crates and backs of cars and taken to the country – a strange pet-recruitment drive dropping city pets or strays into service against the rabbit. This is still having an impact today as cats and dogs went feral, possibly from some of these early releases, and their descendants are still a pest today, targeting native fauna.

It is fascinating how children learned to handle ferrets and dogs, how they discovered which dogs in a town made the best rabbiters, and how they learned tricks to keep the ferrets from having a bite, then a snooze, and staying in the warren, unable to be recovered. The stories

Rabbit coursing in Australia. Coursing is the hunting of game with dogs that follow their quarry by sight.

here honour the best dogs, cats and ferrets, and show us some of the fabulous four-legged legends of the great Australian rabbit story.

A CONTRIBUTION TO BEATING THE BASTARDS

ROB CALDWELL

My mate Rossy Peters had a couple of dogs he reckoned were good rabbiters. My dog had no speed, but a good nose. We rode about town on our bikes to discuss rabbiting with some locals and soon learned which dogs were good rabbiters and which were useless. So, with the permission of dog owners, we rode around town early on Saturday or Sunday morning, whistling up the good dogs and leaving the useless ones. Our bikes were equipped with a long-handled shovel, a mattock and a billy can. By about 7.30 am we'd be heading out of town with a pack of eight to eleven dogs, for a day's rabbiting.

This was in the mid-1950s, when rabbit infestations around Blayney had reached a point where farming was becoming impossible. I can recall opening gates and, if the gate was pushed with a bit of force, it could knock over half-a-dozen rabbits. We heard of prices of two and six a pair at the local chiller, a coolroom where rabbits were stored before transport to the meatworks. That's a quid for eight pairs, if you could catch 'em, kill 'em, bleed 'em, gut 'em and get 'em to the chiller!

Often we rode up to 5 miles before the dogs put up rabbits in a nearby paddock. We had two dogs that could run down a rabbit in open grassland, pick it up by the head, shake it and kill it without bruising the body. There were plenty of dogs in town that could run down a rabbit, but they would pick it up by the body, resulting in severe bruising and ultimate rejection at the chiller. Those dogs were declared useless and therefore stayed in town.

If a rabbit ran into a blackberry bush, we had a couple of smaller dogs who would go in after them. All the other dogs would surround the bush in case the rabbits tried to escape. No chance, Br'er Rabbit! When we saw rabbits running in one direction to a warren, we made camp. After blocking all but one of the entry holes to the warren, we started digging. My slow dog, with the good nose, would show us which tunnel to follow at each junction, while 'potter' dogs scanned the surface around the warren looking for the 'pothole'. This is a part of the tunnel system that comes very close to the surface so that rabbits can dig through quickly, for an emergency escape.

The process of digging out a warren could take several hours, but the reward of up to twenty pair of rabbits made the hard work worth it. The dogs too, got their reward with treats of heart, lung, liver and kittens. We often arrived back at the chiller after dark, but the haul was good. The borrowed dogs were delivered back to their respective homes before we arrived back on our own doorsteps.

MEGS THE KLEPTOMANIAC

BRUCE BOWMAN

Lyn and I live in Ainslie, ACT, near the 'mountain'. While walking the other day, we noticed that in spite of all the recent rain, there is still little grass, but a major infestation of a tall, woody weed with a yellow flower. Also infesting the place is a population made up of roos and rabbits. It seems that they are keeping the grass down, while letting the less palatable weed take off. Not good I think!

When I was young, in the late 1930s and early 1940s, we hardly saw Dad, and late in life he told me that one of the great sorrows of his life was that he did not get to know his family while we were young. He would be out round his traps at first light every morning, to beat the crows and foxes to the free feed offering. He would then do another patrol in the evening. This frequency was necessary, as a skin damaged by a bird peck or dog bite was useless, and Mother told us once that for the first few years of their marriage, she and Dad lived on the money from rabbiting.

Every now and again one would catch a bird; usually a crow or magpie. The crows would be dispatched rapidly, but maggies were let go. The result was always that the bird lost a leg and had difficulty hunting. Being rather smart birds, they would turn up at our home for feeding. At one time we were feeding around fifteen maggies. They shared the cat food and were the bosses too!

As rural electricity spread through the bush, so did portable cool rooms for rabbits. The town of Barraba in north-west NSW, where I grew up, had one and during the cooler months, trappers were encouraged to bring gutted, but unskinned, rabbits into town. The chiller operator would pay per pair, I think on a weight basis.

Now and again the operator would have so many rabbits that the chiller was full. He would then store them overnight on the screens.

These were lengths of fencing wire arranged like the old-fashioned clothes lines, with props to hold them up.

Friends of mine, 'Rob' and 'Marge' (not their real names), who lived a couple of hundred metres from the chiller, had adopted an Irish setter dog called Megs. Megs was a kleptomaniac, meaning she would proudly bring home all sorts of things belonging to local households. Even a used plaster cast from the hospital!

One winter morning Rob and Marge woke to find what appeared to be a very heavy frost on the front lawn. Further inspection, though, showed that the 'frost' was fence-to-house rabbits! 'Megs' must have worked all night to transfer several hundred rabbits from the screen wires to her front yard!

FIGURING OUT FERRETS, THE HARD WAY

J. R. FITZWILLIAMS

As thirteen-year-olds, a mate and I bought our first ferret from a man who told us how to look after him. This was important, because he didn't have a muzzle to give us. To put the ferret down a hole, the escape hole had to be covered with our other net.

The first time we went out, we netted the one hole only, but this rabbit exploded through the surface of the earth, which must have been burrowed millimetres from the surface (smart rabbit)!

The second time we went out, a baby rabbit shot into the net; in releasing him, I took my eye off where I was supposed to grab our ferret (behind the neck). Bang! He put his fang through my thumbnail and halfway through the meat. I screamed in agony, telling my so-called mate to light the match, which we were told to do in case of an accident; we needed to put the flame near the ferret's face, so he'd let go.

The third time, we looked over the rise and saw all these rabbits in a bunch. We were warned never to put the ferret down a warren, because we had no muzzle. But we were that excited we couldn't resist. We blew our whistle for the rest of the day, trying to get him out (you blow the whistle before you feed, to train them). We rode our bikes back to town. We went back for two days with mattocks, frantically digging. Finally success; he didn't want to come home, naturally.

We searched all Wagga for a muzzle; we had learned a lesson. We bought more nets. We would give away rabbits to neighbours and friends. Rabbits were popular eating at the time. There was also the rabbit man, who would sell rabbits from his horse and cart every week. Then myxo came. All finished. I broke so many rabbit necks over the years, but if I was asked to do it now – NO WAY!

DOGS ON THE ROOF RACKS

CHARLES BEAMISH

As a child in the 1950s, I would often visit my grandparents' farm. I remember the stories told as we sat around the fire after tea. My uncles loved to tell tales because as a child, I was such a fascinated listener.

My uncle Jack, like me, was reared in town, but his father was a shepherd at Gretna and drove sheep backwards and forwards to the Tasmanian high country. They would've probably made more money from the rabbits than their shepherd wages in those days. Such was the use for dogs at the time, that (Jack told me), as a school-age boy, he would catch stray dogs in his district and send them to his dad in the lake country, via a ride to Bronte on the roof rack of the bus! I remember Jack's old dad telling me he got some very good rabbiting dogs that way. He lived well into his nineties and he, too, was a great storyteller.

He told me of a time he and Jack had a bet on who had the best hunting dog. As I recall, the old bloke was the winner, with his dog catching ninety-seven rabbits, and Jack's catching seventy-nine. Dogs were pretty prized possessions at that time and they were swapped and traded a fair bit.

My uncle Jack had a number of hunting dogs. One of them was this little white pup with brown markings from somewhere, named Trix. It was so small it could sit in the palm of his hand and I tell you she did not get much bigger as she grew, but she still thought she was a sheepdog and was as good a hunter as I ever saw. Her size didn't stop her going down the burrows after the rabbits, nor did the fact that they would often end up dragging her about the paddock trying to get away, but she wouldn't let them go. Sometimes a big buck rabbit would bounce Trix about like a rubber ball!

She wasn't big enough to kill a rabbit herself, but one old sheepdog bitch Jack had, called Jill, would kill the rabbits for her. Jill had become too old and slow to catch the rabbits herself, but Trix slowed them up enough for Jill to nail them. So the tandem combination worked well. Occasionally a big rabbit would drag Trix down a burrow – sometimes up to 3 feet – so Jack would put his arm up the hole, grab Trix by the tail and pull her out, with the rabbit always in her teeth; she'd never let them go! I loved this little bitch so much that I pleaded with my uncle to give her to me. But he loved her just as much as I did, as I never got her.

FLASH'S LAST LAUGH

DIANNE WRIGGLESWORTH

We had been droving a mob of sheep all day. The dogs: Sally, an old reliable, and Flash, the young energetic dog. We were nearly home: the sheep had slowed down, the dogs' tongues were nearly touching the ground; we had all had enough.

The sheep yards were in sight and the job was nearly done. Then Flash was off like a bolt of lightning chasing something. There he goes; it's a rabbit. The rabbit takes a line and heads straight for the sheep. The mob gets split and sheep go everywhere. Sally and I get them back together and finally into the yards. 'Good job done, Sally,' I say.

Flash is nowhere to be seen. Sally and I go for a drink around at the tank and who do we see coming around the corner but Flash. He has caught that rabbit and is parading it around for all to see. Flash has the last laugh and has a nice rabbit for dinner.

THE BOLT

NOEL THOMAS

Part of the fact that my childhood was happy was due to rabbits! My brother, much older than I, often dreamed up schemes for money-making. One such scheme concerned the purchase of ferrets for the purpose of rabbiting. At this stage it is important to state that the aforesaid elder brother had intestinal problems, and he was under the treatment of a 'quack'. His medication necessitated taking an elixir that contained kerosene.

While my brother was on this medication we went ferreting, his wife and my younger brother included in the party. We found a rabbit warren, a large burrow complex which was the home of many rabbits, and very common in those days. We pegged nets over each of the entrances to the warren, and then set the ferrets into it. We then awaited the rumble, the noise made by the rabbits fleeing their burrow to escape the ferrets.

The rumble noise was known as a 'bolt' – a very appropriate name! All was quiet, then – rumble, rumble. Hooray, the ferrets were working; the rabbits would soon be in our nets! Nothing; dead quiet! Then another rumble, but this time we became aware that it was my brother's intestines! The kerosene was working, but the ferrets weren't. Finally we had to dig them out; they had caught a rabbit, gorged themselves and gone to sleep. Brother eventually went to a proper doctor.

FERRET-QUAKES

KEVIN MORROW

It was 1950, the Korean War was still going, and my family lived at Warrayure in the western district of Victoria. There were eight children in the family, six boys and two girls. My eldest brother and two sisters worked with Mum and Dad, and my younger brothers and I went by horse and cart to the Lutheran school, where there were stables for the horse.

A rabbiter's pack, Darling Downs, circa 1885–1900. Rabbiters' packs often included an assortment of dog breeds, with each breed having different skills.

During this time, there was a rabbit plague, and thousands of rabbits were eating valuable sheep feed – not that I was worried about the sheep feed; all I could see was a great opportunity to catch them and sell the skins. We asked Dad to buy us some ferrets and nets, and Dad would sit at night making more nets. Some of the warrens were so large, even 100 nets weren't enough to cover all the holes. Dad made a cage for the ferrets and I would feed them on bread cut into squares, sprinkled with sugar and soaked in milk, but never when we were putting them to work.

We covered all the holes with nets, put the ferrets in, then only had to wait twenty seconds and the ground would rumble like a small earthquake. We would shake with anticipation, running to the first net with a rabbit in it, quickly putting our foot over the hole while taking the rabbit out of the net, putting it to sleep and resetting the net.

Sometimes we would get a white or black rabbit, or a bandicoot. They have a sharp, pointy nose not unlike one of our past prime ministers, but when they run they look quite comical, zigzagging as they go – just like they had a stick stuck up their diff.

Most weekends we would catch up to 300 rabbits. Dad would come out after tea with the Tilley lamp and help us skin them and we would put them on wires and hang them up in the shed to dry. When they were ready for sale we would take them to town to the skin buyer and get eightpence a pound. It was good money for us; the hardest work was digging a hole to bury the rabbits.

In those days things were very hard going, but we didn't go hungry because, as Dad would say, we had plenty of underground mutton. My mother had many ways of cooking rabbits, but my favourite was stuffed and roasted. There was also curried, boiled, potted and minced – we had so much rabbit I now don't eat it, but would if I was going hungry. My younger brothers and I had great fun earning our pocket money and it brings back wonderful memories. I must be going soft as I now try to avoid killing them when they run in front of the car. 'Rabbit Ho!'

DAD'S BREEDING FERRETS

CAROLE FURLOW

When I was a child, around 1951 in Western Australia, my father used to breed ferrets to use for rabbiting. He made a large wire cage in our backyard under a big tree. As I remember, the cage stood on legs about 6 inches, or fifteen centimetres, off the ground. It was made of bird wire, with small holes so that it was easy for the ferrets to walk on, and easy to keep clean. The ferrets always did their poos in one place. The other end of the cage had their 'house' and it had a lift-up lid so that we could put fresh straw into it, and when there were babies, we could check on them.

We had two ferrets, their names were Suzie and Freddie. Suzie was a gold colour, and Freddie was black and white. Suzie was ferocious when she had babies, and Freddie had to be housed elsewhere because he would have killed them. I always helped Dad clean the cages and had a real soft spot for Suzie until she attacked my hand, and I still have the scars to show where her long sharp teeth bit right through my hand. After that I used to stay right out of her way.

Sunday mornings we'd be up very early, Mum having packed our picnic lunch the night before, and Dad would have the nets that would cover the exit holes from the warrens, along with everything else he might need. The last to go in the car were our ferrets, and off we'd go.

Dad would drive down the Great Eastern Highway towards Pinjarra, probably about an hour from Armadale, until we came to his special spot. In those days there were only a few farms in that area, and the farmers were very pleased to have people come and go rabbiting on their properties. While Dad scouted around looking for fresh burrows, my brother and I would play in the little creeks that seemed to be all over the place.

Once Dad had found the burrows, we all had to be very quiet while the nets were placed over the holes before the ferrets were put in. Dad put muzzles on the ferrets, which were like round steel rings which fitted over the nose with a screw that went from one side of their mouth to the other. I think it fitted behind their back teeth. That was because if the ferrets weren't muzzled and they caught and killed, then ate, they would lie down and go to sleep. After losing

Ferrets have been used for many years to manage wild pest rabbits. Here a breeder from Victoria shows off his ferrets at a family day held at Barwon Park in 2009.

ferrets that way, Dad always used muzzles, because the ferrets needed to be hungry to work.

One needed to be very careful and watch where you were putting your feet in the paddocks because the old and new rabbit holes were everywhere. Once the nets were over the holes (and there could be ten or fifteen holes to cover), Dad would put a ferret down and we'd stand very still and listen. You could hear the rabbits running around under the ground and it was exciting wondering which hole they would fly out of. I could never watch as Dad would break their necks, and I would run away when the gutting started. I can still remember the smell. I liked all the fun bits, but didn't like to know about them dying. Mind you, I still use my grandmother's recipe if I get hold of a fresh rabbit. She used to brown the pieces, add bacon, garlic, onions and carrots and cook it slowly in the oven: we'd have it with mashed potatoes and peas.

I can't remember how many rabbits we would take home, but there were always many to share with family, friends and neighbours. Dad used to take them into work as well; we didn't have freezers in those days, and they wouldn't keep too long in a cooler. I live on the east coast of Tasmania now, and where we walk along a track onto our beach we always see rabbits. The bush is so dense just here that one couldn't use ferrets.

STINKING THINGS, REALLY!

WAYNE JARVIE

Forty odd years ago – I am now sixty-two – I was rabbiting with my father, Ron (still kicking at ninety), walking the Pentland Hills on the way to Ballarat in Victoria. We always had one ferret; stinking things, really. I do not know how people can have them as house pets. Bloody things bite like a tiger.

Anyway, we had been walking these damn hills all day with nets and a spade to dig Rufus out if he held us up. He was simply too smart for most rabbits and had a knack of catching them in the burrow and then holding us up for an hour or two. We often fed him before taking him out but you ran the risk of him going to sleep down a big hole. We'd had a few catches and netted the next big warren. We put Rufus in to do his job. After many rumbles and crashes, all went silent. I suspect we waited for a couple of hours and, as it was getting very dark, we decided to push all the openings in with the spade and leave the bugger there.

We thought we would take our other ferret up again to the same place a couple of weeks later. We netted up a burrow and sat down to wait for the action, when who should come scuttling down the side of the hill, none the worse for wear and large as life, but our old mate Rufus.

A COUPLE OF BLOKES AND A PACK OF DOGS

BILL SKELLY

In 1950, my mate Jack Davidson and I were looking for station work in the Riverina area of NSW. At the Stock and Station Agent we were told that they needed a 'couple of blokes' to work at Bonooke Station east of Deniliquin. We were signed on and told to start work tomorrow. 'Be under the big peppercorn tree at 7.30 am sharp.' This was the usual mustering spot for the day's work.

Our first job was poisoning rabbits. There were millions of them. It seemed as if the ground was moving. They ate everything in sight, even the bark off the trees. We had no choice but to exterminate them. To help us we had fifty dogs. There were dogs of all sizes, breeds and colours. They were a wild-looking bunch but all pretty well-educated as to how to round up rabbits. We were supplied with a horse and cart, cyanide powder, a large long-handled spoon and a couple of shovels. Off we would go each day with twenty-five dogs at a time.

The rabbits built their warrens wherever they found softer ground, as the black soil plains were too hard and they could only dig about a foot deep, and were overcrowded with 'kittens'. They weren't hard to find; there were millions of them. The dogs knew exactly what to do. The big dogs would scout out wide and chase rabbits in towards the warrens, where the smaller dogs would take over and chase them into the holes. Once all the rabbits were in, it was then our job to put the cyanide in the holes and cover them with shovels. There would be squealing and then deadly silence. We had no protective gear back then, and we would often wonder why we had such headaches at the end of the day.

This process would be repeated all day and after three or four weeks we would be back to where we started from. Believe it or not after exterminating thousands of rabbits, they would be back in virtually the same numbers. The smell of dead rabbits was everywhere and they would even reuse the warrens with dead rabbits in them. There were so many there was nowhere else to go.

One day we noticed some sick rabbits on the property. We found out it was a new way of killing rabbits. This was called myxo, or myxomatosis, which was a virus deadly to rabbits. This had been released on the Victorian border south of Deniliquin and was spreading. In no time at all there were no rabbits on the property. It was absolutely amazing. All the rabbiting we had done was nowhere near as effective as that myxo virus. It was a great scientific achievement. We went back to being station hands.

The most incredible part of the myxo campaign, to anyone who was around in the 1950s, was seeing the land gradually return to how it was before the devastating rabbit.

MORE CATS THAN RABBITS

MARGARET, CLUNES COMMUNITY CONVERSATIONS

When we first came to Australia from England and lived in Melbourne (1934–35), people would come to the door with live rabbits. You bought a pair and they wrung their necks and skinned them for you, right there and then. Later, when we were on the farm at Casterton, in the western district of Victoria, people used to dump their cats, and when we fumigated the rabbit burrows among the bracken we would get more cats than rabbits, as the feral cats lived on the rabbits.

THE LOST DOGS' HOME

ELIZABETH (BETTY) ALISON GOLDSWORTHY

My real life experience with the rabbit plague in 1950–1951 began when my late husband, Maurice Goldsworthy, was allotted a soldier settlement block of 640 acres in the Darlington–Dundonnell district of Victoria.

The six settlers on the Barnie Bolac Estate firstly erected a rabbit-proof fence to stop any more entering from adjacent properties. Materials were supplied by the Soldier Settlement Office in Mortlake. The men then erected a netting enclosure with wide wings. Rabbit drives were arranged regularly, with men and dogs making as much noise as possible. When the rabbits were trapped in the enclosure, the wings were quickly closed and the slaughter began. The rabbits were gutted and taken to a point to be picked up by the rabbit buyer, who travelled the district on certain days. The Commission paid the settler two pounds a week to rid the pest, so the extra money from the Buyer was very handy – and I might add we ate rabbit stew, rabbit patties and roast rabbit with bacon. As a result, I hate rabbit!

The dogs were obtained from the lost dogs' home in Geelong. They came by train to Camperdown railway station and were picked up by the settler. All kinds of breeds arrived. I remember riding in the cart drawn by Katie, a half draughthorse, with my husband and two small daughters. It was evening time and, as we approached a swamp area, the ground seemed to be moving in front of us and rabbits were jumping in the water to escape the dogs.

Later, a poisoning program was started. Firstly by laying a trail of minced carrots; this was termed a free feed. On the next day, another trail was laid with the poison added. This was very successful. All dead rabbits were gathered and buried. Only when the supervisor was satisfied were the settlers able to buy in sheep and get their lives in order, to become graziers. Shortly after all the hard work of these men came the discovery of myxomatosis. It was too late for them, but was the answer to the rabbit plague in all parts of Australia.

6.

RUN, RABBIT, RUN: THE GREAT RABBIT DRIVES

Do you need to fund the building of a hall, a school or a footy club? Perhaps a step back in time to the days of the great rabbit drives might inspire a new approach to the fundraising cake stall. These stories are disturbing in the numbers of rabbits needing to be rounded up and killed, and the fact that the whole community had to take part in what was a gruesome but necessary task. None of those involved enjoyed rabbit drives, but found ways to endure them. Sometimes kids seemed to have some fun but it was mostly short-lived, as they soon realised the whole process was a huge and tiresome activity.

Rabbit drives had elements of a modern-day Landcare tree planting or other community-benefit activity. There was always a social side, a lot of planning, and the engagement of the whole community, particularly women. Some drives were initiated by women as this was something they could do, with the aid of a few noisy kitchen items and a round-up of kids and neighbours.

What lies behind the stories is the pure desperation of the farmers and communities faced with the relentlessly plaguing animals. Reflecting today, we need to understand the very real, rapid and constant population growth of the rabbit (without an effective virus control about) and its devastating impact, with the rabbit's ability to thrive so well in a wide range of conditions.

KEEPING THE SCHOOL OPEN

DENISE HANLIHAN

Back in the early 1950s, I'd just turned twenty, just completed my first year as head teacher of a rural school, and had just heard that my school had been condemned and would not be replaced by the Education Department. A very anxious local asked if I would be willing to teach in a woolshed while the people tried to find the money to build a school. I'd become very close to this community, so readily agreed.

Late in the autumn, word came that a rabbit drive would be held to raise some money, as the country was overrun with the little monsters that were destroying all before them. These drives had become opportunities for social gathering at weekends, as well as fundraisers.

On the appointed day I joined dozens of people of all ages as they gathered at the main road with tins full of stones, tins with sticks to bang on them, whistles, toy trumpets – anything that would make a noise. Dress was not as you'd expect to see today: skirts rather than pants, woollen jumpers, long woollen coats, leather shoes with ankle socks; scarcely a rubber boot in sight, though the paddocks were very wet. Men who knew the lay of the land rode on horseback marshalling the drivers. A line was formed right across the paddock, which was fenced with wire netting.

At the signal, bedlam broke out! Banging, rattling, whistling and yelling as the line moved steadily forwards terrified the rabbits so that they just ran ahead in waves of thousands. An unbelievable sight: the whole ground seemed to be a moving carpet. Most were so confused that they didn't even try to enter the burrows or hide in the creeks, but just kept running. A few did manage, or else turned back and escaped through the line as it slowly advanced to the far corner of the paddock.

Here, a length of wire netting had been laid out on the ground, long enough to reach diagonally across the corner. When the rabbits finally hit the corner in their thousands, this netting was pulled upright so they couldn't escape. Men quickly moved in to kill and gut them.

Now came the best part: some locals had lit a huge log fire, had water boiling for tea, and an array of sandwiches and cakes spread out to feed the hungry hunters as we warmed up and dried out a bit. This was a time to socialise, catch up on local news and share stories of the drive.

Triumphantly, the organisers announced they'd hung 3200 gutted rabbits on the fence! A buyer would come with a truck that night. This proved to be more than enough money for the new school.

Even the removal of so many rabbits made little difference overall. Full-time rabbiters were employed for years to trap, poison, fumigate, fill in burrows and remove the habitat. This work was a great boost to the local community and economy, as well as eventually depleting the rabbit numbers.

FOOTY FAN'S RABBIT DRIVE

MARGARET PULLEN

On a sunny Sunday in May 1951, there was a rabbit drive with thousands of rabbits as the target. My father, a keen supporter of the Wangaratta Football Club, always participated in club fundraising activities: rabbit drives, wood days and dances. Rabbits were in abundance, so rabbit drives were organised along country lanes between Springhurst and Rutherglen, crabhole country off the Three Chain Road, a long straight road north of Wangaratta in north-eastern Victoria. At the chosen paddock, before ten o'clock, a small contingent of committee members set up the corral and two holding pens. Shortly after, men and boys arrived on tray trucks and in the backs of utes. Families arrived in cars, as did we in our shiny black Vauxhall UR 058, named Blackie.

Everyone gathered at the given area while Mr Coe, travelling around the perimeter, dropped off men at herding points. One-mile-square parcels of land surrounded by lanes made this an easy task. Prior to the chase, excited supporters, friends, dads, mums and kids gathered together. On sounding the horn on Mr Coe's truck, everyone immediately began the banging and clanging of metal spoons on old saucepans and kerosene tins, the piercing sounds from whistles, and much yelling.

The startled grey army of running, hopping and jumping rabbits was chased towards the corral, into the wings, then drafted off into two pens. The temporary wire fence over 4 feet high with steel droppers was quickly drawn across to prevent a massive escape. The fittest men and boys would grab a rabbit and, in a flash, twist the rabbit's head and pull down the body by putting pressure on their legs, a rapid death.

With a sharpened pocketknife I can see my dad's action right now: a slit was made revealing the gut, and with a firm flick of the wrists, the entrails were flung on a heap and eventually buried in a deep hole which had been prepared by the advance party. Next, a slit was made to the tendon of a rabbit's hind leg and the hind leg of another rabbit was pushed through the slit, forming a firm X-shaped pair of grey rabbits. These paired rabbits were hung over a designated section of fence then covered with hessian bags to keep off flies. I recall this image looking like an old-fashioned clothes line full of children's grey trousers.

Then it was time for light refreshments: morning tea, a cuppa, scones, pikelets and nutloaves before the next chase. After the second drive, it was time for lunch and refreshments provided by the football club. Stories were exchanged about the drives, children played chasey or kicked footies and those wearing gumboots slid on the greasy ground. Yes, it rained back then.

By day's end and the third drive, 1000 pairs of rabbits were taken to the Wangaratta Butter Factory coolroom and eventually transported to Melbourne. The club was paid one shilling a pair and these funds were put towards building the new club rooms. What a day for a little seven-year-old.

Rabbiters turn-out, Cobar district, New South Wales, 1907.

RABBIT PLAGUES

TINKERBELL

Here in the mallee country, where red dust devils spiral high into the glaring heavens and cruel thistles spike the eyes of cattle, the land seems to despair under the crushing burden of drought. Prosperous crows and hawks grow fat on dying rabbits. They perch on branches like greedy black undertakers, swooping to pick up a rabbit as it totters to gain a little moisture from the drip-safe tray right in front of my eyes. The wretched birds pick the heart and liver out and fling the mutilated carcass down with a sickening thump. I hate the carrion birds as they caw, watch and wait.

My husband and I camp in tents on a property, cleaning out large, oblong, ground tanks with a D9 bulldozer. These tanks are common in this part of Australia and are dry because of the drought.

Kerosene lanterns, camp-ovens, a Coolgardie safe, bore water and canvas stretchers are our 'mod cons' of the day.

One Saturday evening a group of ten or so young men arrive by table-top truck to the one remaining tank still containing some muddy water. This tank was fenced with wire netting a few weeks previously. Funnels in the netting facing outward are of sufficient diameter to allow easy entry for thirsty rabbits, however once the rabbits are inside, holes are too small for them to exit, effectively imprisoning the starving bunnies.

As evening falls, hundreds of emaciated rabbits creep to the dam to drink. The men's job is to club the unfortunate animals to death, remove and burn them. The slaughter becomes frenzied, as terrified rabbits try to escape. Men urge each other on, shouting encouragement, much to my dismay.

Rabbit plagues were common during the 1940s in NSW and Victoria. They eat their own weight in fodder very quickly, thus depriving stock of nourishment. Grass, thistles and weeds were nibbled down, roots and all. Of course what followed was soil erosion and eventual collapse of grazing land.

In May 1950, the rabbit virus myxomatosis was released at Gunbower in the Murray Valley. Heavy rains built up the mosquito population necessary to spread the virus and there was a general epidemic by February 1951. Rabbits died by the million along the lagoon and river reaches. However, by 1964, myxomatosis had become less virulent and rabbit numbers began to climb as resistance to the virus increased.

Before the virus was introduced, many country folk made good money trapping rabbits for their skins, or for mobile freezing plants. Indeed, during the Great Depression and hard times in my youth, rabbits were a welcome addition to the table. We ate rabbit two or three times a week.

During the 1930s and 1940s, men would wheel a barrow-full of dressed rabbits along city streets calling loudly, 'Rabbits … rabbits … eighteen pence a pair; fat clean rabbits.' I was glad when the rains came and we moved away from rabbit plagues, red dust devils and the Mallee country.

TANKING RABBITS

ARCHIBALD MACKINNON

In the mid-1940s, our family property was 70 miles from Cobar in central-western NSW. A soldier settler block drawn by my father after the 1914 to 1918 war, it was 24,000 acres, but not enough to provide a reasonable living for a family. At this time, rabbits were in plague proportions and did a great deal of damage to whatever grass was available for stock.

A ground tank – called dams in some areas – was selected, several miles from alternative sources of water for animals. A secure wire-netting fence was then erected right around the water, about 6 feet from the water's edge. Netting funnels were attached to the bottom of the fence at intervals, the narrow end of the funnel inside the fence.

When rabbits came to drink at night they found the large end of the funnel easily but, when trying to escape after drinking, they could not find the narrow end which was some 2 feet from the fence. At daylight next morning we would find live rabbits covering the ground inside the fence, sometimes two or three deep. One person climbed inside the fence to wring the neck of each rabbit and throw the body over. Several others outside the fence then gutted and paired the rabbit carcasses. A truck from a nearby mobile freezer picked up the rabbits each morning and paid one shilling a pair.

This gave the family a welcome addition to the income derived from sheep and cattle; there were no crops that grew reliably in this area at that time. This method of rabbit control was much more effective than trapping and shooting, and cost very little to implement. The fence could remain in place until this paddock was required for stock.

SOLDIER SETTLERS

YVONNE WILDASH

After the Second World War, my husband and I and our small daughter moved on to a soldier settlement block near Ando in southern NSW. From the first our lives were dominated by rabbits. During the war years there was very little man-power available. There was one rabbiter on Mount Cooper, of which our block was a portion. As he had only one leg, what he could do was limited. But he was quite amazing, rode everywhere and how on earth he mounted the horse, goodness only knows.

The rabbits had multiplied and multiplied until they moved in a grey blanket across the hills; as we came up one side they moved down the other, white tails bobbing, so we shot, poisoned, trapped, fumigated and in every possible way exterminated rabbits. We smelled of rabbits and my small daughter Anne developed an unendearing habit of jumping on the carcasses just to make sure they were really dead. The most efficient way of killing them was to poison them with scotch thistle roots soaked in a mixture of vanilla, sugar, oil of peppermint and strychnine. They died very quickly. Every evening we laid a trail: John walking ahead and turning a sod with a mattock, Anne and I following with tongs and dropping bait into each hole. Next morning the bodies were collected, skinned, the skin stretched on a bent wire, then hung on a fence to dry. This provided us with a living as we sold the skins each week. But it was non-stop work. None of us has ever been able to eat rabbit.

Our most dramatic moment was a rabbit drive. In one big paddock, badly overrun with rabbits, we had four men digging out the burrows to destroy any harbour. A netting yard with wings, to channel the rabbits into the yard, was built at the end of the paddock. The idea of the drive had excited a great deal of interest locally and every available man was there to help. The drive began!

A line of men walked from the far end of the paddock driving the rabbits in front of them. When the yard was full it was shut off and the slaughter began. It was a scene from hell and the noise, just awful. The rabbits were clubbed and destroyed in every possible way. They piled up so quickly on the back fence that some were able to jump right over their fellows, escaping to breed another day. The slaughter would have seemed too terrible if we had not realised that it was us or the rabbits.

When myxomatosis became available we were able to more or less clean the place of rabbits but always a strict eye had to be kept. It would not have taken long for them to breed up again. Rabbits are an endless battle.

A motor lorry loaded with 1760 pairs of rabbits, circa 1918.

THEY FLOCKED TO TRANGIE FOR 'BUNNY MONEY'

JOHN R SCOTT

Memories of the explosion of the rabbit population and subsequent plague in the Trangie district of central NSW in the early 1950s take me back to my primary school days. Such was the massive population that the burrows could not hold the numbers, so the rabbits were running loose and the paddocks were a moving mass, like maggots on a dead sheep. Coloured rabbits appeared, in keeping with the numbers, and created a patchwork of colour in the distance as they stripped the country bare.

People down on their luck and needing money flocked to Trangie: many on the train; some in old utility trucks; others in horse-drawn carts and sulkies; all in pursuit of the 'bunny money'.

The rabbits were trapped or shot, or trapped on waterholes fenced with wire netting with one-way funnels, or driven like mustering sheep, such were the numbers. As kids, we knew the names of the best shooters and trappers. The best trapper was a local with a big family to feed; he was known far and wide as 'Bunyip Bill O'Neill'. He didn't lay traps where the rabbits were, but where they were going to be!

The rabbits, paired and gutted, were taken to chillers owned by Angliss Company and they paid immediately. Suddenly, new utilities and trucks were everywhere. The 'bunny economy' had taken off; Trangie became a boom town before our startled eyes. The drives were great fun to schoolboys and provided us with pocket money. As we were available, entrepreneurs would organise our pick-up points for Saturday drives.

They would drop us at the bottom of the paddock in a straight line and we would cooee and make as much noise as we could to drive the mob of rabbits towards the top corner. While advancing, we were able to boondy rabbits with our homemade sticks; we would make a pile of rabbits which were picked up by utes. Our shakers, made of boot-polish tins and lids threaded on a wire, made plenty of noise and we called them our 'hand-held dogs'.

When the rabbits were mustered into the corner, a roll of wire netting was drawn across to secure them, then they were driven into a smaller catching pen where we wrung their necks, legs were split and they were paired back to back and then hung on the fence ready for slitting and gutting. An average drive caught about 1000 pairs. We were paid three shillings for a very long day, which was good money, as we were under ten years of age.

I have seen rabbits pile up in a corner so high that some would run up the pile and go over the fence to escape. Our dad was a very good shot with a .22 rifle and, on winding up a drive, three rabbits remained. He asked for three bullets, lined up and fired, killing the three with one shot. We were amazed and told anyone who would listen to us.

The highway to Nevertire and Nyngan was known as 'the fur highway', such was the number of rabbits squashed by cars. As the plague started to weaken, and before myxo arrived, landholders began to reclaim their devastated land by destroying burrows and harbours. Then along came the grey Ferguson tractor and rippers, and there began another boost to the Trangie economy. Ripping warrens began in earnest and Fergies were in such demand that there was a long waiting list of orders to secure one.

It was a very exciting time for us kids, and out of the devastation of natural grasses, crops and land came instant income, employment and a boom time for little Trangie, which we proudly called home.

THE 'RON GOL' RABBIT DRIVE

MISS PATRICIA WHYTE (FROM THE DIARY OF MISS PATRICIA WHYTE, AS CONTRIBUTED BY HER NEPHEW GRAEME WHYTE)

Ron Gol was a property of around 4000 acres situated on the Darling River between Wentworth and Pooncarie in south-west NSW. After the drought years in the early 1940s (lasting up to 1946), rabbit numbers grew rapidly.

On 18 January 1948, around 150 local people – chiefly men – travelled to Ron Gol to help in a rabbit drive. The property, owned then by Mr and Mrs W. Green, was described as 'lousy with rabbits'. Ron Gol's thirty acres of vines and small amount of citrus were without suitable netting and were ringbarked. The property's (short) gordo vines were stripped of foliage and fruit. Other vines on the property were denuded up to 2 feet from the ground, and in some places the rabbits had climbed up the vines and eaten the leaves and fruit.

Following is an extract from the diary of Miss Patricia Whyte (twenty-one years), Wentworth, NSW, one of the few local women who participated in the drive.

Graeme Whyte.

Sunday, Eighteenth January, 1948

Today Dad, John and I went up to 'Ron Gol' for the rabbit drive. The rabbits are on the increase everywhere and at 'Ron Gol' have reached plague proportions.

Originally there was a netting fence surrounding the place, but during the drought the drift sand formed up along it and it was three-quarters buried, so the rabbits find it child's play. Owing to the shortage of wire netting they could not fence in the vines in time – by the time they got the netting it was a question of fencing the rabbits in, which they did, not that the rabbits needed much encouragement.

Dad said he would be disappointed if there were only about 200 rabbits and he expected at least 1000. I said I didn't see how a block could probably harbour 200 rabbits. Dad was not disappointed.

There were thousands of rabbits. The vines were all trimmed off rabbit-high, the trailing runners were stripped, and the gordos, being only low, not much higher than rabbit-high, were a total loss, as regards crop, anyhow. The young orange trees are all ringbarked and will all die. They do not seem to have made any attempt to save them; they haven't even put any netting around them. The rabbits were starting to climb the vines and walk along and eat from the top …

… The expedition gathered at Bill Langdon's at about 9.30 am. We were the first to arrive and tried to convince Lyells and Mr Bond to start out straight away to be in front of the town cars, trucks, etc, due to arrive any minute – we wanted to avoid the dust. In due course the mob arrived. However, we got all aboard like greased lightning and lit out for the horizon and still be in the lead, when there rose from behind a terrible din: 'Flat tyre! Soft tyre!' Unfortunately that referred to us. What a downfall! The first shall be last …

… The road was rotten. The bumps were so bad that Mr Bond went through the floor of the ute – he was sitting right at the very back and what it did to him I can't imagine …

… Arriving at 'Ron Gol' we dispersed to find waddies and gathered near the house for the first drive. It was a chaotic rabble. People charged down the rows like a bushfire, the rabbits were not used to being driven and they all started doubling back. Owing to the vines we could not see them coming and they were very hard to hit. If we had taken an hour for the first drive it would have been different – but we didn't.

At the end of each drive there was a half-hour wait while no one decided what next, and half of us, impatient, scattered to deal with rabbits on our own account, making it far more complicated still. At the end of the first drive we had about twenty rabbits and there were hundreds back in the rows we had been through.

So with breaks for lunch and smoko, we tramped all over the block all day. The ground was heavy and it was hot. After smoko I did not go out with the drive; I took my shoes off and did nothing. I was hopeless at rabbits anyway. My total for the day was four. Two facts emerged: one, rabbits are far more intelligent than people; two, that the Hospital and Food for Britain (who were to share the proceeds) would scarcely benefit. The live rabbits caught in the morning died. The ones that were dead would not keep until the evening. In the afternoon catch a lot were bruised and/or small and these were unacceptable to Gurds (local rabbit buyers). There was no time to skin them.

When we left we had killed about 1000 rabbits. Back in the vines were probably 3000 very tired rabbits – and were we tired!

IN FULL SKIRTS AND APRONS

BENJAMIN CALDWELL

Imagine this ... just on dusk you look out over your farm and the paddocks seem to be moving; the ground appears to be undulating, like a wave coming in to shore. But then you take a closer look, and this undulating wave is in fact thousands of rabbits, a plague of four-legged furry pests, moving across your farm. The dam bank is covered with rabbits, silhouetted against the setting sun. This is what my grandmother and grandfather saw every night.

And every morning they would see the dreadful damage these introduced pests were causing to the Australian land. Rabbits, in their seemingly unfathomable numbers, ate the pasture needed for the farmers' sheep and cattle, digging the roots out so it could never grow back, and ringbarking and killing native shrubs too. This not only left little feed for stock but also caused erosion. These pests,

A house with rabbit pelts hanging from the veranda ceiling, circa 1965.

which seriously did breed like rabbits, were creating semi-desert districts.

My grandmother was one of a group of about twelve farmers' wives who decided to do something about this plague. On each of their properties they built a fenced-off yard, tapering into a V shape at one end, with gates at the opposite end. Every week, while their husbands were out farming, these women would meet for what they regarded as a social get-together, dressed as custom demanded back in the early 1950s, in long dresses, full skirts and aprons. Even in broad daylight rabbits were hopping around the paddocks, which were riddled with rabbit holes. A couple of the wives owned ferrets, which they would send down these holes to 'ferret' the hiding rabbits out into the open. Then these women would flap their dresses and aprons to drive the rabbits into their fenced yard, down to the narrow end, where they would beat them to death with big sticks.

These enterprising Australian women didn't just feel content that they were helping to eradicate these pests – they ensured nothing went to waste. They would skin the rabbits, bale the skins like their husbands did wool, and send them to auction, often to be bought by Akubra, who made their famous hats from them. My grandmother sometimes kept a few of the skins, pegged them fur-side down on the shearing shed floor, and rubbed into them a paste of carb-soda and kerosene every day for two weeks, making them soft and clean. She would sew all the skins together, by hand, to make 'bunny rugs' for her six children, who remember them being very warm and soft. The actual rabbits would be shared among the families for food. My mum remembers, as a youngster, having roast rabbit, stuffed rabbit, boiled rabbit and rabbit stew.

Today, thanks to a group of enterprising Australian scientists, we do not have rabbits in such plague proportions. I am, however, continuing the family tradition: trapping rabbits on our farm, and selling them to my schoolteachers, who regard them as a delicacy and just love roast rabbit.

RABBITS SUPPORTED FOOTY AND CRICKET

LYNDLEY CHOPPING

There were millions of them – rabbits of course – in plague proportions. At Blackwood, we used to have the Ouse and Hamilton football and cricket teams (1953, 1954 and 1955) come up for a rabbit drive. In the morning before daylight, we would line up along the ridge line and then move down across the paddock making as much noise as we could, belting bushes, bashing tins or yelling out, driving this grey, white-tailed, shimmering mass across the 100 acre paddocks to the far corner through a decent hole in the netting fence into a rabbit netting cage on the other side.

Here the rabbits were about a metre deep; then it was all hands to the task of killing the pests (with a rabbit killer, of course), then skinning and pegging out the skins, to dry for sale. This was a well-earned source of revenue for guernseys, bats, pads, boxes, balls and other extras for the various sporting clubs. We'd get six shillings and eightpence per dozen; that is, thirty cents per skin, depending on your skin buyer (Neale Edwards or Wilcox Mofflin).

RABBITS, RABBITS AND MORE RABBITS

PENNY WARNER

I would have been around six or seven years old at the time, around 1948 to 1949. My father's nickname was Bunny Rabbit, our surname being Abbott, you see. The local football clubs used to arrange rabbit drives to make money for their clubs. The rabbits were in plague proportions here in the Wimmera region of Victoria. We lived in Stawell. My father was noted for his bushman's skills, so my uncle Claude, who had a small truck, used to ask him to go to these drives to gut the rabbits. The drive would be arranged with a local farmer to be on his property.

I was my dad's shadow at that time and went with him everywhere. Dad, Uncle Claude and I would head out to the property and place bird wire about 30 yards along a boundary fence at a corner and back along the dividing fence for another 30 yards or so and tie it all the way along.

The football club would hire a bus and the members, players, coach, president and so on, and their wives and children, would all come out and start at the homestead. They would all get in a line and yell and beat the bushes and drive the rabbits before them. They were so thick by the time they got near us that they were a moving mass in front of them. We would sit in the truck and wait till they were shepherded into the corner with the people behind them. Someone else would run another roll of wire behind them till they were cornered in a triangle.

My father would hop into the pen and start grabbing rabbits, cut their throats, gut them then pair them by the legs. Other men would keep shepherding them by moving the wire in to make a smaller pen. I vividly remember my father sitting by rabbit guts in a pile 4 foot high by 4 foot round, then moving on and making another pile. Sometimes there would be six or seven piles by the finish.

The rabbits were loaded onto Uncle Claude's truck and slung on wooden beams three deep and the length of the tray. Uncle would then drop us off home and then head for Melbourne four hours away. The rabbits were taken to a place that sold them to the meat trade and the skins were sold on to a factory that made men's hats. Every man used to wear a hat made of rabbit fur in those days.

There weren't any refrigerated vans in those days for transporting them to Melbourne; I can't recall much food poisoning then, either. To supplement our food back then, we had quite a few meals of rabbit a week. I can't eat rabbit at all nowadays.

FOUR THOUSAND THEN AND TWO NOW

JOAN, CLUNES COMMUNITY CONVERSATIONS

The Clunes RSL had rabbit drives to raise money for a deposit to buy their building. They had temporary fences and would drive the rabbits using lots of manpower. The rabbits were slaughtered and taken to Collin's Freezing Works, which would hold up to 4000 rabbits in pairs. Trucks would come up from Melbourne, stay overnight, and then take the rabbits back to Melbourne. Today my security light keeps coming on. The cause: two little rabbits playing in my yard.

LIKE LITTLE SAVAGES

ROS, CLUNES COMMUNITY CONVERSATIONS

We sat around as young kids often do; slightly bored. The sort of day when all you want to do is yawn. One of the group, a boy about twelve, said, 'Let's go rabbiting.' So we went rabbiting.

We gathered a net, which we placed over the rabbit's burrow. We knew where all the burrows were and we knew approximately where the rabbit was shivering underground in fear. The creature finally gave up all hope of survival and rushed into the waiting net and hands of the children. To this day I do not know how we selected which burrows to net and which not to net.

Like little savages we clutched the squealing, wriggling rabbit by the neck and stretched it as hard as we could. It didn't survive for long. We put the carcass on the bar of the bike and cycled off, eagerly seeking another victim for our mother's pot. She had commissioned two rabbits for a rabbit pie for dinner that night. Having successfully carried out our mission we were free to be bored once more, or we could help prepare for the next day's big event – the rabbit drive.

So we set about gathering all the bits of rope and a small amount of rags (for wiping hands if necessary) and other such things: bits and pieces of tin, board, stiff cardboard, galvanised iron – anything that would clatter and bang. We wanted to create a loud noise to frighten and confuse the rabbits. We made a neat pile on the woolshed floor, slightly left of centre. The pile looked large and we impressed ourselves.

It was mid-morning by the time all the 'toffs' had gathered at the fray. There would have been between thirty and fifty people milling about, the air of expectation was brimming over and we were nearly ready to take off in pursuit. Men were slapping their thighs with whips made of strips of leather.

'A rabbit battue at North Corack', 1879.

On the outskirts of the town are two hills which, from a certain angle, look as if they are side by side. Using this as a line of sight, the beaters (for want of a better name) made as much noise as possible as they put small dogs into burrows of the increasingly terrified rabbits.

When a certain number of rabbits were reached, the beaters called off the cull. After a drive all the participants were given as much beer as they could drink. A rabbit drive could quite easily turn into a serious drinking session and was therefore not encouraged by the women in the community, who often appeared to be overprotective of the 'old man'. As a child growing up in the bush I was quite familiar with ferreting and trapping rabbits with my brother, ridding the earth of the cursed rabbit.

7.

QUIRKY TALES

Here are some wonderful stories, each one different and so making a stirring mix. These stories have unusual twists, and some describe rabbiting methods different from the ubiquitous trapping and poisoning. In others we see the personal tragedy and heartache that rabbits caused. There are interesting character pieces and stories where rabbits were a catalyst to some other memory. Finally, there are stories about new chums, stories with overseas angles, and even a tale of a tricky relationship with an in-law – the showy display and one-upmanship that the son-in-law simply must endure! And the common denominator, of course – the wild pest rabbit!

A LEGEND OF SUCCESS, RESILIENCE AND COMMUNITY SOUTH SYDNEY – A VERY AUSTRALIAN RABBIT STORY

MARK COURTNEY, FOR THE RABBITOHS

The emblems of sporting teams these days are usually images of aggression. Either ferocious animals like tigers, birds of prey like hawks, human marauders like pirates or feared natural phenomena like storms. You'd have to wonder, then, how an Australian club, engaged in perhaps the toughest collision sport on Earth – rugby league – could have as its emblem a small, white rabbit.

Yet South Sydney, the only professional sporting club in the world whose players run onto the field with a rabbit on their chest, are so closely linked with the term 'Rabbitohs' that it would be unthinkable for them to be represented by any other image. It's an old club – the oldest in the league – and it is steeped in history and tradition and wonderful stories. It's a club that symbolises a lot about what it means to be Australian. And it's a club so loved by its hordes of fans that, a bit like a rabbit plague, it has been impossible to kill.

The South Sydney District Rugby League Football Club came into existence on 17 January 1908, at a packed meeting of local residents at the Redfern Town Hall, in inner Sydney, where the club is still based. Wearing horizontal stripes of cardinal red and myrtle green and representing an overwhelmingly working class area, the team found immediate success, winning the first two competitions of the New South Wales Rugby League in 1908 and 1909.

Yet in was in the mid-1920s – the years leading into the Great Depression – that the club built an aura of invincibility. Souths won seven competitions in eight years from 1925 and the club was dubbed 'The Pride of the League'. And it was during the Depression years that several players used to eke out a living selling rabbits. Legend has it that they would walk the streets of Redfern, often wearing their football jerseys, yelling out 'Rabbitoh, Rabbitoh' to spruik their wares. And so it happened that, on the weekends, the crowds at the matches began to call out 'Come on the Rabbitohs!'. Hence the team had a name and later, in 1959, the players began to wear a leaping white rabbit emblem on their jerseys, forever linking the club with its own community.

In the history of rugby league, no other club has been as successful and no other club is as proud of its heritage. Further golden eras followed in the 1950s (when they won five premierships in six years) and the late 1960s (four premierships in five years).

And great stories abounded. Stories that have been passed down through generations of South Sydney fans. Like the day at Redfern Oval in 1955 when champion fullback Clive Churchill, broken arm hanging limply by his side, kicked a goal from the sideline after the bell to win a game against Manly by a point. That game kept alive a remarkable winning sequence of eleven victories that went all the way to the grand final. Or the incredible courage displayed by captain John Sattler in the 1970 Grand Final, when he played seventy-seven of the eighty minutes with a badly broken jaw, refusing to leave the field and leading the team to another famous premiership win.

Perhaps the most inspiring of all Rabbitoh stories, however, was played out off the field. Its origins lie in significant financial difficulties experienced in the mid-1970s, leading to years of poor performances on the field and culminating in late 1999 when the club was actually expelled from the National Rugby League competition.

Although this was the darkest day in South Sydney's history, it began an extraordinary campaign, waged largely by everyday fans, to get the club reinstated into the competition. As the movement gained momentum, South Sydney fans from all over Australia, from all walks of life, crossing boundaries of religion, race and socio-economic circumstance, were galvanised into action by the loss of something they all loved. On two separate occasions more than 50,000 people marched through the streets of Sydney, millions of dollars were raised at events all around the nation and three court cases were fought, until eventually justice was done in July 2001, when the full bench of the Federal Court ruled that the expulsion of the Rabbitohs had breached the law.

The South Sydney Rabbitohs were back and they rejoined the competition with much fanfare in 2002.

Since then, the club has gradually rebuilt itself into one that can again challenge for the championship crown. And rest assured, when the cardinal and myrtle does lift the trophy, the roar will be heard from Redfern to Broome as the Rabbitoh community celebrates as one. It's a community that remembers its past with pride, appreciates its warriors with respect, and looks to the future with hope.

The mighty South Sydney Rabbitohs. It's a very Australian rabbit story.

BILL THE GIANT RABBIT

SEAN GLASSFORD, MANAGER OF JACK THOMPSON'S HOTEL GEARIN, KATOOMBA, NSW

In the early 1970s my younger brother, Rory, and I lived on Somerlea Park, a cattle station 9 miles out of Trangie, NSW, on the road to Gin Gin Weir on the Macquarie River.

We ran Santa Gertrudis and Brahman cattle. It was massive and was crisscrossed with irrigation channels.

A few things about that time will live with me forever. Flies. Lots of flies! We used to have long yellow sticky fly traps that hung down from the carport. Within twenty-four hours they would go from yellow to black! Thick red dust, also known as bull dust; there was lots of that too. And rabbits: grey and brown ones with fluffy tails, millions of them. Coincidentally, it was about the same time we started supporting the South Sydney Rabbitohs. I was seven and Rory was five.

One day we thought it would be great if we caught a rabbit, not for eating, but to keep as a pet. Around our farmhouse was a 5 foot high brown wooden fence. We decided the best place to make the rabbit trap was 2 feet from the fence. We dug a perfectly square hole about 2 and a half feet deep by one and one half feet square, covered it with inch-thick bark and then covered that with leaves and grass. I believe we even baited the trap with some tasty carrots and crisp iceberg lettuce. We were very proud of our rabbit trap. We excitedly went off to bed that evening thinking that in the morning we would have caught a rabbit!

The next morning we were very disappointed to find that our brilliantly engineered trap had failed to catch anything! But each night for the next few days, we would go to bed hoping that in the morning we would have a pet rabbit to call our own.

What we failed to appreciate was that a whole burrow of rabbits could have been doing a highland fling on top of the trap and still they would not have fallen in.

A week or so had passed and Rory and I returned home from school to be greeted by a very solemn-looking mother. Mum asked us if we had dug a hole beside the fence at the front of the farmhouse and, thinking we had finally caught a rabbit, we excitedly replied, 'Yes.'

Mum was none too happy and informed us that we had in fact snared old Bill the gardener. He was going about his business when to his shock he fell into our well-concealed trap. Unfortunately for old Bill, the unexpected 2-foot fall broke his leg. Being caught in a trap that could only have caught a 200-pound giant rabbit would have come as a complete surprise. Bill was old, very old, well over seventy, which is really old to a seven-year-old. Now that I think about it I'm surprised the shock didn't kill him!

Bill was quite pragmatic about it and, probably having done similar daft things when he was a lad, took it quite well. However his missus was not as happy. Bill was not able to work for a while. So his missus had to wait on him hand and foot.

I don't recall being punished for our efforts but I will never forget the look on my mother's face the day we caught old Bill, the 6-foot rabbit!

My brother and I never did catch any rabbits at Somerlea Park, or for that matter any galahs ... but that's another story.

MY WORST JOB

PETER FORAN

We were moving through a bit of back country, sightseeing really, and taking on whatever work we could, to meet the locals and keep a few quid coming in. I picked up work on a large cattle station in south-western Queensland after putting out a call over the Royal Flying Doctor Service UHF radio. It was sandy country, so horses were used by the blokes employed in working the cattle.

As I'm not much good on a horse, I was given the four-wheel-drive ute to get around and carry gear in. This meant I could keep my camera with me – a real bonus, as recent rains had freshened the country up. It was a photographer's paradise! While the claypans here and there had already dried out, the many wildflowers were still in bloom, and lagoons and billabongs, still holding plenty of water, were attracting a good lot of birdlife. I was amazed to see a pair of brolgas in an ecstatic dance; a raucous flurry of head bobbing, beak chattering, wing shimmering and leg movements.

I managed to photograph an eagle chick in its nest of sticks with its half-eaten meal of ginger-haired rabbit by standing on the roof of the ute; that's how low and scrubby the timber was here. It was a beautiful part of the country and I thoroughly enjoyed the work. However, one of the jobs we did will remain permanently etched, odour and all, in my mind as the worst I have ever had to do.

We drove out one morning to a large concrete tank. It was about 8 metres in diameter and 2 metres high, with no lid. Earth had been pushed halfway up the outside, and rabbits, smelling the water I suppose, had been running up this bank and getting onto the top edge of the open tank, overbalancing, and falling in! There was a foot or so of water in the tank and hundreds of rabbits had drowned in it.

We had to clean them out. With gumboots on, and armed with square-mouth shovels, three of us climbed over the top and dropped down into the foul mess. We shovelled over our shoulders and over the sides of the tank without speaking; preferring to keep our noses and mouths as tightly closed as they could possibly be against the smothering flies and retching stink. It was like a well-done rabbit stew, but less appetising, the meat falling off the bone as we shovelled.

We were soon covered in it, our hats thankfully keeping most of it off our faces. Working without delay until the job was done, we were glad to get out, give ourselves a thorough scrubbing and get on to the next task. As they left me at my caravan that night, dog tired and still carrying the aroma of our work, the overseer dryly commented, 'The cook'll be safe tonight!'

'WHERE ARE THEY, JOSSIE?'

GREG TAYLOR

During the Second World War we had millions of rabbits and hundreds of rabbit burrows, plus half-a-dozen ferrets and a couple of Italian prisoners of war. My father used to let his dogs chase rabbits into burrows and then we would put a ferret in to chase them out into the nets. Often because there would be a blind alley, the rabbits would be stuck with a ferret behind the last one trying to have a free feed; of course the rabbit protests, and thumps his back legs on the ground. By lying on the ground one could almost pick the exact spot to dig.

On this occasion Dad dug down, caught the rabbit and gave it to prisoner Jossie to bag up. He then proceeded to pull out eighteen rabbits which he passed to Jossie to wring their necks. Jossie was fascinated and had his head in the hole also. As the last one came out, Dad said, 'Eighteen eh, Jossie?' He said, 'Yairs boss, eighteen.' Then Dad said, 'Where are they?' Jossie had pressed their head as he had seen Dad do, and not killed one. They all ran away.

Rabbits were everywhere during the war and used to live in big basalt stone heaps on the farm. A well-known Hobart man, a retired bank manager-cum-stockbroker, who had a beautiful sixteen-gauge shot gun and managed to get cartridges for it, used to come to the farm for a shot. My brother and I were detailed to put ferrets in the stone heaps so 'Mr S' could blaze away as they ran out. I cannot ever recall him hitting one, but it was great fun for two very small boys.

'GEE, YOUR OLD MAN COULD SWEAR'

HARRY HILL

In the mid-1930s I was a willing and active junior assistant to my father in trying to control the build-up of rabbits. We shot, trapped, dug out and poisoned them. We put ferrets down their burrows and urged our dogs to catch them.

Some days we saw hundreds of rabbits. I asked Dad if he'd ever seen them in greater numbers. He certainly had. He showed me some places on the boundary fence where he'd been involved in pit-traps in the early 1900s. Rabbits could see what they thought were better pickings on the other side of the netting fence and would establish a well-defined path as they went back and forth.

The humans selected the best spots to put in pit-traps. A large excavation was dug against the fence and the top covered with small tree trunks, boards and some of the earth. Against the fence one board was rigged up to be a trapdoor. An unsuspecting rabbit would start to cross the board, its weight would cause the board to tip and the rabbit would end up in the pit. The board was spring-loaded so that once the rabbit dropped off it moved back to cover the gap, ready for the next rabbit that tried to make a crossing.

A pit-trap was non-discriminating; it could be activated by rabbit, snake, lizard, fox or bird. Pit inhabitants had to put up with one another. Sometimes the company was compatible; at other times, not so. Many animals suffocated.

Often, the next to fear suffocation was the unfortunate family member given the job of cleaning out the pit. Part of the timber cover had to be removed, then the contents thrown or shovelled out with anything showing signs of life being quickly deprived of it.

A few years back I was collecting information to write a memoir about my father. I was deep in conversation with my cousin, Jack, (Dad's nephew) and he surprised me by saying, 'Gee, your old man could swear.' I didn't agree, so Jack felt compelled to tell me of one incident.

One day Dad was cleaning out the pit-traps along the boundary fence and Jack, a teenager, had been assigned to help him. It was mid-summer; hot, dry, thirsty work. The flies were bad and the smell assured the workers that the pit had been effective.

Dad removed a couple of the boards from one of the bigger, deeper pits, sat on the edge, dropped his legs into the pit and let himself fall in. He bent under more boards to be able to reach rabbits that had to be ejected. Dad knew he was standing on rabbit carcasses that were likely to move or roll. With only a couple of the boards removed most of the interior of the pit was still in semi-darkness, but as Dad's eyes adjusted he could see what he was about to grab. It was not a rabbit, but a writhing brown snake, and he could have been standing on it. It only took him a split second to realise it was not one snake, not two, but several. The pit exploded. Boards and dirt flew everywhere as Dad came out of the pit like a jack-in-a-box.

The other aspect vivid in Jack's mind was Dad's flow of profanity. Every snake, rabbit or other animal that had been stupid enough to fall into the pit got a tongue lashing. The complete top of the pit had to be taken off, every moving occupant, especially brown snakes had to be despatched using the operating end of a long-handled shovel, the contents shovelled out and the top replaced. It was not until the whole job had been completed that Dad's language cooled down.

RABBIT HOLES

ROHAN WIGHTMAN

Dad used to say, 'No good ever came from damn rabbits and we sure ain't celebrating 'em'; thus was the Easter Bunny banished. I still follow that edict. We grew up on a farm in western Victoria during the Depression. The dust from the ravaged land blew into the house and settled on everything like a crumbling eiderdown. We farmed sheep on land where the grass was more brown than green. The sheep, emaciated and stained with dust, wandered morosely around the paddocks. Mum tended a vegetable garden that provided greens for our staple of rabbit stew. The rabbits got more vegetables than we ever did. I'd wake in the morning to Mum's daily curse, 'Those blasted rabbits.' Whenever it rained, the fresh green shoots would always be gone before the sheep untangled themselves from their dreams.

I loved rabbiting with Dad. We'd leave before dusk on our two horses, Bobby the bay gelding and Florence, Mum's palomino mare, Snapper and Stumpy our two Jack Russells yipping beside us. Dad would find a warren and carefully place his nets over the various burrows, then send the dogs in. Before long, a rabbit would be struggling in the net and Dad, smiling, would take the squealing beast by the head and crack it like a whip. We'd get at least ten every night and that'd be dinner. He'd then dig up the warren, muttering, 'Blasted holes can cripple a horse and kill its rider.'

Mum'd take the cured skins and make boots, hats, vests and gloves. She even made a full-length coat for herself. Dad laughed and said, 'Those toffs in Toorak'd pay a thousand quid for that and it cost you noth'n'.'

'At least they've got somewhere to wear it,' replied Mum. Dad replied by galloping off with Snapper and Stumpy. That night Mum was worriedly looking at the sky, dogs were howling in the distance. The soft clop, clop of hooves drove her into the night yelling, 'Charlie, love, it's late.'

Bobby was riderless, holding his front foot high and whinnying, his coat a lather of white. Mum screamed, jumped on Florence and galloped off, following Stumpy who'd come back too. Mum came back with Dad slumped over Florence's withers. Mum, stone-faced, eased Dad down, his head lolling about like the rabbits he cracked. Bobby was whinnying in screaming sobs.

Mum never said a word as she grabbed Dad's rifle and jammed five bullets into it with a strange look in her eyes. She looked at me, slammed the rifle butt into her shoulder and fired. An explosion of tears flew out of me as Bobby fell into a heap. Mum turned, dropped the gun, and ran into the house.

Mum lost the farm and after the funeral we moved to a dank one-bedroom cottage in Fitzroy and she worked as a seamstress. Mum tried to sell her rabbit-skin coat but no one wanted it. Dad was right; no good ever did come from damn rabbits.

HEAD FIRST DOWN THE BURROW

KENNETH LITTLEJOHN

During the Second World War years, around 1944, my father worked on a property near Perth in Tasmania, and every weekend my brother and I looked forwards to going rabbiting. Skins were worth about one pound per pound in weight, and it took six good skins to make a pound in weight. In those days this was a lot of money.

While hunting, we noticed that nearly all of the rabbits not caught made their way into a large burrow in a steep, sandy bank below an old farm cottage. This was over a period of months. We decided one day to hunt all round the area and then try to dig and tunnel into this burrow. The plan was for me to be lowered and pushed into the tunnel when we reached the den area. After several hours of digging it was time for me to be pushed into the hole to see if I could reach the rabbits.

On the way in, I noticed it was very hot but I could feel some rabbits. I seized one by the hind legs and on the pre-arranged signal – me kicking one leg – I was pulled up out of the tunnel by my legs with the rabbit.

This went on until seventeen full-grown rabbits were withdrawn. On the eighteenth entry, I was feeling around (as I could not see) when all of a sudden, a rabbit darted passed me and escaped. This so surprised my father and brother that they had no time to take any action, so the eighteenth – and only one – escaped. This was a very successful few hours of rabbiting with all skins salvaged undamaged, and we sold them for three pound.

POP EATS RABBITS

DANNY MACGREGOR

My grandfather loves to eat rabbit. I was never particularly fond of the experience; the strange earthy taste and the unfamiliar, pallid grey colour of the meat did little to endear me to it. Perhaps the most obvious discouragement, however, was its very appearance on the plate. Sitting at the big table if there was enough room, otherwise at one of the fold-out tables or the plastic-covered ironing board on the couch with the other kids, I'd watch Pop eat his rabbits.

All manner of vegetarian-scaring produce from the farm would grace the table, yet it was only ever the rabbit that turned my stomach. Nan would pulled the unfortunate creature crackling from the oven, or steaming from the pot, to place the whole damned thing on a plate before him, looking like one of those creepy fur-less cats with its head fallen off. Pop would pick up his bone-handled cutlery and poke about the critter, assessing its size and apparent good health, as he did all other stock on the farm, before heartily tucking in.

As a boy, I was fascinated with the old ways of the land and invested much time in learning the tricks of the trapping trade like my grandfather and his brothers had before me. Wandering the hills of the district, I would seek out the multitude of warrens dug into the soft, yielding soil, setting iron spring traps. Strictly speaking, I wasn't allowed to use the steel traps, as they were outlawed at the time. I think my mother may have overlooked the whole matter however, recalling the adventure of it all that she herself had revelled in as a youth.

Mum kept ferrets as a child. Sometimes, she said, they had to be dunked in the water trough in order to encourage them to let go, as often they considered humans – especially children – well worth chewing on.

Occasionally, when I was very young, my mother took me ferreting. Her cousins from the other side of the farm still kept ferrets. I was scared of them and none too comfortable with the sensation of carrying a writhing hessian sack full of them jittering and snuffling across my back. Letting them out of the bag, they would slither like furry snakes down the warrens to chase the rabbits into the nets we had placed across the entrances. Sometimes, the ferrets would come across a nest of young rabbits down a burrow and set about enjoying a hearty subterranean lunch. When this happened, one of the adults (usually muttering a procession of words I wasn't allowed to use) would go about the task of digging them out.

On the way home, I would readily swap the bag of feral ferrets for that of the unfortunate rabbits. When we arrived, I would rush the bag up to show Pop. He would then bend over the sack with me, looking inside, poking, prodding and muttering about the size and apparent good health of his dinner.

COLOURFUL TRAVELLERS

COLIN BELL

When we were kids, we lived on the fringes of a little country town along the main southern railway line in NSW. It was the sort of town where, if you lined up all the parents on each side of the road, and all the kids on the centre line, the kids would not be sure who to go to. I think it was because all the people were so friendly.

We lived on my uncle's farm, in his converted hay shed. It was cool (cold) in winter and warm (hot) in summer due to its corrugated iron construction. We were host to 'seasonal' pickers and 'permanent' rabbits.

Uncle grew peas, beans, potatoes, swedes, turnips, oats, corn and sorghum. He did not grow carrots, so as not to encourage the rabbits. There were so many rabbits that you had to kick them out of the way to get a clear shot at them. I ate so much rabbit that Mum thought my ears were getting longer. My eyes were bloodshot from the ploughing dust once, and Mum wanted me checked for myxomatosis.

We had travellers come and pick for Uncle. They had old trucks and big caravans. They made a huge circle near our shed and built a campfire in the middle. They lived on rabbit and 'pickings' from the farm. There was always a cauldron of rabbit stew on the fire and racks of pelts on the fence. They would come and go in twos and threes, with something going on all the time. It was very exciting for me because the only foreign people I knew were my great aunty Mary and uncle Mick, from Scotland.

The traveller boys took my older brother John rabbit trapping one day. I begged them till they let me go too. We went through the enchanted snake-infested forest to the lower dam and set a dozen traps near the bank (shooing the rabbits away so they wouldn't see the traps). We had to rise early in the morning to see what we had caught. We went through the enchanted forest, which was now pure spider webs with dead things in them. I was very brave, until we came to the first rabbit squealing in the trap. The older boys dispatched it with an axe. I ran howling back to camp to be consoled with rabbit stew.

The traveller girls could spin plates on sticks and buzz whizzing cardboard on cotton strings. They wore colourful clothes and head scarves, bangles and earrings, and held noisy parties on Sundays. The ladies told the pickers' fortunes; local townsfolk joined in. I was always going to be a king and ride a big white rabbit.

When the picking season finished, the travellers left with their rabbit pelts and stolen tractor batteries. My brother and I trapped rabbits and my sisters made scarves and told fortunes. All the kids in the middle of the road found someone to go home with, and the rabbit population doubled for the next picking season.

THE URBAN RABBIT, OR, 'ESCAPE FROM COLDITZ'

ANGELA LINEY

He arrived one hot summer afternoon, an unexpected vision sitting under the lush weeping mulberry tree. He was a good size and, I guessed, an adult. His fur was snowy white and well kept, quite an unexpected escapee, nibbling grass in the middle of a green oasis where no dogs or cats reside. I looked up and down the street, expecting soon enough a couple of kids would have noticed him missing and come searching, but nothing. As night fell he disappeared and I decided he had found his way home.

At bedtime I looked out into the street, which was by now very dark, except for the spotlight of the street light on a strange white shape with his tail backed hard against the blue-stone gutter, it was the rabbit. I couldn't believe my eyes; surely he wasn't going to sleep on the road like that!

I had stared at him for some minutes, not believing what I was seeing, when a young guy came up the street from the train. He saw the rabbit and, to my amazement, threw his backpack to the ground and lunged at the rabbit. Grabbing at it wildly, the rabbit slid through his arms and he was left splayed on the nature strip.

Undeterred, the young man made another lunge as the rabbit changed direction and headed down the street. The young commuter laughed, retrieved his backpack and walked on.

An hour later I heard a commotion in the street. A car screeched to a halt and a dad and two kids jumped out of the car leaving mum to watch the same routine. All three grappled the rabbit in the spotlight with no success.

The rabbit had an uneventful night after that and spent the next day eating grass and flowers on my back lawn until the ranger came. He was mesmerised and netted in ten seconds flat.

THE NEW CHUM

GRAHAM NEEDHAM

In the 1960s, Australia was in full flight to increase its population, and as a young migrant from the United Kingdom I was a respondent to that aim. Jobs were plentiful, so I was soon gainfully employed in the airline industry and for the first two years enjoyed weekend and holiday flights to most capital cities. But this was not the full 'on the ground' experience I desired. As a result I quit my job and set off to work around Australia with a group of like-minded mates.

As a new chum with no outback or bush experience I was raw to some of the things that might happen. One early experience in northern Victoria was while working on clearing the irrigation channels that supplied water to the grape growers. I had the pleasure of staying on one of the local farms. This was dry, arid country and survival was tough for all except the rabbit population. At night the open spaces seemed to be literally crawling with these four-legged creatures, errantly introduced for the hunting pleasures of the early settled English aristocracy. A favourite pastime of the local young farmers was rabbit shooting at nighttime with the aid of a ute, spotlight and guns.

One night I was invited to go 'rabbiting' with them. I hesitated because I didn't own a gun, but they quickly assured me that it wasn't necessary because they would chase them on foot. As a new chum in Australia for two years I'd got used to jokes at my expense so decided to take up their offer. Rabbits were in demand for food at that time and also for the manufacture of Akubra hats. Freezer trucks set up in country areas would buy rabbits for this market.

Very soon we spotted a rabbit, so one person jumped off the back of the ute and started the chase. On exhaustion, the second person would take up the chase and the rabbit was run to a standstill, picked up and handed to the lads in the ute, who expertly pulled its neck. I was impressed by the quick, easy and humane way these local lads killed the rabbit and they, with great earnest, tried to teach me the knack, but with little success. This was a great way of hunting successfully with not even a shot fired. Very soon we had a dozen rabbits in the bag and I had done lots of running, but failed miserably with the final act of neck pulling. After lots of ribbing and laughter at my inability, I was determined to prove my manhood with the next bunny. I flexed the muscles of my ego to the maximum and, in defence of my pride, I pulled vigorously. Everyone in the ute, especially me, was astonished to realise I had completely separated the head from the body.

OMEO'S SWIFT ACTION

BARRY HEARD

Many poorer people lived off rabbits, and we fitted that category. In 1955, aged ten, Mum introduced me to rabbit traps. Having just moved from Melbourne to the Omeo district, the traps were dangerous-looking gadgets with a powerful spring and a nasty pair of jaws. Setting the rabbit traps cost me many a bruised finger. Damn things – they would snap shut as I tried to cover them with a fine layer of dirt to conceal their whereabouts. That was the easy bit. The trapped rabbit – a beautiful, fluffy, brown-eyed little creature – was killed, gutted and skinned. That didn't seem right. I thought meat came from a butcher's shop. Consequently, my attempts at killing those first poor bunnies, with their mutilated feet, were pathetic. Most managed to get away. Then the kids at school showed me the 'rabbit killer' action. You had to flatten your palm, hold it rigid, and administer a severe chop behind the poor animal's head. Now I was a rabbit murderer.

By the early 1960s, we had a farm at Tongio. The rabbits were in plague proportions. We tried ripping burrows with the bulldozer, but made no difference. Someone suggested myxo, so I got the ferrets, netted the mouth of the burrows and got twenty, and then visited the Lands Department in Swifts Creek where they inoculated the rabbits with myxomatosis. Initially, there was a good kill. Then, over an eighteen-month period, the number of rabbits was back to where we had started. Then, with the introduction of 1080 bait using carrots, the rabbit problem vanished.

The rabbit has a history in the Omeo Shire. By the year 1909, every week there were dire warnings about the problem in the local rag, the *Omeo Standard*. In 1900, when the 'rabbit plague' problem had first emerged locally, the Shire had formed a committee called the Omeo Rabbit League. It appointed a full-time rabbit hunter called the Rabbit Destroyer. After experimenting with traps, snares and dogs, the Rabbit Destroyer bagged 625 rabbits in his first year. The council declared that the rabbit was under control. Proudly, the Omeo Standard headlined the result: 'Swift action by local council averts potential rabbit plague.'

However, the locals in the Omeo district tell stories of other methods used to eliminate the furry pest. One story, from

Benambra, near Omeo, has it that a local farmer used to wander the paddocks in the moonlight, twanging his guitar and crooning sad, forlorn songs. Distressed by these gloomy, heart-breaking renditions, the rabbits would burst into tears. As the night and the songs wore on, it got colder to the point of freezing. The tears, trickling down the rabbits' cheeks would freeze and the little pests would become frozen to the ground. The singer would then walk around the paddock and twist each rabbit, snapping the icicles and throwing the ice-covered rabbits into a bag. I wish Mum had taught me to sing instead of trapping.

RABBIT Á LA FRANCAISE

PATRICK A. AHERN

My mother prepared rabbit stew often during my childhood in the 1950s and 1960s in rural Victoria. The stew was a marker of the austerity of that time, along with dishes such as lamb's fry, tripe, dumplings and rhubarb.

Rabbits were in plague proportions around Ballarat and they influenced life in many ways. A neighbour made a respectable living as a rabbit trapper. Young boys wore Davy Crockett hats fashioned from rabbit skins as they imitated the American folk hero. A local rule at the golf course allowed for replacement of balls that had entered burrows. The word myxo was heard in many conversations, and signs warning of 1080 poison were attached to fences. The feats of Ron Crawford of Moyston, the world rabbit-skinning champion, were widely admired.

I went ferreting until my teenage years, then I completed the rite of passage of spotlighting with a .22 rifle. After I left for the city to pursue education and work opportunities, my links with rural life weakened. Only major events such as the release of the calicivirus reminded me of the never-ending war. Over forty years I lost all the memory of the taste of that rabbit stew.

In 2006 I was re-connected with the rabbit through assisting Madame Edith Ybert of Paris to interpret her grandfather's memoir of Australia. Captain Ernest Ybert had called here between 1900 and 1915 as a commander of the great French merchant sailing ships. He wrote of a weekend excursion from Melbourne in 1907, when he shot many rabbits.

Other French captains recalled early-morning forays to shoot rabbits at Port Victoria on the Yorke Peninsula of South Australia, and the pursuit of rabbits with sticks at Stockton, opposite Newcastle in NSW; it was not unusual to kill twenty in an hour. Undoubtedly the French mariners ate rabbit during their stays in port, a welcome change from the salted meat, sardines and cod which dominated their diet for month after month of ocean voyages.

An export industry operated in the early 1900s, and steamers left regularly for London with cargoes that included several thousand cases of canned rabbit meat. But exports were never more than a drop in the ocean compared with the proliferation of the animal in the Australian landscape.

Two years of collaboration with Edith Ybert by email culminated in the publication of a book on the French sailing ships; then, in October 2008, the opportunity to meet arose for the first time. As I strolled along the boulevard which led to her residence, I noticed that *lapin* (rabbit) featured in many Parisian restaurants. Perhaps I had never given my mother full credit for her culinary skills!

Edith Ybert was a charming and gracious host, and the menu for the occasion included *lapin*. This most enjoyable meeting proved that – even for an Australian – the rabbit could be associated with good times.

TOUGH TOM

NOEL HIGHAM

It was early 1964 and we had just celebrated our first wedding anniversary. At twenty-five, I was confident, fearless and the world was wonderful.

I had a job as a fitter and machinist at Howard Engineering, a subsidiary of Blue Metal Industries Pty Ltd. This conglomerate existed on about 20 square miles at the base of Prospect Hill, Greystanes, Sydney, which was the largest blue metal deposit in Australia. My hours of employment were 7.00 am to 3.30 pm and sometimes after work I would sneak over to various idle quarry sites and, with my single shot .22 rifle, shoot gourmet rabbits.

It's fair to say these rabbits were on the verge of plague proportions due to their idyllic environment. Their warrens were constructed under huge blue metal boulders and it was a unique industry surrounded by wilderness, which only assisted the survival of Australia's greatest pest.

There were several isolated spots where hopefully my career would not be jeopardised, but to minimise a possible sacking, I only hunted on Thursdays and Fridays when overtime was limited due to union agreements. While I cannot boast about my marksman skills, I always managed five or six 'head kills' which are mandatory for an ideal cooking carcass.

We lived next door to my in-laws, and on one particular afternoon I was skinning and cleaning the six rabbits using their garden table as a work bench. In my routine, precise manner, two carcasses were completed when Tom, the father-in-law, drove in. He was partly inebriated but was about to teach me a lesson, which I still cannot achieve, and shall never forget. In his rather bombastic manner he grabbed an unskinned carcass and said, 'You are taking too long, sonny; this is the way you do it.' Ever so quickly, with his strong fingers he tore the skin on each hind leg, then ripped the whole skin off in a flash; then with the head and back legs as handles, he raised the rabbit above his head and threw it forwards in a stockwhip-cracking action. The intestines scattered across the manicured lawn ready for the dogs to consume. He then cracked the feet off each leg. Total duration: ninety seconds! In true show-pony style he repeated the procedure on the remaining rabbits. I stood there amazed while his wife, Daisy, congratulated him on his unique manly talents. Daisy gathered all the carcasses and pan-fried the lot. During the feast we all agreed that life is great. Most was devoured, while the remainder would be used for the next day's lunch sandwiches.

In the twilight and over a beer, Tom revealed that his unique skill had won him many five-pound notes, but to win you must have warm rabbits and, of course, extremely strong fingers. He reached across the table, cradled both my hands and said, 'Sadly you don't have the strength or skills.'

After forty-five years I would give a million bucks for a repeat performance. But like Tom, Prospect Hill has vanished. It now contains multi-storey homes oblivious of a rabbit empire that once lead to the demonstration of a unique Aussie skill that shall remain just another bushie tale; unless of course you saw it.

RABBIT PARADISE

ELVYNE HOGAN

'Excuse me a moment,' I said to my city friend, Jan, as I got up from the dining room table, grabbed the gun and shot the rabbit from the open window. Jan dined out on that story for many years.

That was one not very effective method of reducing the rabbit population on my property, Casuarina Hill, a granite hill with lots of rock and sandy soils for easy digging and well-drained burrows. 'A rabbit paradise,' my husband, John, would grumble as he tossed in the tablet with wet newspaper and filled in yet another burrow.

That was over twenty years ago and John would be amazed to see the difference today. Some months after John died, I rented out our lovely home and headed to Melbourne to further my studies. Thinking I might have to sell the property, I contacted the Victorian Conservation Trust (now Trust for Nature) about placing a conservation covenant on the 19 hectares of land. Concerned about the rabbit problem, they encouraged me to continue the rabbit netting around the back half of the land which contained the bush. Unfortunately, with the fence completed, the rabbits were still inside the netting!

However, in the mid-1990s, a group of us got together and started the local Landcare group. Rabbits were a high priority in this area of granitic soils, so funding was applied for and a rabbit campaign started. This highly successful campaign was followed by release of the calicivirus and a good bout of myxomatosis. A few rabbits remained, which were dispatched with the help of a friend's dogs.

The result has been no less than amazing. On this land which has been grazed by sheep and rabbits for the past 150 years, all sorts of plants regenerated. Orchids I had never seen on the place before appeared – patches of yellow sun orchids (I refuse to call them by their common name, rabbit ears!), scented sun orchids, golden moths arose in abundance, masses of chocolate and nodding lilies and one plant of another lily, rare in this region, the blue grass-lily.

Shrubs, wattles, hop bush and fringe-myrtle also regenerated providing splashes of yellow and white in spring. Austral indigo, so susceptible to grazing by rabbits (and wallabies), reappeared with its delicate foliage and attractive purple pea flowers. Many native grasses have grown, including spear grasses, several different wallaby grasses, weeping grass (with its edible seeds) and a rare rye-beetle grass. Each year there seems to be some new plant emerging which makes walks on the property quite exciting in spring. I now work for Trust for Nature and have held several open days to show people what a difference having no rabbits makes to our native bush.

WHEN A KID CAN EARN MORE THAN HIS TEACHER

J. P. AND N. M. SHUTE

Snap! Predictably, I jumped. It was May 1946 and I was taking a shortcut across the paddocks towards the lonely, distant, one-teacher school I had just been appointed to. Knowing no better, I had walked on the verge of a rabbit warren on which traps had been set. I was never caught in that predicament again. The country south of Texas was plagued by rabbits. Many farmers and graziers made good money trapping rabbits for the freezing works at Tenterfield. Five days a week a refrigerated truck did the round trip from Tenterfield down the old side of the Dumaresq River back across the NSW side and back to Tenterfield. The freshly trapped rabbits were skinned, gutted and hung on wooden frames covered in hessian, awaiting the daily pick up.

But there was another side to the story. I boarded with a family where the main income was from cattle and tobacco. They earned good money by poisoning rabbits wholesale. The farmer would boil a copper full of wheat to which he would add enough arsenic to cover a five-cent piece. The treated wheat was put into a container; then he would mount his horse and take up a sturdy pole which he dragged behind, making a trail into which he threw handfuls of the poisoned wheat. When he collected, he skinned his catch the next morning; he would leave behind a mountain of carcasses. Saturday morning in Texas was busy, as buyers weighed the skins on scales mounted on the back of that track.

I was earning the princely sum of twenty-one shillings a fortnight so my eyes would pop when I would see 200 shillings on the kitchen table, as the farmer's tax-free income for the period. Even the children trapped rabbits for pocket money. When I enquired why Roger fell asleep in class I discovered that he laid his traps and skinned his catch before school. Roger made more in a week than I did. I could have added more about rabbits being staple food for many; the slaughter on the roads after a dance. I could also have mentioned how my school garden, though it was fenced with netting and securely, was eaten bare overnight when a number of rabbits entered the garden by climbing in down a strainer post, the garden to which much devotion and time were given.

BOWLED!

GLENN McGRATH AM

A short piece from cricketing legend Glenn McGrath AM, who set his sharp eyes to target pests from the farm fields of Narromine to the world's stage.

During my cricket career I've had to deal with pests all over the world – mainly gritty batsmen who have dug in their heels and refused to budge from the crease. But none of those cricketing foes caused anywhere near as much damage as the damage the rabbit has inflicted on Australian soil. All manner of attack on the rabbit population has largely failed to wipe it out completely and it appears as though the numbers are again on the increase.

In 2009, I had cause to reflect on the history of the rabbit in Australia, while helping launch the RabbitScan initiative. RabbitScan involves communities checking their properties, local parks and ovals for rabbits, and, using Google Maps, entering the numbers, location and impacts of rabbits, to help build a new national map of rabbits and their damage.

It took me back to my childhood, as I come from a farm near Narromine in NSW. With my family, we always were and still are vigilant about rabbits on our properties in the region.

As a young fella, I remember chasing rabbits out in the back paddocks on our farm. We knew we had to get on top of the pests then. It was just a part of looking after the land, to keep it productive. It was a great way to grow up in the Australian countryside. But then, as now, we had to be able to see and read the land; to notice what was going on in the paddocks.

Perhaps that early experience, of being able to spot a pest rabbit in the fields out the back of our place was just the training I needed to begin my career, removing opposing batsmen from the crease they wanted to bunker down in. But once I've got my eye on a tricky pest – be it rabbit or batsman – the target is set and I just have to bowl them out!

But in the farming sense, just as you think you are getting on top of the pests, they're back again. I can't help but think it's such a shame that this wonderful country of ours has had to endure this devastating rabbit problem for 150 years. If only the unintended consequences of that innocent action, of releasing rabbits back in 1859, could have been foreseen.

That's a worrying thought, especially for those of us who have witnessed and continue to experience the environmental, social and economic impact of rabbits. As a landowner, I have a vested interest in the long-term sustainability of Australia's agricultural land. Without productive farming land, Australia's proud rural heritage, economy and very way of life would be at threat.

We are a country still very much reliant on our primary production sector. And other countries are also dependent on

Glenn McGrath AM with David Lord at the 2009 launch of RabbitScan, 150 years after the release of wild European rabbits into Australia.

Australian agricultural output, as they don't have the arable land available to feed and support their own populations.

I am also truly concerned about the impact of rabbits on our unique native habitat and fauna. With so many native species already facing extinction, we simply can't allow this rabbit problem to develop any further. The rabbit story in Australia sadly reveals that this pest has taken out too many of our native species already.

Australia and its residents are currently suffering from the ravages of bushfires, floods and ongoing drought in many parts. Our already fragile environment simply could not withstand the debilitating impact of another insidious rabbit plague. In many cases, it would probably be the final straw for farmers and rural communities.

We owe it to those who worked the land before us, as well as future generations, to take action now to prevent an explosion in the rabbit population, before it is too late.

Unlike our forefathers who laboured, often in vain, to keep the rabbit population in check, these days we have science and technology on our side. Complacency and ignorance are not options. We've got to get out there and find whatever it takes to bowl out this pest.

8.

SCIENTISTS, OFFICERS AND OTHER GENTLEFOLK REDUCE THE RABBIT'S FOOTPRINT

The stories in this chapter give some additional context to the collection, being from a range of scientists who have contributed or are still contributing to the science of rabbit management. And these tales show us what they had to endure to understand the rabbit's real impact in Australia and to bring the viruses into Australia and spread them. Laugh along as you read about scientists sticking their heads down burrows to smell whether there were any dead rabbits in them, and getting a head full of fleas as a result. Be surprised to find others risking lives on boats and abseiling cliffs, shooting arrows tipped with phials of fleas, and others combing rabbits to collect fleas, all to help spread the virus.

The controversies find a voice here too – there has never been an animal on which so many, varied and dangerous concoctions – for the handlers as well as the rabbits – have been tried, before scientists were able to develop or bring in more effective solutions. Lately, scientists have helped stop the immense outlay of both the poisons and the money that were used in plague times, and have made things so much safer for landholders and officers, at a relatively minor cost when compared with previous solutions.

But in some areas – rural, regional, urban and coastal areas, and even city parks – rabbits are making a comeback, with some resistance to the last virus controls now appearing. When resistance arises, and until the next effective control is developed and released, the costs and poisons will begin to add up again.

There are only a few scientists working in this field it seems, but their ongoing work appears ever more critical to the future of Australia's biodiversity and productivity and the well-being of rural and urban communities still struggling to contain the rabbit to acceptable levels (no more than one rabbit per hectare). Most of the scientists would agree that Australia will never be free of the rabbit, but we will, with the right understanding, resources and commitments, be able to keep them at acceptable levels and to reduce their ongoing damage and cost. In this chapter you will meet a few of the people who are or have been working on the big rabbit solutions.

THE FIRST GREAT RABBIT CRASH

PROFESSOR FRANK FENNER, IN CONVERSATION WITH THE EDITOR

Most of the stories in this collection talk about myxo or 'mixi', popular forms of the scientific name for the myxomatosis virus. But for something with such a huge impact, little is known about its origins or the stories surrounding its use in Australia. Like the many years of delay between Australia being advised in 1919 of its existence and its ability to infect rabbits, and its arrival here. Or the many years of determination and hard work put in by a dedicated few to bring the virus into Australia to see if it might be an answer to the rabbit problem. But until 1950 myxomatosis and its potential was known only by a few scientists, who were unable to convince various governments – concerned for, and perhaps swayed by, the rabbit industry – to try it out. But by the December of 1950, myxo was well and truly out and active.

Myxo was first noticed as a devastating disease of rabbits in 1896 in Montevideo, Uruguay, in a research institute where work was being carried out on rabbits. It was described then as a 'member of the newly defined group of infectious agents, the "filterable" viruses' (Fenner and Ratcliffe, 1965). The work of Pasteur and Koch on infectious diseases had only been generally accepted in the years between 1886 and 1881. One who knows more than most of this story is Professor Frank Fenner, a virologist now in his nineties, who has studied and added greatly to the world's knowledge of myxomatosis and other animal viruses. Myxomatosis was one of the first viruses ever to be described. He worked on the original Australian release, and as such he is central to the great Australian rabbit story.

Frank Fenner is a name that most Australians should know, but may not. His portrait quite rightly hangs in the National Portrait Gallery in Canberra, inviting those who don't know him to find out more, and those who do to smile back, knowing this man – who really does befit the title 'gentleman' – has achieved remarkable and world-changing scientific advances. Frank and his father both won the David Syme Prize twenty years apart for their achievements, and his proud dad was there when Frank was awarded.

To the global scientific community, Frank is a renowned scientist, having been awarded the prestigious Japan Prize. He most famously worked on smallpox. Many other prize plaques and awards grace his home. But in Australia, he really should be known as one of our great environmentalists as well, such has been the impact of his work. He deserves a great biographer and a heavy book, in keeping with his 'heavyweight' status. His story, while linked to the first massive reduction in rabbit impacts on Australia's agriculture (arguably the prime motivator for his work), is also packed with a fascinating nine-decade lifetime of stories that those national and international prizes only hint at. The impact of his work, and that of his colleagues, both leading to and from his work on myxomatosis from 1950, is still really to be understood in terms of ecological impacts and the critical need to be constantly a generational step ahead of the rabbit and its viral 'predators'.

Professor Fenner worked to achieve the highly successful release of the myxomatosis virus, from 1950, that saw Australia's hugely damaging population of billions of rabbits crash dramatically and quickly. The release saved landscapes, and allowed agricultural industries to get back to business. One startling episode Professor Fenner tells of is the time he and two colleagues injected themselves with the myxomatosis virus, on the suggestion of the Mildura mayor, to allay community alarm about the virus causing disease in humans. Frank's stories are gently told, but powerful in their impact and message for the ongoing battle with the rabbit in Australia.

A couple of people in particular were key to the use of myxomatosis in Australia: firstly Dr Aragao and later Dame Jean Macnamara. Dr H. de Beaurepaire Aragao, from Brazil, was the first to name the myxo virus; he had taken some European rabbits out there to do a series of tests on this new and strange disease, which caused very minor symptoms in American rabbits. They have a lot of different species there and at least five of them do have myxomatosis, but with only the little symptomatic patches. Aragao knew there was a European rabbit pest problem in Australia and in 1919 suggested to the Institute of Tropical Medicine in Queensland (which was the first institute of medicine of any kind in Australia) that they ought to try myxomatosis. But the quarantine authorities said no, fearful of wiping out the rabbit industry, which was deemed too important; rabbits had become a thriving industry with carcasses and skins at the time. That was before the war. But with all the troops away in the war, rabbits really got out of control. So after the war they were very anxious to get something to control them.

Dame Jean Macnamara, the well-known medical scientist, had been on the case since 1934. Aragao had even got a shipment of the virus in, in 1934, but it was not released. Macnamara finally got myxoma in, which began the 1950 trials, that I worked on.

I was involved in all the Australian myxomatosis virology with the CSIRO Australian National Laboratory at Geelong. Ian Clunies Ross was the appointed chief. They looked after any infectious agents of animals or humans. CSIRO did all the fieldwork but they didn't have a virologist there. I was working initially with Macfarlane Burnet, then with F. N. (Francis) Ratcliffe, who was brought out by Clunies Ross to set up a wildlife survey to examine Australian fauna. This later became the division of wildlife research. I knew Burnet well. He gave me two labs in Geelong when I was first appointed Professor of Microbiology because there were no labs up here in Canberra. But Clunies Ross had said to him, 'You have to get onto the rabbits first.' He couldn't look for native fauna until we'd worked on rabbits.

Myxoma was tried in a number of dry places where there were not mosquitoes about and it just died out. But from Christmas 1950 to the New Year there was very heavy rain. There were two big impacts: firstly, it brought a lot of mosquitoes down the Murray basin. With these particular rainfall conditions myxomatosis really got away and killed millions of rabbits all down the Murray Valley at this time. But also it brought the birds that were ordinarily resident in Queensland down; the ones that were the hosts of what they called Murray Valley Encephalitis. That bird came down and they had a number of cases of encephalitis in the Murray Valley. That was why there was this worry, although it was shown to be totally different to the rabbit myxomatosis virus. But people thought myxo might be like the human encephalitis and they were worried myxoma was going to jump to the human population.

The mayor of Mildura said: 'If you are so sure that that is a different virus, you better inject yourself with it!' Burnet and I injected each other with doses, enough to infect one rabbit, ten rabbits and even 100 rabbits with myxomatosis. When Clunies Ross heard about it he said, 'Well, I have got to have that as well.' So I injected him! It was absolutely safe. We don't do anything like that nowadays. People would be very reluctant to allow anything like that to happen.

Before myxoma got away, where we were doing some earlier work near a dry lake just the other side of the Murray River, there were rabbits along about a mile front; we counted 5000 rabbits. Then they injected some with myxomatosis, which they had got from Brazil and the numbers there went down to fifty. But later, those fifty set up an epidemic of their own. Already after the first year the virus had mutated; the ones that survived had a virus that was less virulent than the one they were injected with, and that went on and so on.

Ratcliffe was deeply involved in this work. After the release he and I co-authored our book put out by Cambridge University Press, called *Myxomatosis*, in 1965. He lived just up the road and we'd often get together after work to work on the book. I spent a year in Cambridge around 1962 and I spent a good deal of time in Europe; I got a little car and drove around and looked at rabbits all over Europe.

Myxo is very useful in the arid area, because flies are still numerous there. I think it is still killing a lot of rabbits in those areas in Australia. It is better than nothing and it does work in the arid areas very well. But there are some rabbits that are already immune. Presumably there is a rare form of it that is transmissible because it must have been in those original twenty or so rabbits that were brought out by Thomas Austin. There must have been enough there for it to be transmitted, so that some of them are immune even though they haven't been exposed to the fly.

Before myxoma was introduced, if you drove on any country road, for every mile there would be two or three dead rabbits on the road. An early memory I have is of Adelaide just after the First World War, when there was twenty per cent unemployment. Swaggies would go out catching rabbits, selling rabbit skins, selling rabbits. I remember them going past our place, trying to get people to buy a rabbit.

THE WEIRDEST RABBITER

PETER COYNE

Given the task of eradicating rabbits from uninhabited Phillip Island, about 200 hectares of land halfway between Sydney and Fiji, I embarked on what might be the most unusual anti-rabbit campaign anywhere. Apart from Norfolk Island 6 kilometres away, Phillip Island is alone in the vast area of the ocean. Incredibly rugged, parts are 250 metres above the sea, but maybe 50 metres from the sea horizontally. Almost the whole perimeter of the island is cliff. Wild seas often made boat access to the island impossible; similarly difficult was returning to the boat. Everything to be used had to be unloaded onto slippery rocks from a small moving boat and then carried up the cliffs and across the rugged landscape. Thirty-five kilogram loads were standard. Life was not meant to be easy. As if logistics were not a sufficient challenge, the work involved life-threatening hazards. Fortunately occupational health and safety had not been invented; otherwise my work would have been impossible. Instead it was just plain scary.

Boat trips could be exciting. Several seemed sure to end in fatalities, but mere broken bones were the worst outcome. One trip, in the face of an approaching cyclone, involved racing along wave troughs seeking a way over the breaking waves which towered 12 metres above our small undecked boat. Time after time, we found a spot where the crest was not breaking and climbed the almost-vertical wave face to drop into the next trough. But the trickiest part began when we had to travel with the waves! The engine roared in reverse as the boatman tried to prevent the open bow being buried in the wave trough while the following wave pushed the bow down. And that was just commuting to or from the rabbits.

I was nearly killed early on, when a heavy roll of wire netting fell down the cliff to where I was standing tying on another roll to be hauled up. The netting missed my head by millimetres and was crushed flat by the impact of hitting the ground on which I stood. Reprieve, but apparently only temporarily.

Distributing rabbit fleas and myxo was somewhat challenging. One area was inaccessible even by boat, repeatedly I had to swim, carrying the fleas, hundreds of metres through notoriously shark-infested ocean to land in surf among huge rocks.

Another large area was considered inaccessible as a 1904 earthquake demolished part of the previously narrow razorback-connecting ridge. We had to abseil the top section of a 230-metre cliff, waves crashing directly beneath, and then use ropes all day to move around. Returning hastily, I forgot to tie-on as I worked on a narrow ledge, my back to the sea and the 230-metre drop, happily thinking I was secured and just 15 centimetres from eternity.

To treat some inaccessible slopes below the cliffs we launched infected fleas in glass phials attached to the heads of arrows which we shot with a long bow. Primitive, but effective.

Yes, we did eradicate the rabbits. Eventually! Plants and animals are returning spectacularly. The island is reborn.

RABBITING OFF!

KAY BARLOW

During the 1950s my husband, Harry, his sister, Helen, and his parents, Val and Georgina, lived in Birdsville, an outback town near the border of Queensland and South Australia. An article in a newspaper at the time was titled 'ONE MAN HAS EIGHTEEN JOBS'. What follows is the extract about Harry's dad.

Police sergeant Val Barlow, of Birdsville, Queensland, never has a dull moment, as he has seventeen other jobs. They are: Receiver of Taxes, Clerk of Petty Sessions, Protector of Aborigines, Acting Stock Inspector, Inspector of Slaughter Houses, Commonwealth Bank Agent, Observer of Irrigation and Water Supply, Public Curator's Agent, Meteorological Observer, Assistant District Registrar of Births and Deaths, State Government Insurance Office Agent, Labour and National Service Agent, Electoral Poll Field Agent, Registrar of Firms, Licensing Inspector, Inspector of Brands and Postmaster. What does he do in his spare time? Well, when a Trans-Australia Airlines aircraft lands, he refuels it.

Val's oddest assignment as a policeman was trapping, of all things, forty fleas. The Agriculture and Stock Department wanted them collected from the introduced rabbits to see if the fleas had come from rats. As a result of further research, the CSIRO introduction of myxomatosis was the world's first biological control of a pest mammal. Harry remembers trapping or shooting a number of rabbits with his father and soaking them in a tub to catch the fleas that swam off the fur, then sending them to the Ag and Stock Department. The virus killed most of the infected rabbits. But the ones that did not die produced a high level of antibodies; any female rabbit that survived passed these antibodies onto her kittens.

During the worst of the plague, Harry remembers a day trip just over the South Australian border to Pandi Pandi Station, which was owned by the Moreton family. Most of the townsfolk gathered for the social day to introduce the visiting travelling dentist to a taste of outback hospitality. En route, rifles were fired from the back of the Blitz Wagon into the grey-brown sea of rabbits, where a kill was assured without even aiming the weapon.

During this plague, but before the introduced disease, rabbits were good fresh meat for the isolated locals, but very little vegetation survived their ferocious appetite. Native fauna, as well as cattle, sheep, goats and other livestock, suffered from the loss of fodder. Erosion followed. The rabbits have never again reached such plague proportions, but the battle to eradicate the introduced pests continues.

WHEN WILL THE VIRUS ARRIVE?

DAVID BERMAN

Will Dobbie lay down on his belly and reached into the rabbit burrow where he had smelt a dead rabbit. He pulled the rabbit out and put it on the ground near the burrow. 'Looks very healthy, except it's dead,' said Will. 'Not skinny, no sore eyes. It's nothing like myxomatosis symptoms.'

I stuck my head down into another burrow to see if I could see another dead rabbit. There was a smell of dead rabbit and it felt like millions of fleas jumped onto my head. The fleas must have had no living rabbits to jump onto, so they jumped onto a scientist's head instead.

This is what we had been waiting for since rabbit calicivirus – 'the virus' – escaped from Wardang Island off South Australia in September 1995. It had spread rapidly north through South Australia and I announced, 'It'll be here before Christmas.'

By February 1996, the virus still hadn't arrived. 'When will the virus arrive?' asked a central Australian pastoralist who had been struggling for years to control rabbits. 'We don't know; it should be here by now,' I replied.

To find out where the virus was, Will Dobbie and I drove to Adelaide. We attended a meeting to talk about the virus with other scientists. The new biological control had done an impressive job in the south. 'It hasn't arrived in the Territory yet,' we reported.

While driving back to Alice Springs we stopped at every rabbit warren we saw along the way to see if we could find out where the virus was. Will walked around and at each warren, when he saw a burrow he dropped to the ground like he was doing push-ups and sniffed for dead rabbits. I recorded the result, 'smelly' or 'not smelly', and the location on a GPS. This technique, sniffing for dead rabbits, provided a good indication of the presence or absence of the virus.

Near Marree, which is about the halfway mark between Adelaide and Alice Springs, Will's warren sniffing slowed. The constant smelling of dead rabbits without a break began to take its toll. Fortunately, his spirits lifted when he found a beach fishing rod near a warren, an unusual find in central Australia. He tied the rod to the ute in the hope that we would find a fishing spot. Later, at Lake Eyre, Will untied the rod and wandered across the salt lake, rod over his shoulder, looking for some water to do some fishing. In the middle of this great, dry, salt lake he stopped, cast his imaginary line into the imaginary water and stood fishing. I allowed him to enjoy a few minutes of leisure before gently forcing him back into the ute so we could continue to look for the virus. Somewhat refreshed, Will 'enthusiastically' sniffed warrens for the rest of the way to Alice Springs.

We found the virus had spread as far north as Oodnadatta. There were no smelly warrens and therefore apparently no dead rabbits from there on. Also, since there were fresh rabbit tracks and scats found, we concluded there was no rabbit calicivirus north of Oodnadatta at that time. The drought and hot weather had slowed its spread and delayed its arrival in Alice Springs.

Finally in May 1996, we received reports of rabbits dying 100 kilometres north-east of Alice Springs. So there we were on that historic day, in the dust, sniffing warrens and brushing fleas off our heads. Will placed the dead rabbit he found in a plastic bag which he disinfected, then in another and then a third plastic bag, which was also disinfected, so it could be sent to Adelaide for testing. At that time it was illegal to spread the virus so we had to disinfect everything. The results from the test in Adelaide, as expected, were positive. The virus had arrived. Within what seemed a few days, rabbit numbers crashed.

In many places the warrens are still now, thirteen years later, overgrown and caved in. But if you look closely in some places, a few holes are being cleaned out; new evidence of rabbit activity. Rabbit numbers are increasing. Are they developing resistance? How long will 'the virus' work? Will rabbits re-open all the caved-in warrens? What will we do if they do? When will another virus arrive?

A BAD CASE OF WIND

DENNIS AARTSEN

I'm not sure why this trip was going ahead. Was it simply because no-one said, 'Let's postpone?' The tops of the pine trees were already starting to sway as we loaded the live rabbits, our camping gear and food, and checked that the fleas were still secure. The gusty wind was riffling like shivers across the broad, tidal river as we headed south to the bay. We had visited this offshore island, the destination of this current trip, a number of times in an attempt to reduce the rabbit population. Just accessing the island by helicopter was a challenge. The aircraft was balanced on one skid as you unceremoniously dumped the gear out of the cockpit, then you followed, also in a less-than-dignified fashion.

By boat, seas would have to be relatively calm, and on approaching the island, we would bolt a plank to the bow. The boat would then be nosed in towards the rocks as you balanced on the plank. When the rise and fall of the sea was favourable you would jump from the plank onto the slippery rocks that formed the shoreline. All of the gear was transferred the same way.

The vegetation was certainly one issue on the island, but the main concern was the fact that this same island was host to a rare and beautiful migratory bird. Its nesting viability was seriously compromised by the rabbit population. The lack of pooling water on the island meant that the mosquito population was low. That in turn greatly reduced the effectiveness of mosquito-borne myxo, hence the fleas. All they needed was a nice, warm, snuggly group of rabbits to survive and breed in.

As we navigated through the sandbanks at the river mouth, we were hit by the westerly blow that was whipping up sizeable whitecaps on the normally placid bay. The boat yawed and lurched and plunged its way to the southern shore where some disembarked and called for transport assistance from our clerk. She instantly locked the office and headed our way for a welcome change to her administrative toil.

We struggled for over thirty minutes to safely secure the boat to a mooring buoy and had just made shore when she arrived. As we were discussing who would travel around the bay to collect the vehicles, a shout alerted us to the fact that the mooring had broken under the strain and the boat was being blown towards the rocks.

The clerk covered her eyes with splayed fingers as the youngest and fittest of our group sprinted down the beach, leaving a trail of discarded clothes in his wake as he plunged into the water. Once again the motors were started and a new mooring located. We agreed to re-schedule the work for later in the year. For now, I'm off to visit Berrima's Magpie Cafe in the Southern Tablelands of NSW. There I'll enjoy another delicious meal of Shredded Rabbit and Linguine with Speck Thyme and Cream Sauce.

A LIFETIME OF WORK

GEOFFREY CHARLES COOKE

Although I was only four in 1946, my memories of the rabbit plagues of this era are still very vivid. We lived at a small Victorian town named Meredith, about halfway between Ballarat and Geelong on the Midland Highway. My parents owned the local garage and on my father's days off he would go rabbit shooting with his .22 rifle on Henry and Edith Bolte's farm at Bamganie. Henry was later to go into politics and become Sir Henry Bolte, Premier of Victoria.

This day was usually a Saturday, as you were not allowed to shoot on a Sunday in those days. My father had an unusual approach: he only shot coloured rabbits. In those days black, white, ginger, black with white collars, piebald and skewbald rabbits were quite common sights. At the end of the day he would return home with about a dozen pairs of coloured rabbits and proceed to skin them and place the skins onto extended U-shaped pieces of wire to stretch and dry the skins and make them suitable for sale. The rabbit carcasses were used to feed our dogs and for meat for ourselves.

Spotlighting rabbits was a common method of making extra money in tight times. As my father had an old utility, he and his mates would go to Bolte's farm at night and proceed to shoot rabbits with both rifle and shotgun. Using this method was rather expensive as the cost of ammunition was not cheap. My dad and his mates then worked out a unique method of catching rabbits: one person would stand on the running-board of the ute and, holding on with his left hand, manoeuvre a 9-foot pole with a scoop net in his right arm. It was critical that the driver was able to line up the running rabbit for the netter to scoop up and pass over to the back of the ute, for another person to remove the rabbit and wring its neck. This was cost- and time-saving; they did not have to stop to pick up the rabbit, as with shot rabbits. As I was only four, I was made to sit in the middle, between the driver and the passenger, where I would not be in any danger.

One thing that stays firmly in my memory was the size and number of rabbit warrens, sometimes consisting of between twenty to over 100 holes. Sometimes paddocks could be virtually covered with these warrens, thereby making the paddock useless for the grazing of sheep or anything else. On approaching, these paddocks looked as if they were themselves getting up and moving, as the rabbits scurried to get into their underground homes.

Four years later my father became an inspector for the Vermin and Noxious Weeds Destruction Board, followed by me some twenty years later.

NOT THE RABBIT INSPECTOR!

MARY FINLAYSON

In the 1940s, our local Rabbit Inspector had the surname Nott; he arrived at a local property to do an inspection of rabbit numbers. A fine usually resulted if property owners had not made an effort to get rid of rabbits. Mr Nott knocked on the house door and said he was 'Nott, the Rabbit Inspector'. The property owner gave a sigh of relief: 'Thank goodness, this place is crawling with rabbits. I am dreading a visit from the Inspector.' Mr Nott repeated, 'I am NOTT, the Rabbit Inspector.' The owner replied, 'Yes, you told me.' Mr Nott then gave his full name. The property owner realised the difference between NOTT and not. No doubt a fine resulted!

CAN'T BE CRUEL TO A RABBIT? A BRIEF FAMILY HISTORY

DONNA SMITHYMAN

For a family that never lived on the land but has had a long association with rabbits, this may sound strange. My dad joined the Lands Department in the early 1950s. As was expected of the job, we moved regularly around Victoria to tackle rabbits in areas prone to rabbit colonisation. The Mallee was very susceptible. Western Victoria was different; they were harder to get out due to the volcanic rock that dominates the landscape.

Dad ran baiting campaigns on a yearly basis. He would bring home carrots he'd taken off the top of bags before being cut, poisoned and distributed to farmers. For us, late summer led to beta-carotene overload. Myxo days were arranged where rabbits were ferreted out to be inoculated with myxo through a slight scratching of the eye-ball with steel wool. The rabbits were released back to the warrens where they'd been caught. Myxo, my dad said, 'that was where we let it slip; we had them on the ropes.'

In the 1970s, my brother completed training at the Keith Turnbull Research Institute to become a Lands Inspector. He recalled that one of the worst jobs was combing the rabbits to collect fleas for a study into a better myxo vector. Cleaning the trays below their cages wasn't much fun either. My brother moved around a little, but the expectation to do so had gone, as the

Poison carts like this one lay idle now that we have more environmentally friendly and precise tools for rabbit management.

department began to change. It changed name (and has many times since); it changed focus. Landcare became the framework on which to base rabbit control works. Rather than getting hands dirty, the role of Catchment Management Officers was education and coordination.

My time fighting the rabbit was spent, like my father and brother, in the department. The 1990s was a time for rabbits to once more gain the spotlight in rural Australia. Rabbit calicivirus disease (rabbit haemhorragic disease – RHD) escaped from the trial site off South Australia and we were on alert to see when it would arrive. We were told that RHD would travel quickly; at approximately 100 kilometres per hour, or sixty through towns!

With RHD came money; large-scale ripping programs, coordinated baiting campaigns and extensive education of Rabbit Action Groups; giddy times! One bonus of that RHD excitement was meeting my husband whose career was, for a short time, dominated by rabbits. He coordinated a baiting program around the You Yangs. He believed it to be a failure, with an eighty per cent kill rate. However the local Landcare group thought it a great success, with more people participating than ever before. He was also the RHD coordinator for the Port Phillip region. As the effectiveness of the virus was questioned in Victoria, the dollars started to dry up and enthusiasm waned. The rabbit won again.

My father, brother, husband and I all dedicated part of our lives to killing rabbits or telling people how to kill rabbits; seventy years altogether. Persistence is the key, something the rabbit taught me.

THE KNOCKOUT BLOW AND TREASON

NICHOLAS NEWLAND AM

My experiences as Program Coordinator for the Australia New Zealand Rabbit Calicivirus Program were as interesting and varied as could be imagined for any job involved in natural resources management. The proponents for the program were all nine sovereign governments in Australia, the government of New Zealand, CSIRO and the Meat Research Corporation, a statutory corporation of the Commonwealth that took on the job of banker for the program. My job was to manage the budget and coordinate the research effort (largely driven through CSIRO's Division of Wildlife and Ecology in Canberra and its high-security Australian Animal Health Laboratory in Geelong); finalise the location for a high-security field testing station and to see it built, including accommodation for research staff; plan all the communication with all stakeholders and the community; and deal with the myriad of legislative and planning requirements prior to a carefully designed and executed release of the virus across the various states and territories. I was also working closely with the Ministry of Agriculture and Fisheries in New Zealand. The release was to have been accompanied by a comprehensive monitoring and surveillance program to assess objectively the effects of the release and to report on its findings.

As with all projects of this magnitude, the management of the human factor was a continual challenge. There were some top-class people involved in the program and the general level of goodwill and excitement among the key individuals was quite palpable, notwithstanding the expected array of problems and difficulties. The question of animal welfare was one that required considerable effort; rabbits are seen by many of the urban community as pet-type animals and detailed negotiations and ultimate agreement were required with the key national and state animal welfare groups. Certain socio-cultural issues, including the Easter Bunny, and a lack of appreciation from many urban people about why we wished to bring a new pathogen into Australia and New Zealand, required enormous efforts to manage and to contain.

With the scene set as described, and with all of the effort to ensure strict quarantine of rabbit haemorraghic disease field trials on Wardang Island, the unplanned escape of the virus from the island's high-security field station confronted us with a worst-case scenario, requiring enormous efforts in damage control and the re-ordering of a carefully crafted program. Accusations of incompetence, poor planning, inter-divisional tensions within CSIRO, concerns about the target specificity of the virus and how to make the best of the unplanned escape were among the matters we had to manage.

Assertions of deliberate release combined with the jubilation of the rural community as millions of rabbits succumbed to the virus attracted worldwide media attention. We had to develop a revised communication strategy and the majority of media issues were dealt with by me. I was the subject of death threats from elements of the wild rabbit harvesting industry which saw its livelihood disappearing before its eyes. I was accused of treason in Western Australia, with associated correspondence being referred from state to Commonwealth, to governor-general and on to Buckingham Palace and back again!

There are many stories involving both joy and anguish surrounding this program. Knowing the insuperable difficulties that faced us to gain formal approval to release the virus, and given the wide range of jurisdictions each with their own statutory means, it is arguable that the escape of the virus was the only way that it could have made it into Australia's rabbit-infested lands and thereby have the effect it had. For an overall program investment of less than 10 million dollars, Australia reaped a 120-million dollar benefit that could be accounted for, not including all the non-quantifiable biodiversity values that were gained.

The greatest disappointment was the lack of interest and foresight to institute a serious follow-up program targeting residual populations left after RHD had killed so many rabbits. This was not for want of trying on our part, but we were unable to gain the support we sought. If this follow-up had occurred, we would have been so much further advanced in dealing a knockout blow to Australia's worst vertebrate pest. With the current lack of interest, we stand to lose most of the gains made by the enormous efforts of a relatively few people. Our primary industries and the natural environment will feel the serious consequences of this incapacity to see the obvious.

AUSTRALIA'S TRAGIC RESPONSE

DAVID LORD, WOOLGROWER, CHAIRMAN RABBIT MANAGEMENT ADVISORY GROUP

Australia's response to the invasion by rabbits has been mostly tragic and frustrating, particularly when we know that the myxoma virus was discovered in Uruguay in 1896. It was seen then by scientists as an answer to Australia's rabbit problem and was offered as such in 1919.

However, it was not released in Australia for another thirty-one years, in 1950, and only because of the determination by industry and Dame Jean Macnamara. Only a very limited number of Australians would know that name; even fewer would have any idea of the positive influence she had, not only on the nation's agricultural wealth but, perhaps more importantly, on the environment through her pushing for the release of myxo. It is very sobering and shameful that we delayed the release, when you consider the environmental implications of that. One of the reasons for not pursuing research into myxo was that the trade from rabbit fur was too valuable; they didn't consider the environment in that debate.

During that period there was tremendous effort put in to try to control the rabbit using other methods. Part of the dingo barrier fence, which is the longest fence in the world and stretches for over 5000 kilometres, was originally a rabbit-proof fence funded by the Queensland Government in a vain attempt to stop rabbits reaching Queensland. Most of that effort was by the agricultural sector, both private and government. I suspect that there was little understanding at the time for the environmental catastrophe that was occurring.

As rabbits began to develop some resistance to myxo, the search was on for a new vector to carry the virus. Much of that research was done by Dr Brian Cooke and his colleagues, a small band of quiet achievers who have dedicated a lifetime of work to the problem. Dr Cooke's dedication and commitment is outstanding, and his contribution to Australia through his rabbit research is immeasurable. That said, we actually lost him for a while to the Galapagos Islands, after the programs he was working on were wound down by the CSIRO.

In 1988, Dr Cooke stumbled on RHD in Spain, saw this as another rare opportunity for Australia and was the principal scientist behind its release; this in my opinion is the most significant environmental event in Australia since 1950.

Despite all the very clear warnings from Dr Cooke and others on the team that this was not the 'silver bullet' which would once and forever remove the rabbit threat, and that we may have a window of only seven years to capitalise on the gains made through this release,

Surveyor Canning and party on a survey trip to mark out the line of the rabbit-proof fence, Western Australia, circa 1901.

much of the research and extension capacity in Australia was allowed to crumble.

With all the wisdom gathered from 150 years of rabbits in Australia and brilliant scientific minds in the community, we find ourselves in the situation that the rabbit is again winning. We have done very little to capitalise on the RHD-led respite from rabbits. There are options for other controls. We know the damage from rabbits to agricultural production is one billion dollars every five years, so even now, while rabbit numbers are nowhere near the levels of the pre-myxo days, we should all be alarmed and encouraged to action.

There has been, over the last twenty years, some useful and generous Australian Government funding for rabbit control, which we at Thackaringa have been assisted by. This has seen rabbit populations reduced to a very low base over quite significant areas. While that kind of rabbit control is vitally important, it is not the panacea for all; in the larger private holdings, Aboriginal lands and national parks, boundary-to-boundary habitat destruction programs are not an option, simply because of the enormity of the area involved. Many of the soil types of inland Australia are not suitable for that kind of approach either. Likewise the closely settled and coastal districts have particular challenges. We need to assist these areas with solutions and resources too.

Rabbits not only compete with native animals for food but they are a prime food source for cats and foxes and they elevate the population of natural predators such as dingos and raptors. It is these predators which have had such a devastating effect on our native fauna, as well as agriculture.

The loss of native vegetation which has occurred during the last twenty-year rainfall deficit would not have been so severe had it not been for rabbits. Many species have had their succession stopped; rabbits have been eating seedlings before they are barely visible. The combination of age and moisture stress has killed a very high percentage of the remaining plants; we are in real danger of a forever-changed landscape.

If trees could talk (and argue their plight), there would be coolibahs around Innamincka, mulgas around the Barrier Ranges (Broken Hill region), eucalypts around the Western Australian goldfields, and river reds in the West MacDonnells all crying out the same thing: 'Get off your backsides and do something; too much has been lost already by too little action.'

I found it unbelievable at the time and am still staggered by the attitude of many, during the period when RHD was first giving relief to the environment. Instead of front-page articles celebrating this event, the cry went up on prey-switching (that is, that the loss of rabbits would mean more native animals would be lost to predators). We needed to celebrate the significance of what Dr Cooke and his team had achieved. Just think of all the native plants and animals lost because of the rabbit; a very sobering thought. We have to continue the science and the controls and do this together.

Now we have some control of the rabbit, agriculture will survive in Australia; its fortunes or failures will be largely determined by commodity prices, seasons and the natural resources we depend on. But the science is quite clear that the environment cannot survive continued rabbit impacts even at today's low densities.

HOW WE GOT CALICI

BRIAN COOKE

Dr Brian Cooke has been involved in rabbit research for decades, which might sound dull for some. But to spend a couple of hours listening to Brian is to have a privileged insight into the most considered, holistic and heartfelt understanding of the rabbit and its ecological, agricultural and social impact on Australia. His view seems an essential guiding hand in understanding the Australian rabbit story to date, based on years of research, and about where to go from here to limit the immense damage currently being experienced across Australia from the rabbit's impact. It is a fascinating story, with Brian following the rabbit and its own flea and virus consorts, across Australia – and the world on occasion: from bringing in the Spanish fleas and breeding them up for release to spread the myxo virus, to being in the right place and stumbling over calicivirus, and to the unexpected release of that from Wardang Island. His story is told from the view-point of being one of the key scientists who was in the whirlwind at the very centre of some of Australia's greatest ecological, agricultural and political intrigues, dramas and achievements.

In a recent interview Brian talked about the book he is writing, which will be widely welcomed. For now, Brian is clear about the lack of focus on the environmental impacts of the rabbit, something which he says

Dr Brian Cooke and Dr David Berman taking local government officers from the Atherton Tablelands out to spot for rabbits.

is akin to us 'kissing goodbye to 600 million years of Australia's ecology'. Brian sees a critical need for leadership now, and for using the knowledge and evidence we have to keep rabbit numbers and impact low. Listening to Brian, one feels we are in the midst of an unacknowledged rabbit plague – not like the billions of the past that we inexpertly mismanaged until (and at times following) the successes of the bio-controls of 1950 and 1995 – but a plague nonetheless, given the evidence he has uncovered, that as few as one rabbit per hectare is taking out new seedlings, new growth and life across our landscapes. He is keen for us all to understand the continued need for our best efforts to bring about 'self-sustaining ecological systems' that can bear the brunt of the resilient rabbit and its relentless chomping of Australia's living heart. Here are just a few light-hearted bits. Bring on the book, Brian!

Lots of the stories in this collection talk about how the rabbit provided meat and money from skins, because these were such desperate times. But myxomatosis, plus the Korean war which led to a huge demand for wool, meant more money was being channelled into education and science, and into CSIRO. Until the 1950s, people were rabbiting, but without the benefit of science. No one took any notice of the environmental impacts. It was really Francis Ratcliffe from Britain, who in 1938 wrote the book *Flying Fox and Drifting Sand*, and who commented about the rabbit impact on the environment in a meaningful way.

WORKING IN THE FIELD – LEADS TO ELECTRIC SOLES!

Initially we started rabbit field research in Australia so we knew something about what rabbits were doing; we had a series of rolling experiments, in South Australia particularly. We sampled in all these sites every six weeks for three years and built up a view of what rabbits were doing in different parts of the state. Rabbits were coming up again after myxomatosis.

We used to work really long hours. We would drive from Adelaide up to the Flinders Ranges, set our traps or set up our camp and cook a meal, then we'd go out until two or three o'clock in all sorts of weather, getting samples of rabbits. Sometimes you would be going around and there would be frost on the grass when you are looking for rabbits and trying to shoot. One of the guys really had major problems once his feet got cold at night. So he invented a pair of electric boots; he had a little plug on the tongue, and a lead coming out of the vehicle in a couple of places, so he could plug it into his boots. He had this electric circuit of resistance wire under an inner sole; it warmed up his whole foot. When one boot started to get a bit hot he would unplug it and plug it into the next boot. It had a huge effect because instead of him complaining at one o'clock in the morning that he was cold and wanted to knock off, he was suddenly a very different person.

We needed to shoot and dissect fifty rabbits, and once you got your sample of fifty collected you could relax a bit more. We had daytime work to do, but it was the long night work that you really had to psych yourself up to do. It was all good fun for a while; on warm nights it was good, but they were seldom. The long, cold nights and the wet nights, we'd think, 'We could go home, but if we go home now we'll just have to come back the next night.' So we just kept going.

One time our Toyota was broken down so we took a Holden ute out instead and not only did we run the battery down because we were using spotlights and the generator wasn't charging enough to keep everything going, but we got down in a creek and stalled the damn thing so there was effectively no battery and we couldn't push it. So this guy who had invented the electric boots said, 'I know how to fix it.' He jacked the car up with the back wheels off the ground, and put sticks in the wheels so we could turn them. We got the wheels going as fast as we could and let the clutch out and there was just enough momentum to start the motor again. It worked!

FASCINATING FLEA CIRCUS LEADS TO CALICIVIRUS

With myxo not being as effective as it had been, we were looking for other solutions – other vectors that might make the disease more effective over a greater area. The CSIRO tried to get European rabbit fleas in, because they are vectors in England, but it did not work; they didn't know enough about flea biology. In the meantime, some English people, including Dame Miriam Rothschild, figured out what would work. Her father, the banker Lord Rothschild, maintained a private museum collection of fleas and she followed his footsteps. She worked out the fleas needed the hormones of a pregnant female rabbit to stimulate their own production. If they link their breeding in with the breeding of rabbits, they succeed. Dame Miriam worked that out and suddenly we knew how to breed the fleas in labs and bring them into Australia.

I was helping Bill Sobey from CSIRO by releasing fleas in South Australia, but they only ever took over in the wetter areas. Bill was close to retirement and said, 'Brian, if we could get some rabbit fleas in from other parts of Europe, from Spain in particular, they could act as vectors in the arid zone.' So we ended up in a meeting in Melbourne a couple of months later and talked to a few guys there and got funding to go to Spain to work on rabbit fleas.

That's what led into finding the calicivirus (now known as rabbit haemorrhagic disease virus or RHD). I was funded by Meat and Livestock Australia at the time to do the rabbit flea work; it took over a decade to get those fleas in. I was in Spain instead of another fellow. I didn't anticipate Adelaide's Portuguese millipede invasion, so my entomologist was off to Portugal to look for biological controls for millipedes. I did the job instead. On the way to Spain I spent some time with Miriam Rothschild and other flea experts and found out about what they knew about European fleas. I ended up in Spain, grovelling around in the fields, and shooting rabbits to get the fleas. We finally got them into Australia and bred over a million Spanish rabbit fleas. They were released all around Southern Australia.

On my last 'flea' trip to Spain, I went out shooting with a game guard; we were taking regular three-monthly samples to look at the biology of the fleas. He said to me, 'There is not much point going over there to shoot; look out on the hills; there has been some terrible disease come through the rabbits and killed them.'

I was with a Spanish scientist, Ramon, looking at these dead rabbits. I said, 'Must have had some form of myxomatosis or something.' But the game guard intervened and said scornfully, 'That's not myxomatosis,' and he turned out to be right. It turned out to be RHD. It suddenly occurred to me, why bother mucking around with a little flea, that would marginally improve myxo, when you have a disease which works in an arid country and it is affecting over eighty per cent of the population. Back in Australia, I got in touch with Brian Walker, the CSIRO Chief of Wildlife Research, and suggested we start looking at this.

At the time the people in National Parks in South Australia were a bit desperate about rabbits in some of their parks. They arranged for me and one of the parks people to attend a meeting in New Zealand of the New Zealand and Australian conservation ministers. We put the case to them that they should actually be looking at the calicivirus. Brian Walker from CSIRO was there advising Barry Jones, who was the federal minister.

THE WAY TO WARDANG

We got the money to investigate RHD further, and did this at the big CSIRO lab in Geelong. Then that led to Wardang Island for the testing, where the original myxomatosis trials were held. I ended up being a key scientist there.

We obviously knew that myxoma was transmitted by insects, yet hadn't got off Wardang Island and we had very little evidence of insect transmission of RHD, so the island seemed a safe bet. Still we had fly traps and sprayed areas to control insects as much as we could. But the bloody thing still took off!

I was then right in the middle of what was treated like an exotic disease outbreak. Personally it was pretty terrible. But I just had to keep going. I was out looking for infected rabbits, trying to find out how it spread and document what was going on.

At night we would go back and have a debriefing; we were meeting in the pub. A chief came up to me on the night following the release, when everyone was assembling to see what was going to happen next and said, 'Brian, if I were you I would make myself very scarce from now on!' Suddenly the responsibility was passed to the Australian New Zealand Rabbit Calicivirus Program, led by Nicholas Newland. We took the brunt of the publicity. I was out working in a paddock one day when a TV helicopter landed, trying to interview me, in an infected virus area! Another time, two journalists sneaked round all the quarantine barriers to where I was working; I had infected rabbits in bags in my hands. I had to escort them out past the shed, where I put the rabbits I had been handling in sealed boxes before I took the journalist off the area. Then they went to Yunta and talked to a rabbit industry guy; you couldn't have thought of a place that had more rabbits at the time than Yunta. So they went from an infected area, straight into the heaviest rabbit infestation in Australia. Two days later RHD broke out there, which was 350 kilometres from the island, and of course, they were right in the firing line. Soon after there was another equivalent outbreak 200 kilometres north of that in the Flinders Ranges, and this is when we suddenly understood that insects were taking the virus around.

THIRTY MILLION IN THE FIRST MONTH

When the calicivirus took off, probably within the first month, it killed 30 million rabbits.

We travelled around the north-east of South Australia to find out how far the virus had gone and to set up study sites. It was just phenomenal; in areas we knew had rabbits running everywhere, there were none or just one rabbit was sitting on a warren. It was unreal, sort of uncanny to be there, because it was such a change. Of course all the dead rabbits generated a huge fly wave. Green blowflies went down in the burrows, laid eggs on the dead rabbits and their progeny came roaring out, so around a lot of the homesteads and cooler spots around water tanks and backdoors, the walls would be green with flies. One lady said to me, 'It is nice to be rid of the rabbits but where are all these flies coming from?'

People aren't terribly observant. For that reason things repeat themselves, like after myxomatosis. As rabbits began to build up again, people had to be almost re-alerted to the fact that rabbits were coming back. They did not notice it themselves. It was the same after calicivirus. The only thing that changed, I think, is we are setting slightly different standards for control, in as much as it is not just an agricultural problem; there is a general interest in rabbits. That means we need an even higher, tougher standard of rabbit control. A lot of the management techniques were basically designed around farmland so when a National Park ranger says rabbits have increased to the point that they are chomping through the gains we made with RHD, it is not always appropriate to give them techniques that farmers used fifty years ago. We are in that stage of trying to revamp techniques to the point where we can meet these other targets.

Within the agriculture and lands departments, which usually ended up with responsibility for rabbit control, there was no real culture for conservation issues. If you started talking about those sorts of things to those fellows they would switch off pretty fast. They did not get involved with people in the urban fringes either as it was too complex. Their job was running extension programs for big farmers, not trying to handle hundreds of little landholders. That is why we have this peri-urban rabbit problem, because no one has ever wanted to tackle it.

You can find some groups that are dealing with their rabbit issues very well, but a lot of others who do not want to know about them. What that has tended to do is make any rabbit control work very patchy across Australia; there is absolutely no leadership. That's got to change.

9.

POETIC VOICES

No collection of stories about the Australian bush can pretend to be representative without a selection of poetry. Most of these poets have never before had their work published. Their poems take us into the rhythm of the rabbit story – at times lilting and sad, at others frivolous and fun, but all with a serious intent and message.

I'd have loved to include C. J. Dennis' 'Grimbles and the Gnad' (see bibliography), but will leave that for the intrepid readers to chase up for themselves. It is a reminder of what we often lose sight of, in our quest to conquer pests.

The first poem listed, by David Berman, was read by the author on ABC Radio National's 'Macca All Over', to great feedback.

A RABBIT AND A FARMER

DAVID BERMAN

I'm a rabbit and I scurry, because I'm in a hurry
I'm heading to a party in the cool warren by the creek
Right across Australia we are celebrating failure
Of eradication methods that the humans (desperately) seek

I'm a farmer in a hurry, but I'll get there don't you worry
I'm running late for a party at the local show
To celebrate our (farms') survival since the rabbit's first arrival
One hundred and fifty years ago

I'm a rabbit under piles of logs, avoiding eagles and wild dogs
Diving into burrows, built by bilbies, years ago
There lives my second cousins, they've had kittens by the dozens
But where the bilbies went to, we don't really know

I'm a farmer and I'm driving, through my country that I'm striving
To stop the bank from taking because I can't pay the loan
We struggled through the drought and there's very little doubt
Rabbits helped us almost lose everything we own

I'm a rabbit eating seedlings, in between the poisonous weedlings
The parent tree is dying, full of mistletoe
Seedlings are so very nice, but they can not be eaten twice
I wonder when the tree will flower, and make more seeds to grow

I'm a farmer in me ute, done up in me tie and suit
Driving through the new estates on the edge of town
Once precious cultivation growing food for the nation
Now just houses, fences, concrete and tarred roads up and down

I'm a rabbit and I found there wasn't any sound
At the party at the creek, party noises should be loud
No open active burrows, just loose dirt and long furrows
The cool, deep creek warren had been ploughed

I'm a farmer feeling hearty as I left the celebration party
I had a real good time, a bit tipsy, had a few
Drivin slowly home across the creek flat's sandy loam
I saw a blurry rabbit in fact it looked like two

I'm a rabbit and I scurry, because I'm in a hurry
Running from a roaring ute with headlights on high beam
Running off the side of the track behind a tree to hide
The ute close behind crashing, steam!

The radiator's split and the bonnet's bent a bit
And the rabbit's sitting looking at me ute
Loud I starts to shout, 'I'll get you!' I scrambles out
Bloody nose and starts off after the rabbit in me suit!

I'm a rabbit and I scurry, because I'm in a hurry
Running from the farmer who stops to have a leak
Running to the rocky hill where I know there is a burrow still
Running from the shouting near the ripped warren by the creek

WHITE TALES

ERIC RILEY

In the sing-song voice
of a perplexed five-year-old she asks why the need
for an engineered extermination
of the long-eared burrowing lagomorphs
whose warrens pock the landscape
and voracious habits
destroy and defoliate all with their
secateur-like teeth.

Brittle stubbled grass cracks
as we wearily wander
hand in folded palm
across the untidy holey landscape
where mummifying carcasses seep
staining the tunnelled soil
while putty-coloured skeleton racks
bleach further beneath an unsentimental sun
that stings limp gum leaves.

Questions about the reality
of eye-averting death compared to
the gentle legacy of Beatrix Potter's brush
there are no simple dovetail answers
sufficient to quell the white-hot curiosity
combining with bristling anger of
a fantasy-intoxicated mind
where jacketed rabbits run contentedly
carrying baskets brimming
with casually gathered blackberries.

Through season-wearied eyes
that scan the scorched soil
where fragile stalks and wilting crops wither
beneath a merciless snivelling sun
the rabbit is the grim reaper
that burrows into bank balances
and furrows wind-swept brows
beneath wide felt brims
as raven-black despondency
shadows soul-biting destitution.

My loose grip
tightens and moist lips arc widely
as she determinedly demands to know
the sand bank and fir tree location
where Flopsy, Mopsy , Cottontail
and the curious Peter Rabbit reside
with their white-aproned mother
who lovingly tucks in bed sheets
in a reassuring room of contentment.

A ruminating pause
gives voice to shuffling stalks
teased by a toying breeze
and the grainy texture of life
challenges the wisdom of crosshatching
an unrestricted fertile imagination
with closely woven shades of truth
distilled in a biased brain
and forever being
an agent of disillusion.

Cinnamon eyes of five summers
pierce and plead
as my piston-like heart pounds
while confusion sucks my tongue dry
and words lodge like uninvited guests
in a throat scoured by the sands
of soul-searching
as fleet-footed vermin vibrate
across the untidy landscape.

Viewing the testament of
grazing ravenous rabbits
while acutely aware of dismantling beliefs
thoughts transfer into hinged words
which finally fall onto
innocent ears and a grumbling breeze
describing the predatory nature
of unloved nocturnal dogs
that shred apart parent rabbits
orphaning the young at home.
Within the complex burrows I attest
are bundles of carrots and bowls of berries
upon which the cuddly bunnies feed
and jugs of milk and plates of bread
are shared among them all
just as the eccentric Potter described
in the brown-cornered book repeatedly read which
allows the unharnessed imagination flight
and clamps the cinnamon eyes closed.
There is a shy hope of belief.

'TWAS NOT ONE OF MY HABITS

MIKE O'CALLAGHAN

It may look a gentle creature, some may deem its habits cute
Some may feel my anti-bunny stance reveals a latent brute
My gentle city rellies raised their eyebrows, shook their heads
And muttered at the weaponry they saw around my sheds
The fiendish traps, the poison carts, the rip-tines on the grader
For raking out the warrens of my oh-so-cute invader
From clapped-out utes, monoxide fumes through hoses thick and
thin
Sneaked snakelike with their lethal loads, my shovels sealed them in

Well, my years stacked up, the rabbits won, my paddocks got
infested
My sheep died off, my crops were stuffed, my stubbornness was
bested
And old and ill and sick at heart I sought myself a haven:
Carinya Village took me in. Then scrubbed and freshly shaven,
I went off in the hostel bus from Sea Lake in the Mallee
Our day trip was a visit to a kind of 'Save The' ... rally.
Could well have been koala bears, or gumtrees they inhabit
But 'stone the crows' and 'strike me pink'
They'd come to save the rabbit

Some bleeding hearts had got aggrieved, all kinda sad and funny,
They'd mustered in their hundreds to protect the blasted bunny!
I voiced my sentiments aloud, 'twas time someone protested ...
But rabbits won the final round when I wound up arrested!
They locked me up for seven days and fed me bread and water
For language they described as FAR less civil than it oughta
They could not know that down the years 'twas not one of my habits,
Beleaguered on my Mallee farm, to be polite to rabbits!

WHEN I WAS A LAD

BILL CLARKE

Long years ago, when I was a boy
I had a recreation that brought me much joy
Some folks get their fun from a wide range of habits
I got mine from ... hunting rabbits!
We chased them on foot and we chased them with dogs
We pulled them from burrows and from hollow logs
We once had a record that I think we might keep
Sixty-two rabbits from beneath one stone heap!
The fences in those days were usually netting
We would herd rabbits against these to wings we'd been setting
These were closed in quickly with rabbits inside
Then we'd gather them up – they had nowhere to hide
Their warrens were ripped and poison was laid
But no noticeable reduction to rabbits was made
They continued to dig and to eat lots of crop
It seemed this destruction would never stop
We used traps as well, manufactured by Lane
They were set in the burrows, held there by a chain
The plate and the jaws were covered with sand
These worked well, but were cruel and have long since been banned
A bonus for catching the destructive bunny
Was selling the skins for good pocket money
To have undamaged pelts was always our aim
Skins were carefully removed and stretched on wire frame
Sometimes there were hundreds hung on a rail
Then when dry, packed in bundles and sent off for sale
For additional money, we would skin them with care
And sell them for meat at two shillings a pair

With little money around and bills being due
We often survived on just rabbit stew
If we complained about how we were fed
A luxury was served – bunny, baked – instead!
Our dogs ate rabbit when it was time for a feed
Tinned Chum and Pal, they didn't need
Fresh food hopped around, they just had to grab it
They loved their meals of bread and rabbit
Then myxomatosis and calici were introduced
The rabbit population was quickly reduced
The disease spread widely throughout the land
Results were as successful as ever was planned
The mosquito isn't something we normally admire
But it helped spread the virus – like wildfire
The effect of these saviours is now on the wane
Rabbits are back in large numbers again
They're invading our lawns and gardens in force
What is worse, they're digging up our local golf course
Now, I've been a farmer for many long years
And the damage they've done has almost brought me to tears
Though my thoughts of the rabbit are mostly bad
They did give me pleasure when I was a lad!

A BUSH CHRISTMAS

MELVA GRAHAM

'Twas Christmas Eve in '38,
The rain was pourin' down
Bert and I were carting rabbits
We were miles from any town.
There were rabbits in their millions
So the trappers were there, too
We had twenty trappers on our round
A few rough diamonds 'mongst the crew
One wore a wheat bag for a shirt
With holes for arms and head
And a pocket pinned for trap papers
Another wheat bag was his bed
We used to take supplies to them
When we went to get their catch
One complained we brought him two 'crossed ribs'
And a hat, his 'clothes don't match!'
Way north of Port Augusta
When the big creeks came on down
We'd put rabbits on a flying fox
To load the truck to get to town
This Christmas Eve we'd not noticed
A shallow creek had grown quite deep
And now our laden truck was bogged
We could be here all week
'I'm sorry, luv,' Bert said to me
'Christmas turkey's off this year
And with you pregnant now, as well
Damn! I'm gunna miss me beer!'
'Just as well I'm not too far gone

'Cos there's no donkeys here around
And as for inns or dry stables
They're pretty thin on ground!'
Bert said, 'There's nothing for it but
I'll skin all the rabbits right away
They'll smell like high heaven, soon
And for this lot we'll get no pay'
I gathered wood from off the trees
And made a campfire bright
With a lump of bark to cover it
While Bert worked through the night
He skun the load of rabbits
Stretched their skins on hoops of wire
I thought they looked like Tombstones
As they glowed white near the fire
When the last skin was stretched
Bert lay back, 'That's the lot!'
I covered up the carcasses
But saved one for the pot
Next morning a bright sunrise
Heralded Christmas Day
As we stretched out in our tent
To hear the bird choir's roundelay
Our Christmas haute cuisine
Was a camp oven rabbit stew
Washed down with billy tea
And a ripe quandong or two
Arms round each other by the fire
That night we gazed above
At a sky awash with Christmas stars
In a land we'd always love.

RABBITS I HAVE KNOWN

KEVIN MILSON

Back there in New South Wales' Northern Tablelands this boy was born
Just before those dreadful war years, the Depression not long gone
My dad and mum were battlers: a small farm, a few poor sheep
Those days were very tough ones, his small family then to keep

Now rabbits were another thing, in many thousands they were found
And eating all our sheep feed, with no barriers and no bounds
'There must be something done,' Dad said, so got some rabbit traps
To reduce that population, leave the sheep some food perhaps

Wool bringing just twelve pence a pound, the year's cheque just fifty pounds
Can you imagine 'one hundred dollars'? Quite impossible to me it sounds
To pay his debts, try and run a property, let alone the family needs
There must be a way around it; those furry tails may give some leads

Now blackberries, briars and rabbit warrens were the order of the day
So he must try these cottontails to make them pay their way
The old packhorse with rabbit traps was surely loaded down
He'd catch and skin those critters, sell their fur when next in town

It was not a bit uncommon when our mealtimes came around
And yes, Mum cooked up rabbit stew; we ate, didn't make a sound
Let me tell you those prime young rabbits from off the pastures green

Would help sustain our family's needs and be the go-between

As years rolled on, I older grew; guess what this boy would do
To make some pocket money, help support the family too?
I've seen the hillsides move as one, when rabbits made their run
You wouldn't know which one to shoot even if you had a gun

Many farmers hated rabbits, but I couldn't say the same
My teenage years were mostly spent living from this unruly game
'Twas not long before the myxo plague would spread across our
land
And take away my living, I couldn't really understand

Then the mysterious escape of calici virus from down Wardang
Island way
Crossed over to the mainland, the bunnies didn't have a say
Once again they died in thousands from the mountains to the
plains
Where were our animal libbers when rabbits had so many pains?

Now rabbits have come, have nearly gone, extinct will they ever be?
Will we still see little cottontails as they play, skipping merrily?
Next time you see a rabbit, a ball of fluff, some white as snow
Remember they were our lifeline so many years ago.

A RABBIT'S LIFE

DONNA SMITHYMAN

Ten grey rabbits
Out grazing in the night
A light swept across the field
And one of them died of fright.

Nine little rabbits
Snuggling deep in bed
A dozer came and wreaked their home
Now one more rabbit's dead.

Eight furry rabbits
In a warren underground
A ferret dropped in for a snack
Now one cannot be found.

Seven ravenous rabbits
Nibbling on the grass
One of them found some juicy carrots
And ended on his arse.

Six miserable rabbits
Wondering what to expect
One sniffed the smoky air
And breathed his last breath.

Five grey rabbits
Relaxing in the night
Someone forgot the Aerogard
And myxo took their sight.

Four little bunnies
Recovering from disease
One smelled some gas at home
BOOM! It knocked them to their knees.

Three rattled rabbits
Running from the dog
They quickly ran for their safe haven
But the farmer had moved the log.

Two grey rabbits
Do what rabbits do
They got together one moonlit night
And now there's fifty-two!

RABBITING ON

PHYLLIS KHAN

It's mine now
It was hers once
He caught them all
He killed them and made his selection
He caught and killed them to eat but there were so many
He found other uses for them
He could be very selective
There were so many
The family ate well but none will eat rabbit now
You can't disguise it as chicken
Just ask the family
They'll show you the bones

Anyway it's mine now
I inherited it

I'm the only one who didn't eat rabbit
I wasn't there
I value this thing that no one else wanted
It's beautiful and so soft
It fits me because it's small
I'm the family runt and it fits
I like the rich brown colour
The fur is long and the colour suits
Brown goes with everything

And it's mine now
I wonder how the first wearers were caught
Bullets were too costly
He could have used traps
There were too many rabbits for that
He probably used dogs
Dogs that would hold and return the kill
The pelts were not torn or ripped
There were so many
They were caught and all the bits were used
Nothing was thrown away
It was war and then Depression
The carcasses were skinned
The skins were staked to dry
The meat was eaten
Dogs and people ate well and survived
The pelts were drying when the twentieth century was a teenager

And it's mine now
Gran liked the brown pelts best and he sold the others
Selected pelt were sent to the coat maker
The coat maker knew his business
One hundred and fifty pelts

One panel per pelt
It's lined with brown silk and is very warm
In the New England Ranges that was useful
In the Hunter Valley it's too warm to wear
The rest were sold to the highest bidder
All the white and splotched and black and softly sandy pelts were sold
They're probably hats now
The fur could last for one hundred years
My fur did

Yes the coat is mine now
I inherited it
I valued it when others did not
I hold it close
I can smell the land and see and feel the culture
Feral rabbits today do not know this fur
Their ancestors are un-recognisable
Knowledge passed on
My grandparents would not know me
I never knew my grandfather
He ruled with a stockwhip and a gun
He died before I was born
Grandma died when I was young
I know them by their stories
The stories my parents told
I have this soft brown memory that I can touch and feel and smell
My little piece of history
It keeps them all alive
My roots in the land of ancestry
Conquerors and conquered
This life pattern repeated forever
All rabbiting on

'BUNNIES' BY MYXO

KEITH GREENFIELD

I'm a fluffy little bunny, some people think I'm cute
But the plain and simple fact is, that I'm a country-killing brute
For I ringbark all the branches, then I chew up every leaf
And to the native creatures, I'm a terror and a thief

It's not just farm and station, where we like to make our home
For on national parks and Crown Land, we're most always free to roam
When my friends and I have finished, though, the country should look grand
There's nothing left to look at, but gibbers, rocks and sand

Though I worry about myxo, I'm sure I won't die soon
For my mummy and my daddy tell me, they were both immune
I've heard a nasty rumour of a fellow with a flea
And an even worse concoction – a bug called RHD

And just the thought of 'SIRO is enough to make you ill
For the trick that they are trying is like a lifetime on the pill
But to bring them here to kill us, it would cost a lot of dough
So the people in the cities, they don't really want to know

For there's no votes in the Simpson, and on the Cooper very few
So we're left in peace and quiet, to just chew and chew and chew!
Through this decade of Landcare – I'm pretty safe you see
For the Parliamentary people are all bunnies – just like me!

FORGET THEM NOT

JENNY QUEALY

I know the rabbitohs of old
would love to hear their stories told
to keep the legendary feats
alive through tales, and then repeats
and so we bring their tales to youse
forget them not! (like weathered shoes)
discard them not! those folk true blue
deserve their feats retold anew
for bilbies, birds all threatened fauna
may (in droves) be lost just 'round the corner
if those pesky rabbits thrive
our native species will nosedive
tell the tales to any mate
for the rabbiter of old, it is too late
I commend the stories as a whole
and read them loud; they must be told!

MAGGIE BEER'S RABBIT SCALOPPINI WITH EGGPLANT

Serves 4

This recipe has been kindly provided by Maggie Beer. It originally appeared in her book *Maggie's Farm*, published in 1994 by Allen & Unwin.

6 double fillets rabbit
Flour, for coating
Salt
Cracked black pepper
3 medium eggplant
Olive oil, for frying
1 garlic clove, chopped
3 tablespoons extra virgin olive oil
2 tablespoons red wine vinegar
8 anchovy fillets, soaked in milk for 20 minutes
3 large green olives, sliced
1 tablespoon flat-leaf parsley leaves picked from the stem but left whole
Butter, for frying

Trim the fillets from the rabbit saddle and, using a sharp knife, remove the sinew as if it were a beef fillet. Wrap each fillet in plastic wrap and 'bash' it into a scaloppini shape (an even, flattened fillet).

Season the flour with salt and pepper. Cut the eggplant into 1 cm slices, discarding the outside pieces. Salt the slices if necessary – if it is the natural season and the fruit is not too large, you shouldn't need to. In a heavy-based pan heat some olive oil until very hot and fry the eggplant slices until brown on both sides. Place on absorbent paper.

Vinaigrette: In a pan, gently warm the garlic in the extra virgin olive oil and then add the red wine vinegar, anchovies, olives and parsley. Keep just warm.

Bring a little butter to nut-brown stage in a heavy pan and take off the heat for a second while you toss the rabbit fillets in the seasoned flour. Put the pan back on the heat for a moment and then seal each fillet for about 30 seconds on each side. Remove the fillets and rest.

Warm the eggplant slices on a tray in the oven and then interleave the rabbit with the eggplant, using 3 pieces of eggplant to 3 scaloppini of rabbit. Serve with the warm vinaigrette or anchovy mayonnaise.

INDEX OF STORYTELLERS

GLOSSARY

1080 – a poison used to kill pest animals; sodium fluoroacetate

.22, a twenty-two – a 0.22 gauge rifle, a popular gun used in hunting

44-gallon drum – a well-known and common drum size, often primarily used to transport fuel but finding many other uses subsequently, including as a fire bin in which to burn waste

Akubra – iconic Australian brand of hat made from felt sourced from rabbit fur

Barwon Park – the property of Thomas Austin, in Winchelsea, Victoria; Austin is renowned, or perhaps more rightly described as infamous, as the importer of the first twenty-four wild pest rabbits from which Australia's plague rabbits are probably descended, although other imports and releases of rabbits also occurred; the property, in original condition, is now a National Trust mansion open to the public

billycart – a cart made (generally by kids) from wooden fruit boxes, rope and old pram wheels, and used for fun, and for carting rabbits, dogs, siblings, mates and lunches!

blowies – blowflies or flies

boondy, boondie – seems mostly to refer to a rock or stick used to kill a rabbit, where alternate methods have not worked

calicivirus, calici – the popularly known name of RHD (see below)

chiller – a cold room or refrigerated room for storing fresh meat (eg freshly killed rabbits) before being bought, transported and tinned or otherwise processed

CSIRO – Commonwealth Scientific and Industrial Research Organisation

dunny – an outdoor toilet

free feed – the practice of putting out unadulterated carrots or other rabbit-attracting food for two or three nights, to get the rabbits used to it, before following on the third or fourth night with food that has been poisoned

gig – a two-wheeler carriage pulled behind a horse

kelpie – a breed of dog; typically works well with stock like sheep

kero – kerosene

kitten – a baby rabbit

Lavacide – a poison used to kill pest animals

lignum – a native shrub found in some low-lying areas

myxo, mixi, myxi, myxoma – shortened forms of myxomatosis, a virus specific to the rabbit; first released from late 1950 in Australia

party-line – telephone line shared by at least two families/ properties

phosphorus – a chemical used as a rabbit poison

pindone – anticoagulant used to poison rabbits and rats

poison cart – a horse-drawn cart that a trapper or farmer used to lay poisoned oats, carrots or other bait for rabbits

pollard – a by-product of wheat milling used as chicken feed

Pommy – colloquial term for someone of British origins

rabbitoh, rabbito, rabbiter – a person selling rabbits, usually in cities or suburban areas; they would yell out 'Rabbito!' to alert householders that they were about; also, a footballer from the South Sydney Football Club, the Rabbitohs – named after the early rabbiters and rabbitohs. Many original footballers in the club were rabbiters

rellies, rellos – relatives

rabbit haemorraghic disease virus, RHD, RHDV – a virus specific to rabbits which can cause swift death; first released in 1995 in Australia after extensive testing

setter – a tool used in setting rabbit traps

shanghai – a slingshot: a Y-shaped branch made into a weapon with a 'sling' made of rubber banding; used with a 'shot', usually a stone or other easily found object

soak – a wet (or soaked) area, usually shallow; commonly used as a site at which to trap and/or poison rabbits, especially in drier areas where rabbits, unable to find enough vegetation to eat (i.e. where they would usually get enough moisture from), would come to drink

SP bookie – colloquial term for an unlicensed bookmaker, usually associated with betting on the racing of animals; SP stands for 'starting price'

skun – a form of skinned, meaning to take the skin off a rabbit

soldier settler block – land granted to returned soldiers; usually small acreage blocks

Tilley lamp – common brand of kerosene lamp

two-up – a game using a coin flipped to reveal 'heads' or 'tails' when it lands, and on which punters would place a bet; most often played on Anzac Day in Australia, illegal at other times now

underground mutton – a term meaning rabbit; usually a term describing a menu item; probably comes from the rabbit being as extensively eaten and widespread as sheep (mutton); people used different terms to avoid having to say 'rabbit' or to pretend the meat was something other than rabbit meat; rabbits were also known as 'underground chicken' when cooked

Wardang Island – the place where myxomatosis and RHD science trials were held.

BIBLIOGRAPHY

Coman, Brian, *Tooth and Nail, The Story of the Rabbit in Australia,* Text Publishing, Melbourne Australia, 1999

Cooke, Brian, (with Steve McPhee and Quentin Hart), *Rabbits: A threat to conservation & natural resource management*, Australian Government Bureau of Rural Sciences, Canberra, undated

Dennis, C. J., 'Grimbles and the Gnad', *The Weekly Times Annual*, 4 November 1915, p18 (An early tale of pest control, remembered and referred to by Brian Cooke)

Department of the Environment, Water, Heritage and the Arts, *Threat Abatement Plan 2008: For competition and land degradation by rabbits.* Background Document, Commonwealth of Australia, 2008

Fenner, Frank and Fantini, Bernadino, *Biological Control of Vertebrate Pests: The history of Myxomatosis, an Experiment in Evolution*, CABI Publishing, USA, 1999

Fenner, Frank and Ratcliffe, F. N., *Myxomatosis*, Cambridge University Press, Cambridge, 1965, Library of Congress Catalogue Card Number 65–17207

Invasive Animals Cooperative Research Centre, *The Feral Flyer Invasive Animals e-newsletter*, contact@invasiveanimals.com

Ratcliffe, Francis, *Flying Fox and Drifting Sand – The Adventures of a Biologist in Australia*, Pacific Books, 1938

Rolls, Eric C., *Running Wild*, illustrated by Marianne Yamaguchi, Angus and Robertson Publishers, Sydney, 1973. Entirely rewritten for young readers

Rolls, Eric C., *They All Ran Wild*, Angus and Robertson Publishers, Australia, 1969

Williams, Kent, Parer, Ian, Coman, Brian, Burley, John and Braysher, Mike, *Managing Vertebrate Pests: Rabbits*, Bureau of Resource Sciences and CSIRO Division of Wildlife and Ecology Australian Government Publishing Service, Canberra, 1995

ACKNOWLEDGEMENTS

Thanks, firstly, go to the many hundreds of great Australian rabbit storytellers – our contributors. This is a fascinating history, which you've helped create. I didn't manage to fit all the stories in, but hope I have collected a fine and representative group that all will enjoy. Thanks, next, to the wonderful Sarina Locke (honorary rabbiter) from ABC Rural, to the judges and organisers of the ABC Rural 'Rabbiting On' story competition and to the Invasive Animals Cooperative Research Centre for the prize of a trip to Scotia Sanctuary, run by Australian Wildlife Conservancy, to winners Barry Hadlow and Elyse Svanberg.

Thanks, also, to the Rabbit Scan 150-Year Steering Committee, the 'inner team', for their guidance, stories and leadership; a better team of Rabbitohs one will never find: David Lord, Dr David Berman, Dr Brian Cooke, Nicholas Newland and Professor Tony Peacock (supported by Chris Lane and Dr Glenn Saunders). Australia's environment and productivity would be lost without them.

Special thanks to David Lord, Thackaringa Station, for insisting that someone had to collect the rabbit stories of the old timers, before it was too late.

Thanks, closer to home, to my ever-inspiring son, Zephyr Pavey, and the memories of his dad, Antony Pavey, and my dad, Walter Patrick Quealy, who inspired my love of story from the very beginning. Thanks, Mum (Marie), for your constant love and flowers to your middle-of-seven daughter!

PICTURE CREDITS

Burrumbuttock Public School (page 112).

David Lord (pages 8, 289).

National Library of Australia:

Photograph by Cliff Bottomley: An ICI researcher examines carbon-monoxide foam used for rabbit control, 1963 [picture] 1963. 1 photograph : b&w ; image 12 x 9.3 cm., on card 20.9 x 25.4 cm. nla.pic-vn4835993 (page 14).

Photograph by Bill Brindle: Jean and Ken Crawford and their children, the Hardham youngsters, and Phillip Gilmour, with their rabbit catch at Tidbinbilla near Canberra, 1959 [picture] 1959. 1 photograph : b&w ; image 11.3 x 9.2 cm., on card 20.9 x 25.4 cm. nla.pic-vn4836027 (page 136).

Photograph by F. H. (Frank H.) Broomhall: Boundary rider, Harry Reynolds with his supply cart, Burracoppin Depot, Western Australian, 1926 [picture] 1926. 1 negative : b&w ; 10 x 12.5 cm. Part of Photographs of the Western Australian rabbit proof fence [picture] [1926–1927] nla.pic-vn4836190 (page 21).

National Library of Australia (*continued*)

Photograph by F. H. (Frank H.) Broomhall: Boundary riders, Ovens and team, Dromedary Hills, Western Australian, 1926 [picture] 1926. 1 photograph : b&w ; 16.4 x 21.7 cm. Part of Photographs of the Western Australian rabbit proof fence [picture] [1926–1927] nla.pic-vn4836210 (page 42).

Photograph by Jeff Carter, 1928–: Amateur shooters with shotguns and rabbits, Winchelsea area, Victoria, ca. 1958 [picture] ca. 1958. 1 photograph : b&w ; 48.2 x 33 cm. nla.pic-vn3991140 (page 35).

Photograph by Jeff Carter, 1928–: Father and son, Nyngan, New South Wales, 1959 [picture] 1959. 1 photograph : gelatin silver ; 26.3 x 27 cm. Part of Outback series, Australia, 1953–1995 [picture] 1953–1995. nla.pic-an24716973 (page 73).

Photograph by Jeff Carter, 1928–: Two men processing rabbit meat at McGrath's, Melbourne, 1957 [picture] 1957. 1 photograph : b&w ; 20.3 x 25.7 cm. Part of Jeff Carter vintage print archive, 1952–1974 [picture] between 1952 and 1974. nla.pic-vn4548598 (page 49).

Photograph by Jeff Carter, 1928–: A young boy puts a rabbit in a bag, Nyngan area, New South Wales, ca. 1958 [picture] ca. 1958. 1 photograph : b&w ; 48.2 x 33 cm. nla.pic-vn3991158 (page 86).

Photograph by Rennie Ellis, 1940–2003: Rabbit skinner, Victoria Market, Melbourne, ca. 1970 [picture] ca. 1970. 1 photograph : silver gelatin ; image 24.4 x 16.4 cm., on sheet 25.4 x 17.2 cm. nla.pic-vn4505190 (page 101).

National Library of Australia (*continued*)

Experimental fencing against rabbits, Nekarboo Station, New South Wales, ca. 1895 [picture]. ca. 1895. 1 negative : b&w ; 10 x 12.5 cm. nla.pic-vn4831360 (page 182).

A good sulky load of rabbits, Moruya, New South Wales, ca. 1890 [picture]. ca. 1890. 1 negative : b&w ; 10 x 12.5 cm. nla.pic-vn4835986 (page 28).

Photograph by Charles H. (Charles Henry) Kerry, 1858–1928: A rabbiter's pack, Darling Downs [picture] [between 1885 and 1900] 1 photograph : b&w ; 20.3 x 25.4 cm. nla.pic-an24092167 (page 214).

Photograph by Andrew Leslie McKay, 1909–1976: House with rabbit pelts hanging from the veranda ceiling [transparency] 1965? 1 slide : col. ; 2.3 x 3.3 cm. Part of McKay, Andrew Leslie, 1909–1976 The Reverend Andrew Leslie McKay collection of photographs relating to Inland Australia, 1950–1976 [transparency] 1950–1976. nla.pic-an24716973 (page 237).

Motor lorry loaded with 1,760 pairs rabbits, drawn from depot 30 miles from nearest railway station [picture]. [1918?] 1 photograph : albumen ; 15.1 x 20.4 cm. Part of The Country Freezing Company Limited [picture]. nla.pic-an24664485 (page 232).

Prince Alfred, Duke of Edinburgh at Barwon Park. Engraving after Nicholas Chevalier in : Illustrated Australian news, 27 December, 1867 p4 (page 3).

Rabbit coursing in Australia. Engraving In: Booth, Edwin Carton. Australia. London : Virtue & Co., [1874-1876?]. Volume 3, p1458 (page 207).

National Library of Australia (*continued*)

Rabbiters turn-out, Cobar district, New South Wales, 1907 [picture]. 1907. 1 photograph : b&w ; image 7.8 x 12.5 cm., on card 9.4 x 14.2 cm. nla.pic-vn4836124 (page 227).

Engraving by F. A. Sleap: A rabbit battue at North Corack [picture] [Melbourne : Illustrated Australasian news, Apr. 1879] 1 print : wood engraving ; 21.2 x 34.7 cm. nla.pic-an8926649 (page 242).

Surveyor Canning and party on the survey trip to mark out the line of the rabbit-proof fence, Western Australia, ca. 1901 [picture]. ca. 1901–1902. 1 photograph : sepia toned ; 15.2 x 20.6 cm., mounted on card 19.8 x 24.2 cm. nla.pic-vn3997481 (page 294).

Photograph by Michael Terry, 1899–1981: Jack with rabbits [picture] 1932. 1 negative : nitrate, b&w ; 11.3 x 8.5 cm. Part of Michael Terry collection of negatives [picture] 1918–1969. nla.pic-vn3543972 (page 56).

Norman Plant (page 271).

Jenny Quealy (pages 11, 217, 297).